Never Left Behind

Copyright © 2019 Paul Barthel

NEVER LEFT BEHIND. Copyright © 2019 by Paul Barthel.

All rights reserved. Printed in the United States of America.

No part of this book may be used or reproduced in any manner whatsoever without written permission except in the case of brief quotations embodied in critical articles and reviews.

FIRST EDITION

First Dog House Publishing paperback edition published 2019
Book Design by Voices for Pets / Peppers Tale

Dog House Publishing
ISBN: 978-0-578-55499 paperback
Book print set in 12 point Garamond

Never Left Behind : one man's refusal for status quo how we treat animals / Barthel, Paul — 1st ed.
p. cm

All brand names and product names used in this book are trademarks, registered trademarks, or trade names of their respective holders. Dog House Publishing is not associated with any product or vendor in this book.

ISBN: 978-0-578-55499-0

Printed and bound in the United States of America

10 9 8 7 6 5 4 3 2 1

TO PEPPER

FOR WHOM THIS BOOK WOULD NOT HAVE BEEN POSSIBLE

NEVER LEFT BEHIND

ONE MAN'S REFUSAL FOR STATUS QUO HOW WE TREAT ANIMALS

PAUL BARTHEL

DOG HOUSE PUBLISHING

CONTENTS

	Preface	i
	Introduction	1
ONE	Piperaceae (Pepper)	21
TWO	Rude Awakening	47
THREE	Trial By fire	61
FOUR	The Forest	81
FIVE	On The Line	97
SIX	Holding It Together	111
SEVEN	Head Chef	139
EIGHT	In The Eyes	175
NINE	Losing Pepper	195
TEN	Growing A Backbone	223
ELEVEN	Inaptitude	261
TWELVE	Going All In	281
THIRTEEN	Coming Home	303
	Acknowledgements	

PREFACE

"I don't believe in the concept of hell, but if I did, I would think of it as filled with people who were cruel to animals."

~ Gary Larson ~

And here we have yet another dog salvation book and how their presence incredibly rescues another lost soul. Contrary and further from the truth, after thirty years toiling in kitchens, entrapped within cinder block walls for fourteen hours a day, it would take a four-legged furry creature accompanied by a bitter divorce that would ultimately lead me to question my path in life and how we choose to treat animals. Feeding tens of thousands of people in some of the most derelict of kitchens, decades would pass and what was once a job to pay bills eventually became a career as a chef, only to question my path once faced with losing my companion forever.

I had always felt a natural affinity and kinship towards animals, and not just dogs but rather most that I would encounter, be it in the wild, held captive or used for exploitation. I recall before the age of ten fishing with my father and brothers, not knowing what I'd do had I actually caught a fish, rather simply wanting to enjoy the ride in the outboard, just us guys. Later in life, I would be the odd guy removing turtles off the road, dead carcasses, and shooing those deer away that had wandered to close to the edge of a highway. Often questioning our role, we subscribe to as humans, I had always held contempt for our assumed superiority merely because we yield a higher intellect or brandish a larger stick.

Clearly, I understand the irony of a chef capable of empathy for nonhuman creatures. However, I am not ashamed to divulge with absolution that I question our relevant alliance and lack of assimilation. Hell, it would take weeks before I could grasp the difference between animal welfare and animal rights. How in fact can we claim to provide "welfare," when we decidedly place a piece of them on our dinner plate each night, hold them captive, or willfully choose treating animals as a commodity?

A chef-owner of a restaurant myself, I would witness failure upon failure of restaurant owners with their infamous lasagna recipe handed down from grandma *destined* to make them millions, however, most eventually becoming a statistic. Four out of five restaurants failing within the first five years, depending on what you read. An industry underbelly plagued with chefs and owners coked out, driven by greed or the lure of fame, and many willing to exchange sex for hierarchy.

Embezzlement rampant and turnover notorious; those who survive are damned forsaking their own life, forced to work grueling hours in some of the most hostile of conditions. Bankruptcies, divorce, closures and dreams shattered, and the occasional suicide remain commonplace. Dreamers who drain their bank accounts and risk their entire 401k's romanticizing of owning their own restaurant, where everyone can eat grandma's secret hand-me-down lasagna recipe.

When sitting down to write this book, I made it imperative abstaining from blame, but rather focus on the inequality I would experience and lack of resources available. Even to this day in most states our pets are still viewed as mere property, an object, similar to a table or lamp. It would take grassroots efforts, and a compassionate animal loving Senator from the State of Illinois to recognize the disparity.

Finally, a trending new law in the State of Illinois would be indoctrinated prescribing the most formative measures when determining the fate and custody of those creatures, setting self-interest aside. However, for me, it became much more than pet recognition and my case alone that would awaken and once again germinate that connection I had always held close for those creatures.

Through research for my own case, and the overwhelming support I would receive, I was appalled by the enormity of suffering and abuse prevalent, however, conveniently hidden. So much that it would haunt my inactions, stir my inner emotions, and paralyze my thoughts to an obsession.

Opening this Pandora's Box brought to light the connection that I had always felt and direction in my life so needed at the time. Not enough to idly stand aside until my own issues were resolved, I would ultimately choose to put down my kitchen knives after thirty-odd years, come to terms with my age, and satisfy that urgency. Not as a burden, but perhaps as an opportunity provided to me — a must, that it was time to give back, or at the very least save a life or two.

Do not fret. By no means is this yet another animal liberation book, or page after page of me laminating over my love for a dog, but rather my story and the path leading to my own inspiration and realization for a larger calling at a time that could not have been more pertinent. From these words hereinafter, at the very least I hope that you too may find an altruism or moment of reflection that may offer you pause.

Had it not been for those gruesome years in the kitchen and the stamina it would require, I cannot say for certain I would have been able to summon the courage I would later be forced to call upon. In these writings you will get a glimpse of life on the line inside the bowels of some the most unforsaken kitchens, accompanied by those transients who populate the industry with compelling kitchen anecdotes and behind the scenes revelations. From the vagrants, addicts, and divas, to those choosing to sacrifice their life in exchange for meager wages and experience the endorphin induced rush of kitchen life on the line.

A cliché and familiar story for many of us; forgetting to stop and smell the roses while enjoying the little things that life has to offer. Rarely when someone is on their deathbed will you hear them profess to wishing they would have spent more time at the office. I would be reminded of these passages thirty years later, only after selling my restaurant and navigating through an arduous divorce compounded by losing my Labrador Retriever. It would take losing my best friend ultimately causing me to question my own direction and those rights of our kindred.

From those kitchens described herein and the grueling fourteen-hour days, Pepper would wait for my return each night for years on end. Once home, he would then proceed to hog the bed, cramping my legs, turning and shifting throughout the night, and waking me during the most ungodly hours insisting to be let outside. I wouldn't have had it any other way.

Consider this: A multi-billion-dollar industry; we lavish our companions with expensive gourmet pet food, pampering day spas, costly grooming, and pet "play dates." They accompany us on our vacations, muddy our bamboo wood floors, shed profusely in all corners of the house, and on occasion surprise us with a mistake on our new Berber carpeting, unable to make it outside in time to conduct their business.

We conscientiously follow them around with our saved-up plastic grocery bags waiting for them to defecate, open our wallets to astronomical veterinarian fees ensuring they remain healthy, and finally allow them to break our hearts when leaving us after sharing their brief time here on earth. Loyal and uncomplaining, they never utter a word during their whisper of a moment by our sides. Where else do we spend so much of our time, energy, and love for such a meager return?

Never Left Behind describes the compelling story of a man who, when involved in a highly contested divorce making headlines, refused to let his pet Labrador Retriever be taken away. A contentious lawyer and a refusing litigant; they would part ways on the midnight hour of the impending trial. Ultimately, he would choose going pro se, representing himself, with only weeks to prepare for trial before an overbearing no-nonsense judge.

Never Left Behind is a compelling memoir that delves the reader into behind the scenes restaurant experiences, both amusing and alarming. You will be taken on the line into the candid minds of chefs as they make their way through each day feeding the unknowing, exposing what takes place behind those kitchen walls separating the unassuming diner. Driven by daily pressure and survival, those same traits would be used to mount a campaign in effort to be reunited with his companion.

Three years of a dog's life. Why? Why not merely get another one? He would face those questions and the scrutiny of many. From these trials, he would discover a new world brought on by helping to defend those without a voice, forsaking those years on the line and never letting go.

Introduction

Precariously filling with rainwater over a party of eight diners, the popcorn ceiling tile was prepared to collapse at any given moment. Each diner immersed in their food and conversation, oblivious what was about to rain down on them. Requiring me to scale a ladder in front of a packed restaurant in my chef whites, I could only wait and pray. With the dining room full, I took a chance and chose not to close off the section, risking potential embarrassment in the hope that the rain outside would subside.

Toilets backing up, employee no-shows, compressor failures at $900 each, HVAC breakdowns, sprinkled with the occasional customer driving through our front window; this was merely just another day. On what would be the busiest day of the week, nonetheless. Today, it seemed, would be no different; almost predictable, I had grown accustomed to each obstacle forced to navigate.

Sunday in most family restaurants, easily the most hectic, can also be the most prosperous. So discernible that failing to hit one Sunday pecuniary quota in any given month can cripple your cash flow and probability for survival. Should a host of additional determinant factors such as inclement weather, a struggling economy, competition, or perhaps a negative review that paralyzes foot traffic somehow fail to deter your Sunday, you still had the busiest day to contend with.

Unable to afford any sleep last night after a hopeful Saturday, I was faced with the possibility that my strongest lead cook would pull a no-show. Paid on Friday, it was now becoming common for him to go on a bender, only to return on Monday, head down, tail between legs, remorseful for his actions. Again. *Note to self: switch week-ending payroll to Monday.*

After fourteen hours yesterday I arrived back at 5:00 a.m., following four hours of sleep, faced with the longest day of the week. If fortunate, I may be home by 11 p.m. First thing: coffee. Before any intrusion I would need my fuel and choice of drug. The unmistakable freshly ground coffee smell wafting in the air as the black gold streamed into my mug. A habit I had fallen into by removing the coffee pot when brewing to avoid the watered-down version, I would place my cup directly under the filter delivering the most potent blend. My own quick version espresso. A vice that had become my prescription providing me both solace and warmth, would allow for pause, and a sense of calm before the impending storm.

Introduction

Routinely going through the opening procedures, I unconsciously glanced at my watch, now 5:45 a.m. and no Miguel, despite opening in fifteen minutes. Thankfully the other two cooks were here, however, they were unqualified to prepare the three different soup offerings made fresh daily, in addition, the variety of sauces, needed for a day on the line.

Rare that a customer would crave soup this early in the morning, however, similar to wine, soups demand time to simmer, mature, and for their body of flavor to develop. As a chef, you don't want your twelve-burner stove crammed with three overbearing 32-quart pots, all simmering when hit with the ensuing breakfast rush, commanding all available burner space. Stock preparation, cleaning the vegetables, uniformed chopping, spice adjustments, and constant monitoring, bringing all the elements of a full-bodied soup together, can take hours.

While most restaurants today are guilty of using bag in the box soups coming frozen, for those restaurants that remain true, the subtle art of soup preparation is typically the start of each day before the thousands of additional tasks performed in kitchens everywhere. I have always considered the preparation of soups to be one of my strongest traits as a chef, using a combination of flavors, various ingredients, and the idea of creating something from scratch that is both warm and comforting on a cold winter day, shared with others.

Six a.m.; it was now clear he wasn't coming, my strongest man on the line. While I was the chef proprietor of Peppercorns, I also employed a qualified chef as well to help oversee kitchen operations.

When he decided to come in of course. Begrudgingly, I was now forced to put on my whites and go on the line in Miguel's absence.

While the kitchen was my home and place of solace, this could not have happened at a worse time. Sunday had become my one day of reprieve off the line allowing me to greet, seat, and interact with my daily customers, placing a face behind the food.

As the owner, I understood the gravity that it wasn't merely about preparing each dish, rather getting to know my customers and their families demonstrating gratitude in exchange for their business. Besides, I had begun looking forward to Sundays, affording me the time to step back off the line and work on front-house operations. Too often a wall divides the kitchen from the dining room leaving the customer questioning, who's preparing their food. I too find comfort with familiarity in restaurants and wanted Peppercorns to be no different.

Pissed off as I changed into my whites, I could only imagine what kind of fucking mess was waiting for me inside the kitchen. Not only was the restaurant open, but having to work the kitchen, left the front house vulnerable without a hostess, leaving me with only two options: the first asking one of my servers to assume hostess responsibility, while the other would be begging one of my family members to come in and help.

Requesting a server on our busiest day to now hostess is no match in wages compared to her earnings if she served tables. My request would certainly be met with attitude. Relenting, I promised to swap out a day she needed off in exchange for filling the role today. It was

Introduction

far better than being forced asking one of my own family members for a favor, whom I would undoubtedly be indebted to. Problem solved.

During any given hour on the line, waiting on wire shelves, or tucked away behind spices, one could find half-empty coffee cups that once offered repose midst the madness; each cup placed within arm's reach on the line. Under pressure, I would crash without it. Like a crack addict needing their spoon, coffee was my needle. With the printer and its tiresome clicking noises spitting out ticket after ticket, table after table, the adrenaline it would necessitate, the robotic nature of each chefs movements; all time-controlled, every detail like that of a ballet would not be possible were it not for coffee.

To the unknowing eye, the orderly chaos on the line would appear unhinged. Voices talking over one another in urgency, servers staring you down waiting for their last plate of an eight top. "Fire table five," "I need more plates," and "a party of 15 wants to be seated without a reservation!" Tickets a foot long spitting out of the printer, plates clattering, the static noise of spatulas hitting metal, tongs clicking, and of course the relentless unforgiving heat coming off bare metal all around you. Grease incessantly airborne, your clothes at the end of the day would smell like a combination of fish, blood, and fryer oil. Taking it home, your hair if left unwashed, leaving the distinct smell of grease on your pillowcase each night.

Entering the kitchen, knowingly, all eyes avoided contact with mine, mindful of my resolute disposition. I immediately assumed the role of sauté, by far the most challenging of stations. Virtually all plates either start or finish with most items on the menu coming off sauté. Stepping onto the line without any notice or chance to inventory my station, already orders begin to trickle in demanding my attention.

Assuming control of the kitchen, I barked out to the cooks insisting they carry the line until I'm needed. Meanwhile, I then assess the condition of my station left from the previous day, scrambling to find soup ingredients knowing I only had a couple of hours before all three must be ready. Fuck it, I thought; with little time left decide only offering two soups for the day, refusing to block three burners when orders would be coming in at the same time. Not only were there soups to prepare, but we also had gravies, sauces, coulis, and a plethora of other items that would demand burner space.

A gulp of coffee. Pressed for time, I feverishly scour over my hotel pans making mental notes on what else was needed, noticing all omelet ingredients needed to be chopped. Green peppers, onions, tomatoes, sausage, bacon, and fresh spinach, only but a few of items. I then notice that were almost out of pancake batter. What about waffle batter? Crêpe batter? I then question, do we have enough fresh potatoes for hash-browns already cooked and peeled? If so, have they been shredded yet? My mind races in a panic while in the background I can hear the unrelenting printer. Where's my coffee?

Struggling with a mixture of emotions, my mind was on the front of the house and both angry at myself for not having checked the kitchen last night to ensure breakfast would go smoothly.

Introduction

Mistakenly, I had broken my cardinal rule by allowing myself to become dependent on others, assuming Miguel would report for work despite his history.

Focused, I then decided to prepare two of my most fundamental soups; classic chicken dumpling, and three-cheese broccoli gratin; staple soups in most family restaurants, and by far the easiest for me to knock out. I then grabbed one of my dishwashers, who fortunately was cross-trained, delegating that he fills all the pans of sauté ingredients. With my second dishwasher, I instruct him to forget about the dirty plates coming in and instead, begin prepping the potatoes. Slowly the kitchen begins to take shape. Thankfully, at this early hour, there is only the before-church crowd to worry about. In three hours after church, and still not ready? We'd better pray.

Now 9 a.m., the soups have been simmering for a couple of hours, most of the sauces are made, and the line is as ready as ever. A stream of tickets spilling from the printer demanding our attention, my mind wanders while preparing plate after plate, concerned we may not have prepped enough product to make it through lunch. If not ready now, we will be forced to "wing it" at the height of the slam.

Winging it without the essential preparedness, sequentially extends into the dining room leading to unsatisfied customers impatiently waiting or being served unacceptable plates. Dissatisfied customers and long waits for their meal, both ultimately leading to eventual attrition. One of the most common causes for restaurant failures being inconsistency.

In all circumstances, and rightfully so, a customer should never be expected to understand if you're too busy, failed to prep, or that any employee failed to show up for their shift. It's not their business, nor should it be. I remind myself of this every time a customer frequents my restaurant; that a conscious effort was made of them, to get in their car and drive to my establishment among the many choices available for them to spend their hard-earned money.

Like being on a stage, we are here merely for their entertainment and satisfaction, bearing no significance the previous day in sales, how many covers you put out, or how tired you may be from last night's slam. Each day is a new crowd of faces, and they couldn't care less about your yesterday. A paying audience that must be entertained; each day is akin to a new production, demanding excellence.

Back on the line, we momentarily claim victory after reaching terminal velocity with every seat in the restaurant filled to capacity. Despite the line stretching out the front door waiting to be seated, only when one table leaves can another be seated. Thankfully, the tranquility amidst the controlled chaos now affords us time to put out a far superior plate than having to spit out 300 covers all at once when filling up.

A bit of advice: like the plague, avoid going into restaurants with large groups. Your plate will almost certainly – while you may find it acceptable – lose its full attention in the kitchen had the flow of people only been steady. I am referring, of course, to genuine

Introduction

restaurants as opposed to those offering soup-in-a-bag or pre-fabbed and manufactured foods resembling something vaguely edible.

Finding our groove while plates leave the pass one after the other, I notice a light rain began to fall outside. My mind now drawn to my failing HVAC system, with the rain, the inside of the restaurant remained hot and humid from the front door constantly opening and closing. The once-cool restaurant air countered with the humid outdoor air causing the exterior walls of the AC ductwork to condensate. Condensation forming, slowly trickles down into a pan hidden above the ceiling tiles. The pan, ultimately filling up if it remains humid for an extended amount of time, then causes it to overflow. Overflowing where? You got it. Directly onto the ceiling tiles, smack-dab in the center of my main dining room. The drip, if steady, will eventually pool, weakening the tiles, collapsing under the weight onto the unsuspecting diners.

Dealing with my main chef pulling a no-show, a questionable hostess handling all of my cash, and working in a disheveled kitchen, I am now forced to leave the front of the house open to liability, forgetting when was the last time I checked if the pans above the ceiling tiles had been emptied. With the dining room completely full, it would be impossible, never mind humiliating, to climb a ladder popping each tile to check. I could only monitor the rain, imploring it to subside while keeping a watchful eye on the tiles above.

Finding my place back on the line, I hear the phone ring in the distance, and I'm notified that a server scheduled to start at 12:00 p.m. has suffered a death in the family and will not be coming in.

Apparently, her grandfather had died, again. Over the pass, in between dishes, and the clatter of plates, I ask one of the servers if she could pull a double. Met with a huff and shrug of the shoulders, she would mutter some expletives without answering, storming off. It seems today there would be no respite.

Now 11:00 a.m. and still raining outside with the dining room full, once again, I wander out of the kitchen, making my best effort to remain inconspicuous. Looking upwards, I notice what appears to be a large circle on one of the tiles, while a party of eight dines directly below. Having experienced this before, I instinctively knew how much time remained before collapsing.

The circle will enlarge, become a slow drip, then a stream, followed by a noticeable bowing, until finally, it crumbles into a large mass of aluminum framing, asbestos, and rainwater. Gambling, it's only a matter of time. If the rain continues, I'll be forced to bring out a ladder in display of a packed dining room, awkwardly blocking off a section, or even worse, request that the party move in the middle of their meal. Humiliating but necessary to avoid potential collapse, liability, or perhaps even injury.

With the kitchen noises growing louder and the faint clicking of the printer rising to a feverish pitch, demanded that I return. One hand short, within mere minutes of leaving the line my team has once again found themselves in the weeds. A quiet controlled kitchen can quickly turn into a panic of pans slamming down, orders being barked out, dishes rattling, and a flurried scene of hands flying, knives chopping and cooks running.

Introduction

Finding your way through the weeds can be as simple as keeping your head down with intense focus and hammering each ticket out. All too many times, I have witnessed those inevitable Gordon Ramsayesque Oscar worthy performances, someone having a meltdown, cooks arguing, plates smashing, and eventually someone storming out the back door.

Unfortunately, all too many interruptions can hamper your efforts, and it's hardly ever as simple as getting orders out. Between prepping the line, running out of items, or a customer insisting on saying hello, all these distractions encourage shortcuts. It's during these times, that it's inevitable you'll receive "special orders." Typically, I have no problem with custom orders; not only is it necessary, it is a must for customer satisfaction and repeats. Those orders that require an indefinite pause on the line just to read the ticket full of instructions as if it were a fucking novel. The finished plate resembling nothing like what was intended off the menu.

Each menu item made from memory, not only do special orders force you to stop and read the written diatribe, but they irritably require constant reference ensuring its accuracy. And that ticket may be only one of 20-30 additional tickets on the rail at any given time. Unique orders by far, are the ones capable of bringing the line to a halt, negatively affecting every diner. Add onions not shallots, no cheese, green peppers not red peppers, Yukon Gold potatoes as opposed to Idaho, gluten free, egg whites only.

Once in the weeds, special orders encourage shortcuts that the customer will ultimately suffer with the finished product. Shortcuts leading to imperfect plates, imperfect plates leading to inconsistency, inconsistency to erratic experiences each time the customer frequents the property.

Unaware at first, your numbers slowly begin to diminish, leaving you to wonder and only guess the impressions you may have failed to leave upon your customer base. While it may not be that the food was inedible, however, failed to provide that "experience" you strive to offer, setting you apart from the competition. That pause when they first taste your creation, causing an unmistakable reaction. If a chef fails understanding why it's imperative to kill each plate, causing every table to enthusiastically scrutinize your finished work or request to meet you personally, having no aspiration behind each dish, they are better suited opening a hotdog stand.

If it's not in your blood – the notion to please, to blow your customer away with every serving, more often, it cannot be nurtured. It's either something you have, or you don't. Terminally infectious by nature, inconsistency is easily fueled by complacency. Thriving restaurants have no room for contentment.

Understand that despite all the tensity, chefs wouldn't have it any other way. While abhorring the stress, they feed from it at the same time. The constant attention it demands, creativity and quick thinking, and being forced to put out one fire while another continues burning.

Most efforts met with immediate results working on the line, allows us to abstain from obscurity in a four by four cubicle like a rat where any intuitive insight is stifled by constant red tape,

Introduction

backstabbing, and meddling. Each employee struggling to get noticed, meet a deadline, or schedule a meeting, deciding when to have the next meeting in the corporate world.

The inner drive for excellence, satisfaction from serving, and ability to leave an impression on each person with an expression through food is paramount and unlike any other career. Still, nouvelle food trends, rich décor, and gimmick plate presentations are no longer enough for survival. A restaurant's ability to set itself apart extends much further than the kitchen's talent in producing a superior plate.

Three o'clock could not come soon enough. As quickly as the restaurant would fill, like clockwork it would empty out, allowing for a much-needed reprieve. Dodging a bullet, the party of eight seated under the tile has settled their bill and left the restaurant. Outside, the rain, although light, remains unyielding. Realizing it's about to cave at any moment, I curse myself for failing to convey the urgency to my landlord in replacing the faltering $10,000 HVAC unit. My lease leaving me on the hook, would force me to spend thousands in band-aid repairs month after month on the behemoth dinosaur. While restaurants operated for pennies on the dollar making margin, I simply couldn't afford any additional expenditures, nor was my landlord willing to foot the bill for a new unit.

4:00 p.m.; The restaurant slowing, we managed to seat the remaining diners in another section out of view. Racing to find a ladder before the early dinner crowd arrives, fumbling, I hold the ladder with one hand, and grab an empty five-gallon pickle bucket, broom, and two new ceiling tiles with the other. Familiar with the predicament, stashed away are new tiles ready at a moment's notice.

A small audience of staff members begins to form, having witnessed this before, bracing themselves for my tirade of expletives certain to follow. With all eyes watching, I summit the ladder, reassuring myself under my breath: "I got this."

Careful not to puncture the soaked tile and risk a complete collapse, I carefully wiggle and lift a neighboring tile to gain access. Slowly raising my head through the opening, I first notice all the pipes and ductwork surrounding the entire HVAC unit sweating profusely with condensation. Forty-foot-long piping running parallel to the unit perspiring with droplets as far as I could see. The previous owner failing to wrap the ductwork, left me exposed each time a sharp difference in temperature occurred, causing condensation. Defiant, no longer was I going to use my own personal funds band-aiding a building that I didn't own.

Finding it impossible to maneuver a bucket between the conduit, ceiling rebar, and various wires, I scoop out as much water as possible. Unconsciously, I glimpse around down below one last time to see if anyone was recording with their cell phone, only to be uploaded to YouTube later, the spectacle about to unfold.

With one hand holding the garbage can, I slowly begin lifting the tile with the other hand. Pushing through the mush, I accidentally cause all four corners to collapse and the adjacent crossbars to come crashing down in a white crumbling mass of black rain-soot and asbestos-laced debris onto my head, face, and floor. "FUCK," being

Introduction

my response, or some semblance of, spitting out tile while brushing off my snow-laden hair. Below I look to see several staff members scurrying away.

Sunday, a favorite among chefs working in family restaurants, is not only the ending of a long week, but in most cases the busiest. Families dining, children laughing, souls exchanging stories, drinks flowing, servers happy to be earning money, cooks and the camaraderie they share on the line; there is nothing like it when it all comes together. A high of adrenaline, anticipation, and emotions; almost euphoric. A vibe, if you will, like that of a symphony, all the moving parts and people with their own section, working concertedly.

Love and the food we share are two of the simplest universal ingredients that bonds and transcends all cultures. Regardless of politics, religion, or position in life, our daily bread brings us all to the table. Together we share, after long days at work, during holidays, and during lavish correspondence collations between foreign countries bringing world leaders together over one table. Foods fortified and entrenched in traditions and history capable of breaking down barriers of different cultures and societies, bringing us all closer.

Peppercorns, albeit far from fine dining, however, I remained adamant about following all the top chefs; intently watching for new openings, prevailing trends, who was moving where, and what chefs were doing things differently with food. Charlie Trotter, who I had always held in high regard, following his entire career, said it best:

The kitchen, to him, was akin to listening to the great Miles Davis in a drawn-out jazz session. A blend of ingredients, movements, notes, adjustments, and flavors. The various instruments that make up an ensemble and the arrangement of music are likened to each plate prepared by a chef and the intensity on the line. Every session could include the same song in the setlist, and yet is never played the same. Similarly, every day new dishes are prepared, while each plate offers a slight variance.

After having bathed under the tile-shower, I was ecstatic this particular "jazz session" had only a few hours remaining. Tiles replaced, the area cleaned, and tables back in place, I was now looking forward to grabbing a booth, sitting down over my coffee, and perhaps catching up on some paperwork. Still in my bloodstained, crumbled-tile-laden chef whites, I change clothes for the third time.

Either in the front hostessing, in the back chefing, or maybe outside painting, it would not be uncommon to change clothes as many as four times on any given day. A brief acquit off the line, I would sit in one of the booths; my make-shift office strewn with papers, a calculator, stacked invoices, and open laptop. Was it unprofessional? Yes, but it allowed me to keep an eye on the dining room, employees, and most importantly – as I would learn later – the cash register.

Armchair restaurant owners *not* in the business seem to have all the answers for the challenges and choices restaurant owners face daily. Why did you not simply have a busboy repair the ceiling tiles?

Introduction

Why are *you* painting instead of hiring a contractor? Why are *you* on the line cooking, when you should hire a brigade of cooks? These are all great questions, but clearly, I would suspect, they have never been an owner-operator of any business, let alone the beast of a restaurant.

My preferred response is best to answer with a question: Why had Peppercorns operated for eight years, yet after having sold it, witness three different operators in the same location take over and fail in succession in less than three years? Of those eight years' operating Peppercorns, four were during the economic collapse of 2008; one of the most severe economic downturns since the Great Depression where not only restaurants but business closures were rampant, providing a seemingly endless landscape of vacant storefronts.

Knowing many chefs and having numerous acquaintances in the trade, they will all tell you: unless you have deep pockets or an angel investor, you are responsible for *everything* as the owner. In the early weeks, months and perhaps years of opening as a chef-owner, I would have been extremely fortunate had all that was required of me was focusing solely on culinary and food alone. Countless chef entrepreneurs in order they survive, are demanded they take off their chef jackets performing a variety of odd jobs, most having absolutely nothing to do with food.

Business brisk in the early years, however money always tight after having incurred thousands in opening expenses, access to additional funds — while not impossible — I refused digging into my own pockets any longer. Demanding the restaurant sustain itself, it could no longer be a money pit. As any business owner will attest, when in the trenches, many times it can be difficult, finding it hard to pause and look up since you're always "doing." If something needed addressing, it was corrected by myself. Not only was it rewarding, it would meet my own standards and most importantly, be cost effective. Micromanaging? I think not.

A popular story shared among chefs, Trotter, when he first opened his infamous restaurant, he reached out to the city of Chicago, wanting to know when the crumbling, appalling cement sidewalks were scheduled to be repaired in front of his new establishment. While assuring him they were scheduled to be replaced, this was on Chicago time, or years as it were. True to his character, Trotter found it unacceptable. Pleading with his alderman and the city, his urgency would get him nowhere. As the story is rumored, in the middle of the night on city property — no small task — Trotter, jackhammered, removed, and then replaced the sidewalk himself. Using his own money, he then planted young saplings, where each could grow in their own intermittent private island along the freshly poured cement.

To this day, you will see those same trees nestled in front of the building, fully grown, while in other areas down the street you will not find a similar setting. So precise and calculated in providing dining excellence, his vision began at street-level. Rather than enter off the harsh city curb, he offered a welcoming, manicured sidewalk reminiscent of a café, its entry lined with trees. This story always

Introduction

fascinated me; the abrasiveness and determination, not taking no for an answer in getting things accomplished.

While I'm no Trotter by any extent, it was examples like him that fueled my determination, marveling at his convictions and finding inspiration allowing Peppercorns to make it through some of the harshest of economic times.

After two long years and seven days a week nurturing Peppercorns, the business began to find its footing, allowing me to have one day off a week. Not only to re-energize myself, but perhaps to nurture a troubled marriage and welcome into my life this creature, changing it forever.

CHAPTER ONE

Piperaceae (Pepper)

After having first read the introduction, one would think this book is about a troubled chef struggling with the daily challenges unfolding within restaurants. Contrary, the narrative illustrates where I was at the time when this particular creature would enter my life, changing it forever. All those years on the line and the similar determination used in my work, I would be forced to summon later in effort that we be reunited after unwillingly forced apart. Not the first dog in my life, however, our relationship was unlike any other I had experienced before. This creature of course would be Pepper.

Looking back, the timing could not have been more fitting. With the restaurant going on its third year, I had finally begun taking off one day a week, albeit on somewhat of an irregular basis. Those

Mondays, when many restaurants are either closed or the executive chef is granted a day off, had less to do with the success of the restaurant and more so with preserving my sanity. Grateful to finally break away, anxiety had also begun surfacing in my marriage. Perhaps by removing myself from the restaurant at least one day a week, it would allow us a chance to rekindle our relationship.

Entering the marriage with one dog already; she had picked him up at a shelter during a break when we were dating. My affection for dogs would prove to be the catalyst that eventually reunited us. Coincidence? It was no secret, however, that I had always wanted to welcome a puppy into our new home, raising it as we all grew together as a family. Harboring no ill feelings towards her dog, I simply wanted a loyal companion to grow old with, not having had my own in over 15 years. One that would symbolically sit next to me in my chair when reading by a warm fireplace or share hidden forest trails together. Recently married, new home, a functioning business, two cars in the driveway, white picket fence. What else would make it more complete other than a new puppy?

Time passed until it would finally require a bit more persuasion. Both of us consumed in demanding careers, we had to be fair not only for any new member of the family but also the commitment it would require on our behalf. Personally, I preferred to avoid a "canned dog," one that was bred, fed and vendored from a storefront or unscrupulous breeder. Nor was I going to pay $800 for a dog, merely with the intent of boasting my AKC purebred papers to all the neighbors. Somehow, I wanted to make a difference by offering

Piperaceae (Pepper)

a new, innocent life an opportunity outside of the typical boxed store selection and exploitative puppy mills.

Without having to search far, I knew exactly where to find an abundance of strays to choose from all needing a home and a life off the street. Two hours south of Chicago, my mom's house was situated among farmland, corn, scattered housing, and more corn, all nestled in a quaint welcoming farm town. Imagine a town where everyone knows each other by name, where they hold pumpkin fests, summer carnivals, and apple pies are cooling on windowsills.

When time would allow and not at the restaurant, I would fuel up the truck to make the trek, both visiting mom and unapologetically bending her ear like a true son burdening his mother. Incessantly complaining about my business and personal woes, I would reflect during the long rides back home after visiting, shaming myself for how much of a "downer" I must have been to her. God bless her for being mom in all sense of the word, listening to her son and his selfishness. I guess that's what moms do.

Approaching the small town on my visits, I'd notice stray dogs roaming many of the streets. *Who owns all these poor, defenseless animals? How are they getting fed?* I would find myself purposefully slowing down, obsessing about their poor existence. Breeding uncontrollably, they were simply left abandoned on the side of the road, left fending for themselves. It reminded me of Louisiana, Tennessee, and many other southern states where it was common to see dogs aimlessly wandering or in packs scouring for food and struggling for survival. Skittish when they were approached, their ribs visible, starving for scraps that passerby's would toss from their cars. I would become agitated by my inability to help, questioning how anyone who lived there could allow this to happen. It became so heartbreaking and unbearable, that I began taking alternate routes to avoid witnessing the suffering.

Heading home after one visit, passing endless rows of corn in the middle of nowhere, on the side of the road I caught a glimpse of something rustling in the tall grass. A dog. Not just a dog, but a puppy resembling a beagle frolicking around, completely alone, oblivious to the fast-approaching dusk and its potential dangers. Pulling over, I watched from the truck as my mind raced. *How the hell did he get here?* I then considered the consequences waiting back home. This must be someone's dog, I convinced myself, refusing to believe such extreme cruelty could exist. Preferring to circumvent any further confrontations on the home front, I hesitantly drove off after assuring myself he would be fine.

Who would take care of him knowing I'd be back at the restaurant tomorrow, for yet another week straight? Back at home, with everyone's busy lives, I also knew it would be unfair to ask anyone to care for the little guy. Dying inside as I slowly drove away, watching the yellow line in my rearview mirror, I saw its figure emerge from the tall grass, jogging down the street after my truck. That would be enough.

Stopping the truck, I got out, and when he approached without any hesitation, I scooped him up, embracing him in my arms. His wide eyes, floppy ears, and that new puppy smell was unmistakable.

Piperaceae (Pepper)

My emotions taking over, I couldn't help but envision him running in the same manner towards the car that had initially dumped him. I wasn't about to let it happen twice.

My new friend comfortably sleeping in a ball on the passenger seat; the two-hour drive home was a mixture of both joy and anxiety, uncertain what to expect when entering the house. But despite my worthy intentions, as quickly as I brought him into my life, I would be forced into letting him go. Between both our careers, her children in school, and rarely being home, left little time to care for the guy. Alone for several hours a day, he would have several accidents in the house that welcomed me when I got home or someone else who was forced to clean. In all fairness, he deserved a better home, one that could provide for what he needed. Unable to admit it at the time, letting him go was the right thing to do.

On my next Monday off, begrudgingly, I found a no-kill shelter, assured that because he was both cute and a puppy, he would be adopted quickly. His large adorable floppy ears would also help in finding a new home. Before letting him go I checked each pen for standing waste, cleanliness, and obvious signs of neglect. I then checked a couple of the dogs for matting and potential urine burns. Matting caused by improper grooming, and urine burns evidence of prolonged exposure while standing in their own bodily waste.

For weeks after surrendering the little pup, thoughts of him haunted me; *does he think I gave up on him? Did he find a good home?* As a man, I despised my insecurity, oftentimes borderline obsessive after giving him up. Once again, my work would provide me the escape I needed to keep my mind from being totally lost in my thoughts.

The following Monday, satisfying my compulsion, before the adoption agency was even open, I was parked outside the parking lot. Knowing that if he were still in a cage it would absolutely crush me, I found relief that he was gone. Adopted by a family in less than two days, I was told. Little did I know at the time, losing him would be the impetus that would eventually bring Pepper into my life, thus changing it forever.

Months would pass, and the brief encounter with my floppy-eared friend continued to come up in conversation at home. With the right amount of persuasion and relentless reassurance, it was finally agreed by everyone in the family that if we were to get a puppy, a concerted effort would be required by all in the raising, clean-up, and maintenance. Even though our hours at work hadn't changed, we were somehow going to make it work. Besides, my Mondays off had now become almost regular and would give me the entire day to spend with the new family member.

One call to Amanda, my brother Nick's stepdaughter who also lived in the same small farm town as mom, was all it took. Twelve years old, a typical kid, she had connections via Facebook that put us in touch with a neighbor friend only three blocks away from mom's house. Recently giving birth to a litter of nine babies, the owner of the mother and her litter were merely giving them away for a small donation.

Piperaceae (Pepper)

Everyone preoccupied with excitement, our visit to my mom's that day would be the briefest on record. Leaving moms, all five of us packed inside the truck, we passed rows of weathered clapboard homes, many with large wrap-around porches and hanging planters. Each home dimly lit inside, left you to imagine everyone sitting at the kitchen table after a long day of work and school, sharing the events of their day over dinner. Arriving at Sara's house, the short gravel driveway crumbled under the truck's tires, eventually giving way to a large tractor wheel on the front lawn serving as a makeshift planter. Picturesque, the scene couldn't have been more perfect.

Knocking on the door, unable to contain our excitement, all five of us stood there, like waiting for our candy on Halloween. Once introduced to Sara, she told us that all the puppies were being held in the backyard, motioning that we meet her out back. My obsessive nature once again causing pause, I questioned: *The backyard? Even in this mild December, isn't it too cold to have them outside?* I had to remind myself: you're not in Chicago. This is how things are done in many small farm towns, where a scattered bale of hay and a barn is typical in providing a home for a variety of animals. Explaining why you may see dogs wandering the streets due to over-breeding and the lack of spay and neutering resources.

Walking up the remainder of the driveway to the back of the house, eventually gave way to a fenced-in backyard. Still no puppies. Noticing a carport off to the side adjacent to the garage, I caught a glimpse of a small shelter with a fence surrounding it. Silent, other than the crisp December grass crumbling under our shoes, without notice, Sara opened the small gate to the pen. In an instant, what must have been a dozen black and brown Lab puppies came bursting out, along with their proud mother, her tail wagging profusely. What was once a quiet setting was now filled with puppies yapping, running, and clamoring up everyone's legs for attention.

Each of us overwhelmed as the exuberant chaos surrounded us, concerned that they may run off or someone could possibly step on one, as tiny as they were. Sara, knowing better, assured me they wouldn't leave their mother and that the scene was quite common. Taking our turns holding each of them, we then did it all over again; for a moment, we considered taking two, or maybe three? How could we choose one over the other? A lack of time now insisting a decision, we were reminded that two had already been claimed.

In all the mayhem, I noticed this black one, still unclaimed, returning to me each time he was placed back on the ground, while the others either ran off or rolled around with their brothers and sisters. The decision suddenly became easier. Sara, who was originally asking only $25, told us not to worry about the money. However, I insisted, unaware how this small investment in another being would bestow upon me the most substantial returns later, ultimately changing my outlook on life.

It appeared his mother was a Shepherd, while the father, we were told, was a Lab. I wouldn't discover until years later — by chance — that Pepper is primarily an English Labrador. His unmistakable stocky, low posture — more pronounced than the traditional lab —

Piperaceae (Pepper)

and boxed head, all characteristics. And, I could only surmise that his always pointed antenna tail was indicative a bit of Retriever.

Back inside the truck, everyone bustling with excitement and chatter, we then once again thanked Sara and made off with our new-found member of the family. Little did I know at the time, years later I'd call on Sara again for her assistance in my struggle to be reunited with Pepper. To this day we keep in touch, talking occasionally on Facebook; Sara now a grown woman, happily married and the mother of a handsome young boy.

Leaving Sara's house, I found it difficult to leave the others behind. One by one, each puppy was taken from their mother by strangers. Rather than enjoy the rousing ride back home with the others, I obsessed about those we had left behind in the carport. *Should we have taken two?* I convinced myself that it happens every day, besides, if they had not been adopted would be living on the streets, starving for food, similarly like the others. I sold this notion on myself to ease my thoughts and live in the moment with the others. Raised around dogs my entire life, as we drove, my thoughts trailed back decades earlier to my very first dog.

My early memories of Sarge, a reddish-brown Shepherd mix, were of him running around the house, almost as if he were always there even before I was born. Regretfully, before my parents had passed away, I never asked them how Sarge had come into our lives. He truly was a part of the family in every sense of the meaning. Childhood photos of Sarge on family vacations, in boats, cabins, and hiking trails remind me of the closeness we all once shared. Long before the days of doggy daycares, boarding kennels, and babysitting apps when you had no other choice than to take your pet with you, Sarge followed us everywhere, and essentially, *was* family.

Around the age of twelve, we would pack up and leave Chicago destined for Wyoming of all places, uprooting a suburban dog like Sarge, suddenly thrusting him into the surroundings of sheep, horses, cows, and various livestock. Although we weren't farmers, we did manage to find a home directly next to a sprawling, fully functioning ranch. Imagine, one day living in suburbia, each home separated by only a driveway and a manicured patch of grass, now surrounded by thousands of acres of corn, farm animals, and rolling hills of countryside with the inspiring snowcapped Big Horn Mountains in the distant view. Sarge was suddenly living in paradise; a whole new world for him to sniff, explore, and run freely. And run he did.

Driven by curiosity over his new surroundings, Sarge, who rarely left the property, uncharacteristically disappeared for an entire day. Perhaps it was our fault for not watching him, but I recall our fear; being a city dog, unfamiliar with many of the dangers of the wild, he might never find his way home again. Still missing on the second day, while outside, I spotted what appeared to be Sarge in the distance, slowly making his way down the lane.

The lane, as everyone called it, was a gravel road roughly a half mile long that led to other homesteads and farm fields. As he gradually approached, his body slouching and contorted, I ran over to greet him. His back legs dragging on the ground behind him, he was pulling his entire body with only the use of his two working front

Piperaceae (Pepper)

legs. *How far did he walk? Did he walk all night, pulling his crippled legs behind him?* My mind raced with the disturbing likelihood.

Oblivious to what had happened, nor had I noticed the bullet that entered his body, penetrating his back and into his spine. His reddish-auburn coat masking the blood around the entry point. I recall mom coming out of the house suggesting he had been shot, probably with a farmer's bullet from a .22 long rifle. Any larger caliber would have certainly killed him. The round appeared to have severed his spine; left for dead, however, miraculously our precious boy found his way home. Although he was able to survive, was now indefinitely paralyzed, and his bladder left uncontrollable. Before they could say anything, I read my parents' minds. *"Mom, we can get him some wheels,"* I pleaded. Having seen another dog suffer a similar injury, I begged for us to do the same. My dad wouldn't have any of it, while my brothers and I held no leverage in the matter.

The next morning dad and Sarge were gone, mom suggesting he had driven into town with Sarge to have him euthanized. In a moment, here one day and gone the next, someone who we had shared our lives and grown up with for years, was now gone in mere hours.

At that age, my father seemed like the strongest man on earth, the leader of the house, the definitive patriarch. But as I matured, knowing back then how tight money was, I often wondered how Sarge truly met his fate. Had he died peacefully, or had dad simply drive a mile down the lane out of sight and take care of business on his own terms? Wyoming style.

It was hard to believe my father would've been patient enough with Sarges' condition to place him in the pickup, drive eight miles into town, and then actually *pay* someone to humanely euthanize him. All this, when a .38 slug to the head could just as easily do the job. In Wyoming, everyone had guns. If not cozy on one's hip, each cab of every pickup truck likely had a mounted gun rack with a choice of rifles. My mind incessantly wondered. *Did he choose to put him down quickly with a bullet, or did he maybe take a shovel to the back of Sarge's head?* My father, a "man's man"; I question if he had at least hesitated or experienced any empathy in the end. To this day, I still don't know how Sarge's last moments were spent.

Older and a bit wiser, I now somewhat understand his reasoning. However, I have no sufferance for an animal inhumanely having its life taken away. My brother Jim heard that Sarge was chasing sheep that day, which likely resulted in catching a neighboring farmer's bullet. In Wyoming, there are two unwritten yet steadfast rules: never mess with a man's crop, and never tamper with his livestock. Neither was tolerated and many times swiftly dealt with outside the convenience of a courtroom.

Back inside the truck, the excitement was feverish as names were being tossed around for our new family member. Confessedly, I decided his name long before leaving Sara's house, however, I had to appear fair and open to all suggestions. The name of my restaurant was Peppercorns, the puppy was black, pepper is a black spice used

Piperaceae (Pepper)

in cooking; how clearer could the choice have been? While perhaps not original, Pepper would be his name.

Returning to the restaurant the very next morning, discouraged, an entire week passed before I could spend time with Pepper and get to know him. An eternity, the week dragged until finally, when everyone else was either working or in school, Monday would be ours. Perfect. Unfortunately, it had been snowing relentlessly for the past two days, with more snowfall predicted for the entirety of the day. Shrugging it off, I wasn't about to let it stand in our way, forced to endure waiting an additional week for our alone time.

Sarge and my brothers 1968?

A place I had discovered only a few months earlier, our plan was to hit the isolated woodland preserve that I frequently hiked when time allowed. Bundled up with my coffee mug in one hand and Pepper cradled in the other, we climbed into the truck. Driving in white-out conditions, the snow now blowing sideways, for the next five miles I carefully navigated the snowy, icy roads until we finally reached the entryway. A long curving road under a canopy of trees leaning as the heavy snow weighed on their branches. The road and parking lot unplowed, there was no trace of human intrusion. Once inside the preserve we were surrounded by a landscape of untouched brilliant bleached white snow and covered trees, the scene was breathtaking.

Determined, I pulled myself out of the truck with Pepper in my arms as we made our way to the path before setting him down. Exhilarating, flakes as large as quarters danced around us, the kind so large and light it took them forever to hit the ground. Lost in the deep snow, experiencing for the first time all the splendor it had to offer, Pepper immediately began running and frolicking, consumed. Pepper, no more than six weeks old, I failed to consider his underdeveloped paws and short coat in all the excitement. Despite our wishes to hike the entire mile loop, I quickly surmised based on the conditions it wasn't going to happen. While offering no initial indication as to how cold he was, Pepper was at my legs minutes after being set down, wanting to be carried.

Considering that tomorrow I'd be back at the restaurant and this moment would be only a memory, I decided to march on. Unzipping my jacket, I placed him inside, his tiny black head and wide eyes poking through the top, and together we plodded along. My knees forced high with each step, reaching over the snow; we bravely marched on to eventually finish the hilly terrain. That day, and the heartfelt memories created over the years on that very trail, would remain engraved in my mind forever.

Now part of the family, Pepper would mirror my every movement, following me everywhere. Watching T.V., he'd be on the couch next to me. If I were to go outside, he would be at the door crying to be let out. Preparing for bed each evening, intuitively he knew when it was time to head up and would be waiting on the bed covers before I could even reach the top of the staircase. Exhausted after long days at the restaurant, regardless of the hour arriving home, once he heard the hum of the garage door, would race down the stairs, welcoming me at the front door. His unmistakable antenna-like tail wagging profusely, contorting his body, and his familiar open-mouth smile.

Off to be each night, now almost 50 pounds, Pepper would insist laying at my legs each evening requiring me to sleep in a ball so that "Chub-Chub," as I started calling him, would have room to sprawl. Adjusting, yanking the covers, and fighting over space until both of us were settled in became our nightly ritual. Regardless how tired I was, never did I sleep better, and wouldn't have it any other way. Without the feeling of his body and warmth next to my legs, I found it impossible to sleep.

As the restaurant became increasingly stressful, unfairly, I would insist on bringing it back to the house, sharing my strife with everyone. While the bills were paid at home, those at the restaurant were becoming increasingly difficult to meet. Fighting to remain assertive and vigilant under pressure, I assumed even more roles at the restaurant in effort to save money. Extended hours, cutting staff, scrutinizing food costs, and combining job details; it wouldn't take long before the idea of bailing on the restaurant came up in our conversations at home. Never one to throw in the towel, I resented the notion of giving up, refusing to discuss it as an option.

Chefs, inertly proactive when faced with diversity, are daily faced with troubleshooting problems they must instinctively provide solutions. This was my livelihood and the restaurant my baby; much more than just a business, in many ways it was an expression of who I was. Was it a selfish decision insisting I march on, working all those ungodly hours? Ironically, when *successful* in business, those excruciating long days are much easier for others to understand. However, it's when your struggling and less than prolific, doubt and uncertainty settle in. Once admired, the drive and determination, then becomes labeled as indulgent and selfish. Hmm.

The ambiguity while striving to be in the black, at the same time creating balance between work and home life began driving a wedge between us. Not only had it become a challenge floating the restaurant, suddenly it had become a burden that I refused to let go of. The long hours and struggle for solvency now deemed trivial,

Piperaceae (Pepper)

regardless of how hard I worked. What was once *our* restaurant, was increasingly becoming *my* project that I stubbornly clung on to.

Back at home, our other dog who was older than Pepper painfully hyperextended his rear leg on the slick wood floors running through the house. Because of his torn ACL, coupled with being an older dog, we were faced with the option of surgery, or some —$1900 with no guarantee he would fully recover, or choose to experiment with pain medications for the duration of his sedated life.

Coupled with the torn ACL, the poor guy also began experiencing seizures causing him to rigidly lock his body up on the floor in a fetal position, drooling and trembling, sometimes unable to move for up to ten minutes. Heartbreaking and painful to watch; his helpless, stiff body on the floor, there was little to do except offer comfort during those long, excruciating moments.

Barely a year after his torn ACL he then lost the ability to control his bladder and began having uncontrolled accidents in the house. At the same time, cysts and visible fatty cells had also begun taking over his body. The difficult decision my father once had to make had now come full circle, placed upon me. I had now regained the respect I'd once lost for my father years ago; forced into making a similar decision that certainly must have burdened him when ending the life of our family dog, Sarge. One verity offering little comfort was that he technically was not my dog, therefore, the decision was not solely mine to bear.

Never really making a final determination, the decision seemed to be made on its own without having been thoroughly discussed.

Reluctantly, I surrendered in manning up, stoically unflinching to save face and mask my emotions. To live or die. Deciding what day is *best* to take the life of another being. "*Best*;" a hypocrisy. What day is best, if it were my life? I found no absolution in my rational point of view or solace knowing these decisions took place every day, hundreds or even thousands of times; I was now the one faced with that same crippling burden, unwillingly placed upon me, upon us.

Consciously taking a life while tossing around cliché phrases: "It's for the best," or, "He'll be in a better place," then wrapping a bow around it, all neat and tidy while justifying the means. Nevertheless, I was forced into finding the courage and witness what we were told would be painless. *Sure, it would be, right?* I would offer through my own experience what I was told to be bullshit.

Steadfast in my struggle to contain my emotions, we were led into the veterinarian's office with our boy in tow, the room uncomfortably silent. Earlier, we'd given him a sedative, explained by the veterinarian that it would make it easier. While he lethargically laid between us on the cold floor, the adjacent office door opened where the doctor greeted us offering his condolences as best he could. Performed a thousand times, he then walked us through what would take place during the procedure.

The first injection was to be an additional sedative to slow his breathing and prevent him from feeling pain. The second was the one that would take his life. The doctor then left the room, allowing us to share in his last breaths of life and final moments before administering the final lethal dose.

Piperaceae (Pepper)

When the doctor returned, we looked on as the final injection was administered. Now remember, we were told this was going to be painless. As the poison entered his bloodstream, his lethargic state was abruptly interrupted bringing him out of sedation. Grimacing in pain, he repeatedly opened and closed his mouth, clenching his teeth, lips quivering; struggling for his life. Clearly, the chemical had entered his heart as life was leaving him. Painless? Furious inside, staring down and statuesque in my chair, I said nothing. What seemed like five minutes of hell, he was gone in less than 30 seconds. I already knew what the answer would be if I were to question the doctor about the pain he experienced: "He felt nothing. It was only his nerves reacting."

Paralyzed by what I had witnessed, I remained seated, eyes locked hard at his body on the floor, struggling to stop tears from escaping. Ashamed of the choice I had made going along and angry for consenting to his death. Assuring us there was no longer a pulse, the doctor left us alone for one final moment to collect ourselves. I desperately wanted to leave, to scream, to take it back, the fatal decision we had made. *Should we not have done this? Who are we to have made this choice?* I couldn't have cared less that it only took 30 seconds; I decided then, to never again be an accomplice of such gross exactness. God help me if I'm ever faced with the perverse decision again should Pepper ever fall ill.

Looking back, I now understood my father and that fateful day he faced alone in taking Sarges' life. Not just my dog, he was the family dog and loved by us all. A much stronger man than I, he did it without hesitation, never allowing us to witness the pain he surely must have felt on that fateful day. I can only imagine my father having to take the family dog away from us that morning as we slept, and the difficult decision that assuredly must have weighed on him. Strange, the emotions and resentment burned on our ceilings that we harbor are many times only reconciled years, if not decades, later. Sorry it took so long, Dad. I would be reminded of some lyrics.

> Well I guess we all
> Have these feelings
> We can't leave unreconciled
> Some of them burned on our ceilings
> Some of them learned as a child
> The things that we're concealing
> Will never let us grow
> Time will do its healing
> You've got to let it go, let it go .....
> ~ Neil Peart ~

Piperaceae (Pepper)

Sarge in Wyoming

Resentful of my obsessive actions, as if it were another task to complete, another job, I planned the day *too perfectly* for when he was to be laid at rest. My exact preparedness, down to the particulars; what burial blanket was to be used, remembering a pickaxe to penetrate the ground, and what type of shovel. All loaded into the truck, I couldn't help but think while we drove to the veterinarian office, the very tools that would be used to bury him were but mere inches away from his body. The irony was disturbing. The forest trails explored hundreds of times before with the dogs offered the perfect tranquil setting that would become his final resting place.

Opening the door leading to the lobby, I carried his limp warm body wrapped in his blanket. Having witnessed this a thousand times before, knowingly, the staff at the front desk fell silent, heads turned away making busy while avoiding eye contact. Once in the parking lot, I then solemnly laid him next to the burial tools I had placed in the rear of the truck. Resenting my being forced to be the adult under such conditions, aching to be anywhere else, the silence was deafening between us while driving. Angry, the choice I had made for participating and fighting back tears, I wondered, *should I not be crying?* By not, am I coming across as cold and uncaring? Closed for my protection, risking perceived callousness, I remained committed in my restraint.

The Preserve understandably would not allow any type of burial, so we planned on doing it early Monday morning, my day off, before any hikers would be on the trail and risk being noticed. At sixty pounds, his lifeless body became awkward and cumbersome to carry; shifting and sliding in his blanket. Knowing the forest all too well, I knew of the most perfect and serene resting place. A half-mile trek into the dense forest, the location was adjacent to a large and unassuming rock, surrounded by towering oaks and maples.

The moist forest soil was easily penetrated with that first push of the shovel, and in no time, I dug to a depth of three feet, deep enough to prevent coyotes from disturbing his grave. Digging while keeping an eye out for hikers made it somewhat easier dealing with my grief by providing a diversion to focus on. A trait picked up early

Piperaceae (Pepper)

in my career on the line in the kitchen; when confronted with a crisis, I had always found it much easier to cope by losing myself in work.

With his body wrapped tightly in the blanket as his only protection, I kneeled over lowering him into the cold ground. Reaching down into the grave, I removed the blanket from his head, allowing us to see his face one last time before saying goodbye. His beautiful long white nose, eyes peacefully closed, motionless; surreal he was now gone. I then secured the blanket as my partner stood over him, staring into his grave, weeping. After shoveling the soil back in, we then scattered leaves and brush, concealing the grave.

No words or prayer spoken; we stood in silence within our own thoughts. I've since asked myself why I never said anything aloud or reached over to hold her hand during the trying heartbreak. Unaware due to the strain of the restaurant and struggling marriage, I had become void and hardened any ability of connection. I refused to acknowledge or accept that the restaurant had become a cancer. Disturbingly proud of myself for not having broken down and simultaneously angry for successfully disguising my emotions, together we stood in our guarded raw sentiments, with no one to share them with. Conditioned as men to remain strong, I'd venture to say most of us have tired of masking our strength and perceived lack of empathy. For without solicitude, are we then unmerciful?

Weeks eventually melded into months, alone, Pepper and I would still hike that same trail always taking the time to pause and either visit or glance in the direction of the boulder marking the grave. A couple years later, only 50 yards away from that very same boulder, a freak accident would take the life of a young boy when a large branch broke off a tree, falling on him as he played with his friends below. This location was also marked by a rock inscribed with signatures from the boy's family. While the forest held a tranquil and sublime element, it had developed into a menacing lure that I explore in a later chapter.

Back at the restaurant, while it was consuming my life; any time off was filled by running errands, creating menus, or catching up on things around the house that had been long-forgotten or neglected. Fending off the flames of one fire while fanning another, my demeanor had become increasingly coarse and resentful, starving for downtime and any chance for reprieve. *Where had all my friends gone? When would I see Mom again?*

Years passed in likeness, and summers brutal; looking out the restaurant window during slow times at the busy street, I'd watch convertibles with their tops down, SUVs towing boats, and people bustling while seemingly heading somewhere other than work. Feeling isolated and alone, I'd scoff at people working 40 hours a week having the audacity to complain. *Bitch please, 40 hours is a part-time job!* Religiously by the start of Tuesday I'd be yearning for Monday, and my time to spend with Pepper.

Pepper, now the only dog in the house, seemed unaware of his friend's absence. Our hikes gradually became more remote, many times brazen and reckless. We'd go mostly off trail among various preserves, forests, and fields. Wherever we could be alone is where

Piperaceae (Pepper)

we preferred, unleashing Pepper, allowing him to explore on his own terms unconfined.

We discovered old abandoned farmhouses, carcasses of animals, pining streams, grasslands, and areas seemingly untouched by man. One day we'd be chasing a herd of deer in full stride knowing we could never catch them, while the next day we'd be running through streams and mud, leaping from rocks, or trekking through knee-deep snow. Our time together became coveted, purposefully lost without phone calls, texts, or demands. I needed this, we needed this.

Arriving home, we would have cockleburs and thorns stuck to us, my clothes and his coat covered with the stench of a muddy stream or soaking wet because we refused to allow inclement weather to deter us. We were two guys doing guy things, together, we became inseparable. Regardless of where we found ourselves, Pepper instinctively knew when we neared our destination. The slowing of the vehicle, my body language when driving, or the change from suburbia to forest causing him to spin in his seat, crying uncontrollably with excitement. His head turned sideways, ears up at attention, he'd keenly stare at my left-hand fingers, waiting for the eventual flick of the turn signal. Click, click, click, the sound driving him into a frenzy as we turned into the Preserve lot. He was my partner, and I his guardian.

CHAPTER TWO

Rude Awakening

Rarely was I assured up until Sunday night if my much needed Monday off would be covered. Sporadic and refreshing when time would allow, it was during those hours that our trail outings became the highlight of our week; each excursion rarely the same. With Pepper leading by twenty yards, on occasion I'd intentionally change our course and he would shoot past me, insistent on taking up the front. Heartwarming, he would rhythmically glance back every so often, ensuring I was not only following but intently watching, as if he were a child on a swing set needing attention.

I am fully aware of those critics who state that when a dog leads, suggests they are acting "out of control" or somehow defiant. I am reminded that your dog should always be at your side, both loyal and yielding. Never have I subscribed to that notion, nor have I ever had the inclination to train my dog in such a manner. If by chance were, he to offer his paw or roll over when commanded, then all the merrier. Having nothing to do with the time necessary or cost of having your dog sculpted, I had always felt it intrusive and dominant of another life.

Why must we wrestle to control, train, cage, and ultimately master, simply for our benefit, enjoyment or exploitation? To roll over. Really? While it's true that I am Pepper's guardian, he remains a sentient being in his own right, with self-defining characteristics. What would he be, or would I even know him, had I trained him for anticipated reactions? His quirks, attitude, temperament, character, and his general spirit are what I grew to love unconditionally, without imposed measures or restrictions. Besides, his need to lead made him the protector, watching out for me, for us.

You can keep your stuffy, manicured Westminster Dog Club. Mutant dogs acting, prancing and breathing on command for reward. Countless hours of training, correcting, and forced breeding; what have they become, other than an extension of their owner? Many of the dogs bred via incest to keep the genealogy pure, and freakish breeds genetically designed by man that have become plagued with physical ailments and abnormalities.

Dogs force bred that have genetically become contorted anatomically suffering from a host of indispositions; hip dysplasia, heart disease, obesity and cancer. Breeds that were never intended to exist. "I paid $1500 for my purebred and hold the papers to prove it!" Really? More importantly, did you contribute to any efforts to curb over-breeding or champion a stoppage to the numerous kill shelters across the country? How about donating your efforts placing an end to the estimated 10,000 amoral puppy mills across America? Maybe you could have helped those unfortunate shelters on shoestring budgets unable to afford vaccinations by donating resources? Always remember; *character over pedigree and loyalty over best in show.*

The best of times was those when Pepper was out of control, wrestling on the bed, jumping over forest logs, sprinting through streams and muddy trails. By being himself, he was merely utilizing his keen ancestral skills and naturally inherited tendencies.

One needs to only observe those habits of puppies when separated from birth and the inherited habits they retain regardless never being around their siblings. How they circle and scratch the ground, making their bed before they lie down or how they instinctively mark their territory by leaving their scent to fend of intruders. Demanding Pepper always walk by my side, never chase a squirrel up a tree, or forcing him to bark on command would discourage the Pepper I came to know and love.

Countless times, our excursions would be interrupted, forcing me to race home before 6:00 p.m., thus avoiding any arguments about getting him dirty. Monitoring the time carefully, I would race Pepper up the stairs to shower, leaving a trail of muddy paw tracks from the garage to the tub. I eventually perfected this ritual by keeping a towel in the truck; our hearts both racing, I'd hurriedly wipe his paws to prevent the muddy trail, and then race him into the bath. While Labs are notorious for their excessive shedding; once in the shower, cockleburs, dirt, hair and grass would cover the shower stall. Over time, the joy of having Mondays off had little to do with getting away from the restaurant, rather about spending time with my best friend. Vowing to always protect and be there for him, my promise would soon be challenged.

On Sundays at the restaurant, I would struggle to prevent my demeanor from falling into a funk. Countless families would frequent the restaurant, their laughter erupting from each booth as they were on their way to some festival or dressed in Sunday church clothes. The countless hours coupled with the restaurant's constant need for massaging every operational hour was clearly wearing on my being.

Spending less and less time on the line, my entrepreneurial spirit reminded me that my kitchen skills were being underutilized, and the very reason I wanted to own my own restaurant. Between payroll, scheduling, marketing, menu design, the website, bookkeeping, and training; efforts to remain solvent would take precedence over cooking. Less involved in the food's preparation, I was extremely skeptical of the product escaping from my kitchen prepared by others. Perhaps micromanaging, however, my creative passion was simultaneously being stifled.

My first rude awakening in underestimating the gravity of front house operations happened rather quickly, reminding me it's not always about restaurant fare as the sole determinant of a successful operation. When purchasing the restaurant in my efforts to make a smooth transition, I found myself undecided about keeping any of the old staff around from the previous operator. My concern was the chef and hostess had developed a rapport with many of the existing clientele, making it foolish if I were to estrange them from the existing customer base. My rational decision was to give everyone a fair chance, while evaluating those who shared a similar vision and work ethic. This, regrettably, would turn out to be a huge blunder.

The long hours while no surprise when I first opened, I longed for an opportunity to break away after working for several months straight, from morning until close. Annually, every May in Chicago, takes place the largest food convention in the country. Perfect, I thought. All systems and checks in place, Monday being the slowest day of the week, what the hell, so why not?

The day of the event, like a nervous new mother leaving her newborn, I called the restaurant incessantly, checking in. Met with reassurance the restaurant had not burned down, I felt confident that I had made the right decision. After all, some of the staff were leftovers from the previous proprietor, and fully aware of operational procedures. What could possibly go wrong?

As it turned out, those *leftovers* were mistakenly a little too aware. Arriving refreshed on Tuesday after reviewing receipts from the day before, I found it had been recorded as the lowest revenue capture since I'd taken over the property. Coincidence? Theft, not of goods, but of cold, hard cash, proven by matching each ticket and questioning the cooks on what had been prepared. Each ticket that was presented to the guest was supposed to have a traceable carbon copy for the house. Unable to find the copies and match them to the prepared items, all indications were uncoincidental, you just don't *lose* several tickets by chance.

That Monday versus every other Monday since, was the lowest in covers ever reported since I had assumed ownership. While credit card transactions were in line, since one can't steal from a credit card swipe, however, the cash percentage ratios made no sense in comparison. While we move to a cashless society, never has there been a day where every customer had paid with a credit card. It just never happened.

Always suspicious, it required me to provide solid proof. From employees and customers who found unsettling humor in my suffering, they reminded me of the chef I chose not to fire. There were incriminating stories about how when he managed the property previously, he was essentially responsible for the restaurant's demise, eventually bringing it to its knees.

Upon investigating, I found the walls surrounding the office where the cash was kept were constructed from floor to drop-ceiling in height. Notice how I failed to say floor to *ceiling* in height? That space between the rafters and drop-ceiling, providing just enough space allowing a person to balance on conduit and piping, accessing through a ceiling tile. They could then squeeze over the top of the wall and down into the office. The previous owner foolishly leaving cash in the office overnight, baffled, his settled cash receipts were regularly short but never enough to cause overwhelming concern.

Rude Awakening

On a separate occasion, without any alarm in the building, one of the windows was smashed by that very same cook, staging it as an anonymous robbery. Rumor after rumor haunted me that I'd likely made a colossal mistake by not firing his ass from the start. I later found that he was the very same person who'd served time on a federal offense after forging checks.

The restaurant industry has always been a magnet for attracting transients, requiring little qualifications to flip a burger or wash dishes. Many regularly leave one job for the next, working just long enough for a single check to support their habit of choice. Regardless, I was the one closing each night, counting the drawer, and leaving last; no one had a key to the office besides myself, and I never left cash on the property. How could they possibly steal from me if I was always there yet how would I ever be allowed to have a day off?

To confirm the rumors, I examined the ceiling tiles in the office and the window rumored to have been smashed. Sure enough, the caulk line replacement and glass temperament were different from all the other windows, confirming it had in fact, been replaced. The ceiling tile also had noticeable dirty handprints and was fraying around each of its corners.

That Monday confirmed all my suspicions; the money stolen wasn't so substantial that they could take a vacation, but just enough to go undetected. This, in addition to their time on the clock, made for a nice profit if it were to continue undetected. I was being played for a chump.

A common misconception that all restaurant owners are lavishly profiting; what difference would it make if a few hundred dollars go missing? Most thieves believing, they are owed while more often convolute their reasoning; "my life is harder than yours and you were dealt the better hand," thus justifying their actions. The infectious attitude so prevalent in this nation of self-described "victims" was no secret to me, but I mistakenly overlooked it on that Monday. Most people have no idea that a large percentage of restaurants are barely hanging on, overleveraged, and for many, the average net return is merely a single percentage.

When taking over the restaurant, the very same chef who I suspected of stealing, questioned me; "why in the hell would you leave such a high paying head chef position to own your own restaurant?" I would remind him, that many people are destined to be followers, needing others to survive, unable to forge their own way, while there are those willing to lead and take chances ultimately growing, despite numerous failures. Where would we be as a people if we failed taking chances despite the odds, those doing so exemplifying the courage of that old saying, "fall down seven times and get up eight." Always, set yourself apart to avoid becoming one of the sheep in a flock.

The *sheep* people are destined to follow whenever convenient or how the wind blows. Many, self-proclaimed "victims" in life, when things fail to go their way, or when their own actions cause them to repeatedly get fired from job after job, they conveniently blame others for their misfortune. Their place of employment, always just a job, never a career nor worth any serious effort to excel or set themselves apart. Whether it be mopping the floor or being the most productive mechanic in the shop, they fail to realize it's all the same, regardless of the task.

Putting forth your best effort, knowing you gave it your all with no shortcuts is what allows for success, many entry level jobs assumed by the future CEO of the company. Mary T. Barra at the age of 18 got a job on the assembly line at General Motors, inspecting hoods and fenders, in 2014, Barra was named CEO of General Motors. Doug McMillon loaded trucks at a Wal-Mart distribution center as a teenager, at the time, he earned $6.50 an hour, now the CEO of the retail company. And of course, there is the infamous story of Bob Iger who started as a weatherman on a local ABC news station, today, he is the CEO of the Walt Disney Company.

Having mopped thousands of floors myself, there is no shame ensuring those floors shine better than anyone has mopped them before you. At the end of the day, you can hold onto your self-respect knowing you did the best you could. I've always found it's how you do, rather than what you do, that sets you apart from others regardless of the task. It's no coincidence that the spirited, roll your sleeves up and get the job done conviction, can be infectious for others to mirror those sentiments making most jobs welcome. Remember; character over pedigree.

That Tuesday struck me with a variety of emotions struggling to control. I was both angry at myself for being weak and taking a day off and frightened by the thought that I could never leave my restaurant unprotected again. While I have terminated many people throughout my career, I was now faced with having to fire three at once, all in key role positions.

Point of Sale systems are so much more important than simply entering orders. They track inventory, perform timekeeping, make fake coupons virtually impossible to use, and almost eliminate the opportunity for theft. The problem is they typically start at $5000 for a small restaurant, for only one terminal and one printer.

While Peppercorns was somewhat antiquated, we were still utilizing handwritten checks, creating an easy opportunity for thieves. Handwritten checks leaving you open to rampant theft; they also have their advantages. Let it be said: the next time you go into a restaurant and notice if handwritten checks are still in use versus a POS system, two things are happening 99% of the time. First, is there is theft taking place; the handwritten checks offering several opportunities with minimal means of tracking. Second: the owner is skimming. With the use of paper checks, the only traceable revenue is via credit card transactions, short of an audit.

If an audit were to be performed and 80% of sales were allotted to credit cards, while 20% cash, this would immediately raise a red flag. Percentages are of course changing as we move to a cashless society, however, paper ticket use remains prevalent in thousands of small mom and pop establishments across the country. In most businesses, be it retail or food, if you don't see a POS system, you can bet the owner is cooking the books. Don't believe for a second that your friendly Greek diner down the street lacks a POS system simply because they're computer illiterate.

Hardly discussed, yet common knowledge amongst both restaurant owners and the Internal Revenue Service is the no talk rule. A fine line existing between those who skim to survive and those owners blatantly defiant over the IRS. Skimming, not too much to get noticed, many fraudulent restaurant owners unwisely allow greed to interfere, ultimately getting flagged. Having witnessed this firsthand on several occasions, the IRS does, in fact, come knocking on your door with a pink sticker.

Not uncommon in my early career, when arriving for work I'd find the doors locked or literally chained shut, chains wrapped around the handles with a pink notice on the door. The IRS not known for being shy, the sticker boldly forbids anyone from entering the premises, noting that delinquent back taxes are owed, and that the property is under further investigation. A federal offense, if the property is breached, protects the IRS from the owner removing the dated, crappy, greasy kitchen equipment they assume holds value but most likely will only return pennies on the dollar at auction. The IRS doesn't want your pizza oven, it wants your money.

Commonplace among restaurant owners is the notion that the IRS rarely audits or never has enough employees. Owners emboldened to skim; most are merely fighting to avoid excessive taxation allowing them to stay open yet another month. Let's face it: if every business caught manipulating its books was forced to shutter, where would all the tax revenue eventually come from? Avoiding that pink slip on your door is never allowing either the cash or credit card transactions to exceed that unspoken benchmark. In other words, cash is king.

The Forest

CHAPTER THREE

Trial By Fire

Back in Chicago, like most teens fresh out of high school, I had this unsettling burning desire within me. Uncertain about who I was or what I was going to do with my life, my cousin Ray who had worked at a restaurant aptly titled the Bullmarket, knew the owner and managed to get me in. To this day, I still hold him accountable for introducing me to the restaurant business. While embracing the opportunity to work with food, I'd unfortunately also be introduced to the dregs, transients, alcoholics, drug users and peddlers plaguing the industry.

The pay while only $4.00 an hour, I felt was robbery on my behalf, a far cry from the meager $3.65 an hour I was earning when working during high school; besides I could eat whenever I wanted, was around music and girls, and got to play with food all day.

Dennis, who was the head chef, using the term "chef" loosely, was also the veteran pinball champion at the Bullmarket. He achieved the title because if Dennis wasn't in the kitchen, he could be found in the bar playing Ted Nugents, Wango Tango Pinball and nursing his Jack and Coke.

Sporting a scraggly, unkempt tobacco-stained beard, Dennis, could always be found with a cigarette permanently dangling from his lips; the precarious ash seemingly an inch long, ready at a moment's notice to fall onto an unsuspecting diner's plate that he was preparing. His shirt unbuttoned halfway down and nest of chest hairs protruding, gave way to a potbelly swelling under his shirtwaist.

Long before health department codes and surprise visits from inspectors, this was when anyone who could boil water was allowed to open a restaurant. My job title, which didn't exist, included any menial task wherever I was needed most. Lifting and washing bar mats, scrubbing dishes, running for ice, bussing tables, or merely cleaning the restaurant after hours, I accepted the work with open arms matched with an eagerness to learn. In exchange, I was rewarded with countless hours, minuscule wages, and consistent degradation. Arriving an hour before my shift each day, I immediately felt a sense of belonging, a buoyant energy believing that my efforts mattered in some small way. A glutton for punishment, I grabbed as many hours as they'd toss me.

Keen to my unflinching desire for abuse, it wouldn't take long before management asked me to work in the kitchen; either because one of the cooks was too drunk, coked out from the night before, or

Trial By Fire

simply because they knew I was a magnet for a steady stream of rebuke. Having found likeable characteristics in *chef* Dennis, he demonstrated how to cook virtually everything on the menu in less than an hour. And just like that, I was able to master the kitchen, literally thrown on the line with no previous experience. Now a "chef," qualified after my extensive training, I was working the meat slicer with a broken guard, cooking foods in 350° frying oil, flipping steaks over a 1500° charcoal broiler, and reaching inside 500° pizza ovens.

While Dennis was certainly not the most kempt of chefs, strange that in those early years it seemed sanitation was not a high priority. Never was anyone required to wear gloves, hair restraints, nor instructed the proper etiquette not to scratch their balls or itch their scalps whilst preparing food. It would take years before I understood what the white powder was on the floor in many kitchen storerooms. Assuming flour had been spilled onto the floor, I would learn otherwise when interrupting a colleague "fluffing" his balls with cornstarch due to excessive heat in an effort to prevent chafing.

No longer working in my street clothes, I now proudly adorned my first white chef's apron, my new position made official. Like Dennis, I too would lose my first name, replaced by the same token. Chef, and so, it was. Finding much-needed direction in my life at the time, I welcomed my new position. Before long I was tossing frozen Ms. Paul's batter-dipped fillets into the fryer, flipping frozen burgers, and cooking precut, prefabbed frozen steaks. Each plate carefully crafted and doused with a decorative and excessive dose of parsley ensuring superb culinary authenticity, the more parsley, the better. Parsley being the only biennial fresh herb we used; each dish looked as if someone had shaken a bush over each plate. We did, however, make pizzas from scratch that Dennis – ahem – "Chef" had seemingly mastered, I admit most times were mildly edible.

Out of place on the line and precariously balancing on a set of construction bricks, the double deck pizza oven was eight inches higher than necessary. *Perhaps a giant cook held the position before me?* Its flimsy legs shaking when the oven door was opened, ready to collapse at any moment; your face met with a blast of 500° intense heat each time. Hundreds of times each night, opening and closing the metal door, it would catch my forearm instantly searing my skin off. The smell of burnt skin in the air, each burn would proudly leave a brand mark, the larger, the more bragging rights, my baptism into kitchen life. To this day some 30 years later, I still carry those faint rites of passage christenings at various increments along my forearm.

After some time passed, maybe because I always showed up on time or was merely a warm body, it was ascertained that I was more valuable in the kitchen than bussing tables or lifting beer-stained bar mats. Chef, who was more and more bartending, found it easier to hide his Jack and Coke amongst the many bottles in the speed racks than behind the spice containers in the kitchen.

Between Wango Tango Pinball and making busy at the bar, Chef was rarely inside of what had become *my* kitchen. Purposefully, I worked harder and smarter so that Chef felt I was capable enough, in

Trial By Fire

my effort that I be left alone in my new domain. If he wasn't fucking one of the waitresses in the office, milling at the bar, or playing pinball, it was unlikely he would bother me inside my kitchen.

With my Ms. Paul's frozen fish squares and a tub of chopped parsley, I lived for the weekend, easily packing the house and turning over the dining room twice most evenings. The weekend pace frantic, each order was scribbled on a piece of paper in hieroglyphics and then snapped onto the spinning wheel where it was then pulled down and placed on the ticket rail.

The noise from the dishwashers, clanking plates, hood fans churning, orders being yelled out, and throbbing music from the bar all adding to the excitement. Relishing the solitude of the kitchen, however, I was surrounded by people at the same time. The urgency demanding that I perform — or no one got fed — only further fueled my adrenaline. Rewards while certainly not monetary, rather were from a feeling of satisfaction and achievement at the end of each night after feeding countless droves of the unsuspecting.

Prizing the controlled chaos of the kitchen, I longed for each busy weekend and those moments when I could peer into the packed dining room, watching everyone eating my food. Enter coffee. While always enjoying a cup in the morning, suddenly coffee had become a crutch throughout the day; without it — agitation setting in — prevented me from developing a rhythm on the line. There was also a warm and reassuring comfort knowing a cup was always within arm's reach. At the end of each night it wasn't uncommon to find on shelves or next to spices multiple half-filled, cold mugs throughout the entire kitchen. I later found out that this is a shared habit among many chefs everywhere. Either that, coke, or enough drug of choice to get through yet another crush. Perhaps, in some strange way, toiling around in the kitchen all day with a warm coffee nearby offered some semblance of home.

The Bullmarket in a short time became routine for me; seemingly, they must have been printing money with the amount of business we were doing. On nights when the restaurant was slow, the bar then compensated with its own batch of eccentrics and bizarre characters. Many nights upon completion of my shift, still underage, I would venture into the bar, and watch different live bands as my reward. Amazed, there was a regular cover artist who looked exactly like Cat Stevens, sporting his acoustic guitar and scraggly beard, note for note he consistently nailed "Moonshadow" and "Peace Train." Each night, a menagerie of ne'er-do-well alcoholics would scamper in, each having their own bizarre nicknames, yelled aloud upon scampering in: "Stick!", "Cheese!", and "Blunt!"; however, everyone oblivious their given birth names.

Then there was Stosh. *His real name?* Stosh, a migrant worker from Mexico, was truly my first real friend at the restaurant and responsible for introducing me to "kitchen Spanish," as we called it, that I would later use for the entirety of my career. His job, while it involved any menial task, in exchange was given a small stipend and a booth to sleep in every night. Like a child in a candy store every night, Stosh always had a bottle of whiskey nearby, perhaps tolerated because it was cheaper to keep the labor drunk and insensible.

Trial By Fire

Over time, compounded with the antics of Stosh, the owners often absent, and Chefs excessive drinking, I began to question my future and the solvency of the business; aimless and haphazard at best. The constant bar activity and number of covers we were doing in the dining room was always undermined by hints and whispers that the business was hanging on by a thread.

It became apparent how dire conditions at the restaurant was becoming when frequent squabbles between the two owners eventually escalated into blows. Knowing the restaurant like the back of my hand, however, I rarely ventured into the office as if it were somehow forbidden. I recall needing to speak with Chef once, cautiously opening the office door out of curiosity, it was in complete shambles. Books strewn on the desks, papers upon papers stacked, and unopened bills spread everywhere with "past due" or "final notice" stamped on the envelopes. I then noticed a white powdery substance smeared on the desk. Naïvely, I assumed it was leftover flour that Chef had smeared after leaving the line. Only years later, when I experienced a similar situation, did it all make sense. Common in many restaurants for the plenitude of cash to go right up their noses.

It wasn't long after one of several violent scuffles that the partnership finally dissolved, leaving only one owner; unfortunately, he was the one with the coke habit. Within weeks after the partnership had ended, he began using his van to purchase inventory after being blacklisted by food vendors — clear we were down to our final days. It became so dysfunctional that even Stosh, who'd been a pillar at the Bullmarket since it opened, had finally had enough and failed to return for work one day. My pay eventually became sporadic, even at the low wage of $4.30 an hour; sometimes going weeks between paychecks.

Worried the restaurant would close before I would get my money, relieved, one evening, I was finally paid a portion and now had $300 in my pocket. When arriving to the restaurant the next morning, I entered an eerie silence; the lights dimmed, and the owner and chef mulling in a booth midst serious conversation. Ushering me over, they explained that Friday would be our last day open.

The day has finally come, I thought. This can't be allowed to happen; I was having too much fun. Instructed there wasn't enough money to purchase provisions for even one more night, my visceral reaction was that I couldn't let it happen; reaching into my pocket, I pulled out the $300 they had just given me the night before, laying it on the table. *"Let's open tonight, pack this place, and make enough money to open again tomorrow!"* Initially refusing the money, they eventually accepted and Steve left to fill up the van, returning a few hours later with just enough food supplies to get us through one more night. I would have one last night to sprinkle a few more plates with parsley, in *my* kitchen.

Making just enough money each day, we survived for two weeks, driving the van to the market, until the inevitable. I never did get my money back nor see the owner again. In total, I was owed about $1500 by the time the doors were locked for good. It occurred to me that it's likely I'd been played all along. The two of them sitting earnestly in the booth that day, perfectly timed to prey on my generosity. Fortunately, I was able to get inside the closed restaurant to find Chef packing all the liquor from the bar into milk crates to take home for himself. No surprise that he would value the liquor versus any piece of equipment or other memento.

Inside the restaurant, dark and grim, the pervasive saturating smell of spilled beer, kitchen grease, and overall funk filled the air. The office door now wide open, papers were strewn throughout as if someone had ramshackle it desperate to find any misplaced cash or coke. A perverse scene; in apparent desperation, someone had even pried open each pinball machine door to retrieve the quarters. Bar glasses were either smashed or missing, while chairs were laying on their sides and tables knocked over. *What had taken place in those last hours?*

With feigned consolation, Chef said I could take items in the restaurant in exchange for my lost wages before the doors would be locked permanently. Even after all the money they owed me, I felt guilty removing the two huge, four-foot-tall amplifiers from the rafters. Those speakers and several coffee mugs would go with me out the back door. I didn't care about the money, and never truly wanted the speakers, I just wanted my kitchen back.

Years later, I discovered where Chef was working, and with a bit of curiosity felt compelled to go see him, for old times' sake. Instinctively knowing where the kitchen would be, I passed the hostess station and bar to the back of the house, where I found him behind the line once again. Several years older, he was still rocking the same scraggly beard but with hints of gray. After taking a moment to recognize me, our hellos were strained and awkward suspecting he felt ashamed or maybe uncomfortable, thinking I was after him for my money. The conversation that followed was brief while disappointing at best. A sense of pity arose watching him shuffle behind the line, quite older now, still performing the same menial tasks. Flipping frozen burgers, frying frozen fish, plunking the same shitty, frozen mozzarella sticks into a fryer.

If anything, I'd hoped to share a laugh or reminisce about those absurd experiences on the line that we shared together, the speakers that I had removed and never hooked up, and my trepidation to the sight of parsley. It never took place and for the first time, I felt betrayed. My thoughts trailed to those days alone on the line, spitting out 200 covers, while he yucked it up behind the bar drowning in his Jack and Coke. They should have paid three cooks, or at the very least returned the money I was owed in the end. Years past, it had become water under the bridge, and I was grateful for the experience, despite its misgivings.

A glutton for punishment, despite my experiences at the Bullmarket, like a vagabond, I continued to toil away in several derelict mismanaged properties hopping from one to the next. However, from each property, I was gaining experience and confidence. Working with Seafood that had never seen the inside of a freezer, with vibrant herbs and fresh spices. Foods that were surprisingly not prepackaged, pre-breaded, and precut, would arrive crisp, raw, and green for same-day use. I would experience farm-to-table cooking before it ever became a trend. When one restaurant owner surrendered his business due to either his chemical dependency or fiscal mismanagement, I would pack my knives and jump to the next establishment down the street. It didn't matter to me. There was always another restaurant where I could still get paid to experience that rush of adrenaline.

Single at the time, I was earning money, relishing the camaraderie on the line, constantly meeting new people, and reveling in the high of having customers experience my food. Watching them laugh, enjoying their meal, and pausing to reflect on a dish that I had created was always a humbling compliment. The most flattering times were when those same customers would be so taken aback by their experience, would request to meet the person behind the food. All too satisfying, I began considering whether I should enroll in culinary school to become a real chef with papers or continue haphazardly jumping from one restaurant to the next.

Burning through hours at yet another restaurant, a server noticed my compulsive coffee drinking habit offering to fill my mug over the line. That coffee eventually led us down the aisle and to the birth of our beautiful daughter Amy. No longer could I be selfishly responsible only for myself, earning money for leisure, it then became a necessity as husband and father.

Unaccustomed to my new role, my selfishness gave way to urgency, while money at one time was always plentiful when single, was now paltry. Each restaurant, seemingly operating on a shoestring, offered no stability, and little money as a cook. Did I have what it would take to be a chef responsible for his own kitchen, or should I continue struggling, floating from one defunct restaurant to the next? Striking out on my own in a new restaurant, I landed the gig by presenting their newly designed menu using my own computer at home and presenting it during the interview, knowing this would be a distinct advantage versus merely filling out an application.

Fittingly, the "Three Stooges," owners had no clear concept or direction. While making money from the bar and dance floor, the kitchen remained idle; customers couldn't care less about the food and were more interested in who they would be taking home that night from the meat rack that it was. The steaks eventually spoiled and cost of operating a kitchen became overwhelming among other cancers, shuttering "Stooges" in less than one year.

After the Three Stooges came Tikos, and then Toby's, each one more dysfunctional than the last. Each bearing an abundance of wannabe chefs that couldn't scramble an egg, absentee owners, and amoral temptations that proliferated each property. Most destined to close or change ownership in mere months or at most in a couple of years.

Days from closing yet at another restaurant, before storming out the back door, the head chef proceeded to go through the entire walk-in cooler, intentionally dispensing white pepper into each sauce, soup, and prepared food item. Rendering all product inedible, they had to essentially close the restaurant, this after many of the employees had not been paid in over a month. Taking his entire kitchen brigade with him, he introduced me to his brother, who was also a working head chef.

Formally trained, Kenny, would be my first interaction with a true chef, eventually becoming my mentor ultimately helping me choose my career direction for the next twenty-five years. Commonly working sixty-plus-hour weeks, he taught me how to truss fowl, charcuterie, butcher, break down fresh seafood, champion saucier, use of proper seasonings, master soups, perform inventories, write menus, and understand basic food cost principles. Soups were by far my favorite; the smell, layering of flavors, and the variety of fresh ingredients all brought together with the use of stocks, patience, and time, I went on to understand these principles from my close friend Kenny.

Countless days, Kenny took me off the line and had me watch him fillet a whole fresh salmon, break down and butcher a forequarter of beef, work a consommé, prepare for a buffet, or demonstrate ice carving techniques. Religiously, he'd arrive at 6 a.m. and frequently work until 11 p.m.; I admired his extreme dedication, ludicrous hours, and self-destructive lifestyle with which he succumbed to his craft with total abandon. The endless hours, grueling heat, and the urgency that each day demanded; like a drug, I wanted every bit of what he had. Little did I know at the time, but the same work ethic and determination he instilled in me would become the very foundation of many of my own life's challenges, not only in the kitchen but personally, including the travails I'd soon face with Pepper.

With my new small family in tow, I grabbed as many hours that became available, learning as much as possible. With no clear course of direction, I slowly morphed into a respectable cook, but not arrogant enough to boast chef-level status just yet. Common, I often arrived three hours before my shift began, working the line for free.

Kenny, now a close friend, was finally able to reduce his workload and rekindle his relationship with his own family. Together during the height of the restaurant's success, we'd fill up the dining room night after night, and no other time under any previous ownership was the restaurant as busy; or kitchen as solid. There was no dance floor, no traces of coke on the office desks, frozen Mrs. Paul's fish fillets, steaks pre-cut and shrunk in cryovac, and if parsley was used it was primarily as a spice. Together, we were all about churning out numbers, and our personalities had become a mirror.

Broiler was, by far, the busiest station. I was not only responsible for all items going through the two 140,000 BTU commercial Blodgett broilers, but the ovens as well. Strenuous, however welcomed, the broiler man was also responsible for pulling down every ticket and barking out each order. He was not only required to prepare, season, monitor, and plate food items from his station, but also work in symphony with the entire kitchen as each dish neared completion from all stations; fryers, sauté, garde manger, and grill. In chorus, each plate was placed in the window for the expeditor to examine one last time before leaving the kitchen.

The heat lamp wasn't going to save you if your plate was finished prematurely; at least, not here. While not a race, each cook was

Trial By Fire

aware when a plate should hit the pass and not a minute early, thus, food sits under the heat lamp. A time before political correctness, discriminatory lawsuits, and when snowflakes permeated our culture, when you would be openly scolded by the head chef and literally have the plate thrown back at you if prepared incorrectly. No place for those thin skinned, it wasn't uncommon for chefs to throw pots, threaten your job, or humiliate you in complete display of the entire kitchen staff. Yes, kitchens did exist and operate similarly to what people might see watching celebrity chef Gordon Ramsay during one of his televised, staged tirades.

Every station was in the weeds, the controlled chaos demanding the broiler man to shout out times plates were to hit the pass, instinctively knowing how long each would take to prepare. *"Fire lamb shanks, number 15!"; "Hold on number 12!"* With each chef focused, the broiler was getting the brunt of orders, sometimes thirty tickets deep. Thirty tickets meant thirty tables, with each table anywhere from two to a party of fifteen.

At times so busy, the broilers couldn't accommodate the amount of orders spitting out of the printer. I mentally sectioned off areas on each broiler tray for every steak temperature, add chicken, fish, chops, and ribs. A cup of coffee, sometimes three, always waiting within arm's-reach, each cup half-empty. Each cooks' hands and body in a blurred motion.

As business became rampant and the money flowed in, the owners decided to do a complete remodel. A total gut from top to bottom requiring months renovating. Once finished, the property was adorned with deep cherry woodwork, an elaborate double-sided curved bar, recessed lighting, elegant lighting fixtures and sconces, beautiful hanging stemware, new china, fresh carpeting, a double-sided fireplace, bay windows, and even a piano bar in the main dining room. All servers now had matching white tops with bow ties, and the menus were completely revamped. To compliment the new digs, they even splurged by bringing on a fulltime Sommelier. Everyone knew it would not have been possible without the dedication and relentless hard work that the kitchen had accomplished.

Great friends, Kenny and I had fostered a unique cadence on the line and in our personal conversations. It was a comfortable kinship that made work enjoyable, and each twelve-hour day felt as though there was never enough time getting things accomplished. Entrapped behind the windowless cinderblock walls of the kitchen, I'd occasionally change into a clean set of whites after catching up on the line, stepping out into the dining room where it was common to encounter local celebrities, newscasters, or professional athletes. Unlike many of the other dives I had slaved at previously, we weren't just flipping burgers.

Suffering from chef-relatedness syndrome, between the culinary classes that were consuming my time and the arduous work schedule, it wasn't long before my marriage began to suffer. By striving to become a chef and earn a better wage, I had ironically alienated those closest to me. Failing to achieve that elusive balance while juggling a career in food with a family, commonly haunts chefs their entire work lives. The industry littered with a landscape of divorced, once

Trial By Fire

well-intentioned, compulsive, and driven personalities unable to sustain the demands of both family and career.

Often wrapping up after midnight, I began hanging out with some of the cooks, avoiding the cold and emotionless conditions at home. Celebratory for a job well done in turning over the dining room twice with ease, we ventured out to find our own trouble. While alcohol was never our vice, we found other forms of amusement.

Lifting one of the server's cars, we would angle it so that both the front and rear were in-between the corner of a building, hiding in the distance and watching her unable to maneuver. Other times we climbed expressway billboards, hanging out high above on the catwalks talking for hours. Always out for a good time, we'd drive around in my old Ford Granada on frontage roads while one steered and others would dangerously surf on the hood at 40 mph. While reckless, we were never destructive or harmful to anyone besides ourselves.

Ever more audacious, after our shift on a slow Halloween night, decided we would visit Resurrection Mary cemetery and scale the graveyard fence. Folklore has it that Mary Bregovy was killed in a traffic accident in 1934 in her favorite white dress after a dance, and every few years she is spotted hitchhiking, only to disappear back into the graveyard where she was buried, once let out by the unsuspecting drivers. An infamous graveyard noted not only for being haunted, but also for the beating's trespassers would face once caught. So popular on Halloween, that the groundskeepers were forced into hiring security detail specifically for that night alone.

Trespassers regularly dressed in camouflage gear making it a ceremonious event, running over graves, between trees, and mausoleums. Others would drunkenly get caught on the spiked fence trying to get inside or be forced to hide behind tombstones. Left beaten on one of the cemetery roads, making headlines, one year a trespasser was found the next morning by police clinging to life. Security would never claim responsibility, but everyone knew. Apparently, trespassing was consequential, and security was in no mood to play around on Halloween.

In the darkness, I could faintly see figures dodging and hiding to avoid being caught, their howling and laughter echoing their location. Tommy, a cook I worked with and the mastermind behind our soiree, happened to also be a little slow on foot. Caught in the high beams of a security vehicle, he found himself unable to outrun the lights trailing his moves. Running and ducking between grave markers — security on his tail — he caught the edge of a marble slab with his leg breaking his right femur bone in two places.

Grimacing and balled up in a fetal position behind the tombstone, I found him there shivering, his leg contorted and clearly broken. Undetected by security, I slung Tommy's arm over my shoulder and together we scrambled across the cemetery to the seven-foot wrought iron fence. I then hoisted him over, protecting him from being stabbed by the large spikes on top. We spent that entire night at the hospital where his leg was reset and placed into a cast. Arriving home with no sleep, I had only two hours before I had to be back at work on the line.

Trial By Fire

Part of maintaining a sanitary kitchen, all fresh chicken had to be iced over a drain pan to avoid sitting in its own foul juices. Failing to change the water on a regular basis causes an unmistakable stench to develop. On more than one occasion, I would half-fill a five-gallon bucket with the juice, hiding it out of sight behind a walk-in cooler. Forgetting about the fermenting frap, I was surprised to find it still hidden and untouched after two weeks.

Devising a plan, I ventured down to the basement kitchen where Latrucha, a cook on prep detail, happened to be working. He was to be my first victim. Taking the five-gallon bucket of rancid liquid salmonella, I snuck up behind him and stirred the concoction. The rank odor slowly rising to greet Latrucha's nose, with one unmistakable whiff he ran to a nearby prep-sink, his head inside ready to vomit. I stood there, hunched over from hysterical laughter. The stench so potent that it had climbed the staircase as the kitchen hoods pulled the odor upwards, quickly followed by loud eruptions from the staff, servers gagging, cooks laughing, and midst the turmoil I heard Kenny yell, "Paul must be here with his fucking chicken juice!" The smell so offensive I was worried if I'd overdone it and released it into the dining room full of customers.

Everyone was content it seemed, we were all thriving in a functioning, profitable restaurant, and our paper checks not turning into rubber. For the first time, I was finally comfortable knowing I held a job that wouldn't end with an IRS seizure sticker on the window, or chains placed on the doors.

CHAPTER FOUR

The Forest

Settled back into somewhat discernible regularity, the daily operations at Peppercorns, would never be considered boring nor without challenge. Now open a few years and having gotten my feet wet in my new role as chef-owner, it was consuming more of my time than ever and in constant need of perpetual massaging, like a child that never grows old. Even at home on my Mondays off, my time was primarily spent on the computer working, with Pepper perched on the couch next to me. If out, more often it would be to Kinkos making copies of menus or shopping for restaurant supplies; Pepper sitting patiently in the passenger seat, staring out the window waiting for my return. If not working on restaurant projects at home, any spare time was consumed with household tasks that had long been neglected. Subconsciously, I had become automated, losing my identity to the restaurant and all it required.

When managing to schedule a Monday off, regardless of how preoccupied, I religiously kept an eye out for that sacred three o'clock hour, refusing any intrusion during *our* time. Rarely working out at the gym anymore and having alienated my friends, I came to accept it as part of the sacrifice in addition to the constant hours. Those life experiences and moments people inherently take for granted were but a distant memory for me. Yes, it was our choice to open a restaurant, but hardly my choice to go it alone all those years.

During what time we had before dusk, the next couple of hours on the trail would be ours alone; an abundance of paths all within five miles of the house to hike and explore. Routinely, Pepper would settle into the passenger seat for the ride, instinctively looking for the towering trees in the distance with his head out the window, sniffing profusely for the distinctive smell of lush forest vegetation.

Signaling that we had arrived, the Click, click, click sound when flipping the turn signal, would drive him into a frenzy, circling and crying in his seat, charged with excitement. The winding forest drive was enveloped by a cascading canopy of trees so thick it darkened the sky, leading us to the trail heads that forked in multiple directions to choose from. Our best times, however, were off the path, ostensibly exploring where no one had set foot before.

In the spring, not found on any trail and hidden hundreds of yards tucked out of view, few people knew of the endless rolling hills of

The Forest

bluebells. They took my breath away the first time I happened upon them. Acres upon acres of undisturbed, bluish-purple bell-shaped flowers mother nature had concealed from view, not to be disturbed; their brief, elusive moment during the spring when in full bloom. Pepper, always leading and slightly shorter than the perennials, would be lost had it not been for the shaking flower bulbs consuming him as we carefully navigated through the masterpiece. The scene was both breathtaking and amusing at the same time causing me to reflect how we allow ourselves to live in a pool whilst forgetting about the Sea.

We came upon dried up streams, no larger than puddles, with dozens of fish squirming and fighting to survive. As if he understood, Pepper, crouched over and scratching at the dirt, would watch intently as I scooped as many as possible into an old milk jug, bringing them to a larger pond in an effort they survive. Regularly, we would stumble across carcasses of various animals that had succumbed to death for various reasons, be it age, the elements, or injury. On other occasions, we'd witness herds of mule deer grazing off the forest bed in the distance, their bodies shrouded in a haze of mist from over the lush forest vegetation; I would stare in awe at the magnificence.

On sunny days, penetrating the highest of trees, streams of brilliant rainbow light-refractions filled with pigments and particles of dust danced in the radiance from 100 feet up. Autumn trees that were undoubtedly a century old, and as round and broad as a car at their trunk, with curvatures and deep bark crevices inches deep. I found myself mesmerized by those most mundane observations, consumed with the verity of where my life was at that moment.

Many moments and events I had fortuitously taken for granted or never given a second thought; it now seemed time was no longer on my side. Almost as if I was imprisoned for years, only to be released for two hours on Monday, cramming in a sensory overload of thoughts and moments to experience those things that previously had never mattered. This was our moment, our place, and I couldn't expect anyone to understand or share in its profound allure. I would, however, inadvertently find that the forest also held a menacing, darker side that played upon my emotional vulnerability.

Peppercorns, a purposeful acquisition for several reasons, was chosen amongst several distressed restaurants I surveyed before assuming ownership. A troubled property battling mismanagement and extreme pilferage, there was ample room abound for effortless improvement and opportunity. Directly across the street stood three churches, all part of a small town known for having the most congregations of all counties in the state. This meant diners, primarily *many* Sunday diners.

Never for a moment did I take the previous owner's books seriously about the numbers he claimed to have been churning out before purchasing the restaurant. Armed with my morning thermos of coffee, determined, I'd inconspicuously stake out in my car next to the restaurant and watch the in-and-out foot traffic for hours, counting each head, preferring my own means determining the restaurants solvency. On occasion, I'd venture inside – trying not to

The Forest

arouse suspicion – to have a cup of coffee, taste the food, and observe the staff. The flavoring of the food was unimportant to me since word had already spread that the food left much to be desired; Yelp reviews had trashed the property, and rumors were circulating that the restaurant was weeks away from becoming a statistic. Perfect, I thought. Having already amassed a track-record of taking over distressed properties and turning them around, I would welcome the challenge.

The takeover was relatively painless; however, I found it taxing to understand the pre-existing clientele. Menu development and selections of what to offer rapidly became a thorn in my side when designing each menu. Paralyzed between the stark contrast of what I preferred to serve — leaving room for culinary creativity — versus what the neighborhood palate had grown accustomed. Looking back over that first year, I realize now my largest fault was transitioning with hesitation from what the restaurant was previously, into what I had envisioned it could be.

The first menu, while met with query and rejection from many of the regulars, also managed to capture a new audience and create a buzz about the *new* restaurant in town. Overall, it became a hard sell since frozen mozzarella sticks, chicken tenders, fatty 70%-lean frozen burgers, and breaded poppers were all the norm in the plentitude of sameness at each of the restaurants in the area. The food was all crap leaving no imagination to any culinary creativity. Arriving full circle, the existing clientele had grown accustomed to eating those foods reminiscent of my days back at the Bullmarket. All that was needed was a bucket of parsley to blanket each plate.

The struggle of transitioning became how to avoid alienating the existing paying customers while encouraging a shrewder, welcoming audience, eager to explore their palates. Those customers dining on meatloaf were hard sells getting them to open their wallets wider for filet mignon, in addition, purging those customers who'd nurse the same cup of coffee for three hours was killing me. While I welcomed each customer, their bottomless coffee cups meant endless hours of poured coffee and many times never ordering food. I refused the stigma of being just another coffee shop down the street.

Peppercorns would bleed cash for months in its effort to find its place. It became excruciating having to raise prices in exchange for higher quality food; the backlash from customers experienced verbally and through eventual attrition. Many times, I questioned whether it may have been wiser to perform a build-out rather than take over an existing operation, thus acquiring all the previous owner's baggage and clienteles preconceived assumptions.

Forced to retreat in pricing, I attempted mirroring those restaurants in proximity, while offering a more vibrant food selection. In the end to remain solvent, I would be forced to sacrifice those customers who were previously loyal while attracting those more discernible. It required time, effective marketing, an open wallet on my end, and the patience to float the business before finally hitting stride.

The Forest

Thousands of dollars spent on remodeling, new menus, and upgrades, I foolishly discovered that making customers line up at the door wasn't as simple as me going into the kitchen. People wanted to feel welcomed by the owner, to experience that genuine feeling of community that would keep them coming back. However, my expertise was always drawn to the demands of the kitchen. It became insufferable watching impermissible plates leave the pass when I was working the front. My struggle flamed by those needs of the customer, versus where I was needed most, in the back — overseeing kitchen operations. Meeting and greeting customers all day while resigning my kitchen to another chef was psychologically killing me; something I was later forced to overcome if Peppercorns was to survive.

During those most crucial early years, when not dealing with managerial issues, budgetary concerns remained an incessant burden. Compressors seized almost monthly in one of several refrigeration units and the demand of meeting weekly payroll, combined with the struggle of keeping vendors current remained constant. Maintaining a comfortable climate in the restaurant on hot days became a constant battle. My landlord would always skirt the issue as to who would foot the bill for a new $10,000 HVAC unit and the crane operator required to set in place.

For each repair in the restaurant, I found myself jumping from one technician to the next, each one more dishonest than the last. Each time a call was placed, I was down $150 before they even walked in the door "travel time," they'd say. Like clockwork, breakdowns happened at the worst possible times, either when the restaurant was full, or on weekends when repair costs would double. Peppercorns would continually bleed cash, while one week could do our best numbers, it would then be wiped out by a $1000 HVAC issue, or $800 faulty piece of equipment, many times simultaneously.

Before long, I quickly learned how to troubleshoot most equipment repairs myself. I could swap out a compressor, install a thermocouple connector, and most times diagnose problems before having to call out a technician. Plumbing issues, carpet cleaning services, and other routine maintenance demands, I would purposely call each contractor from my cell phone, concealing my location. Early on I learned to never call from the restaurant landline, giving away the identity as a business. The common assumption, that if you owned a business, must certainly have accumulated wealth, and inexplicably rates would rise.

I would instruct the carpet cleaner, *"The carpet is fifty feet by twenty-five feet,"* when asking for a quote. The response was usually met with surprise about how big a room I had in my house. Strange how the same plumbing issues in a restaurant are four times as costly as those in a home. Rates would either skyrocket, or unnecessary repairs mysteriously created. Similar to taking your car in for an oil change that should cost $25 but leaving with a $600 repair bill. On countless occasions, technicians would quote a job, say for $600 when they arrived, then agree to do it for $300 after haggling; clearly most were con artists, doubling their price for those gullible who never questioned their bill.

The Forest

Back at home, I found it impossible to speak freely about the woes of the business or having lost my identity due to the crushing demands of the restaurant. I would be reminded each time that it was my choice to open a restaurant. Reflecting, the experience reminds me of an old saying I can only loosely paraphrase: "It's when you are suffering that you discover who is truly by your side, willing to work hard and remain committed." Had I successfully opened a second or third location, I'd likely have received an endless readiness of support and encouragement, however, when floundering and merely attempting to keep my head above water, I was left to drown.

To be fair, the restaurant was on my mind constantly, affecting my home life and who I'd allowed myself to become. Even when dining out, I'd obsessively scrutinize and critique the food, ambiance of the restaurant, and even the execution by the staff. How attentive were the servers? How clean were the bathrooms? What type of stemware were they using? I would take any opportunity to leave the table looking for the pass, hoping to catch a glimpse of what was taking place in the kitchen. While the restaurant had taken away the life I had known, strangely, I began to prefer it many ways.

Working with someone having no experience in hospitality or little inner desire to please by serving, is akin to an accountant who has no interest in math. The best employees, who truly appreciate serving others, are those who inherently have a tendency and desire in pleasing people. Unfortunately, most times this skill cannot be taught. Those holding the proclivity and skillset, once bitten by the industry bug, either remain in hospitality for life, or tend to surround themselves with people having some need that can be satisfied with either a service or product.

My best dinner parties or family engagements were those when I was rushing around, plating, opening ovens, whisking food, pouring drinks, or meticulously setting a table. "Sit down, sit down," everyone would profess, "you're working too hard!" More often, I found that working hard is much more enjoyable when expressing oneself with food; the common denominator at every kitchen table, overlapping all cultures. The sustenance, nourishment, and the daily bread we share with friends and family. How it's prepared and presented, and how Grandma's recipes are passed down for generations, her secret ingredient, and those cherished moments, stories told time and again at the dinner table over food. *Show me to the kitchen!*

On Mondays during my reprieve, exhausted and now years into the thick of it, the restaurant was increasingly wearing on my well-being. Aggrieved, I was becoming more and more anxious, struggling to keep the restaurant afloat. Even the forest, once offering the solitude to decompress, had emotionally become overwhelming with its glaring tranquility; deluging my senses.

Alone with Pepper when hiking, we'd come across stray dogs that had either gotten lost or were intentionally dumped left to fend for themselves. Many of the dogs so thin you couldn't help but notice the outline of their protruding ribs and concave stomach. It would take days for those sobering images playing on a loop in my head to fade.

The Forest

Every occasion involved coaxing the shaken, starving dog into my truck, then taking it home despite the inevitable arguments that would follow. Years earlier, I learned to always carry dry dog food in my truck, so I'd be prepared for such predicaments. Briefly, I'd welcome them into my home, feeding and bathing them myself. I'd then nurse them for a day or two until I worked up the strength finding a local no-kill shelter.

Determined in the beginning, I would set out to find their owners, unwilling to take the chance that they might never get adopted. I'd load Pepper and stray into the truck, heading out to hit as many farms as possible in the area. We'd go from house to house, knocking on each door, but in the end, no one would ever claim them, and off to the shelter I would go with yet another misplaced dog.

On a separate occasion we came across a deceased poodle, its body intact and the collar still around his neck, not yet ravaged by coyotes. Removing the collar, I found a first and last name inscribed on the tag. Taking only three calls to local veterinarian offices to successfully locate the owner, my intention was to provide the owner some peace of mind knowing their dog had finally been found, and that they could perhaps provide it with a proper burial.

The vet informed me that the owner had already notified them that the dog had died, and then terminated their account. I questioned, *"so their beloved dog dies, and they choose to dispose of it like trash, exposed on the cold ground, left as food for wild animals? Seriously, with his collar still on him?"* I couldn't help but imagine how the poor dog must have been treated when alive. The only conclusion I could surmise that would pacify my obsessive thoughts, was that the cold February ground might have been too hard for a shovel to penetrate the soil, thus preventing them from completing a proper burial.

On a further hike, we stumbled upon a sizeable, rotting oak tree that had fallen over onto some nearby saplings. The young trees were bent so far over that their highest leaves were touching the ground, looking as if the trunk were ready to snap any minute. Compelled to save them, I chopped away at the dead maple to free the younger trees.

During a separate incident Pepper would come face to face with an elderly buck, frightened and unflinching as he stared Pepper down. The Buck nursing his hind leg, I could clearly see that it was broken. Unable to keep up, the larger herd had moved on leaving him behind. Left to die and unable to run from Pepper or forage for food, he eventually would succumb to a cold, lonely, and painful death. My mind trailed off to all the carcasses and antlers we came across, wondering if they too had suffered a similar fate.

Surrounded by a sea of trees, the three of us alone, I found myself struggling to understand who decides the providence and where is the mercy for those unable to fend for themselves; my mind lost to conjecture. Pepper and I watched the old buck, offering our goodbye, respectfully leaving him to die on his own terms. I was unable to muster the courage to contact forest officials, knowing all too well they would destroy him.

The Forest

The forest, in all its beauty and inviting solitude, suddenly became perverse and malicious, placing my faith in question. Hundreds of people would turn out for a memorial in that very same Preserve when a freak accident made headlines when a large branch silently fell to claim the life of a young boy as he played underneath an unsuspecting diseased tree. The area now blanketed with the mulched remains of those trees reduced to stumps after being met with chainsaws. A painted rock now marks the spot; all the family members names inscribed, offering their goodbyes to their son and brother.

I couldn't understand why that rock affected me so much at the time. I never met the young boy, but somehow the rock seemed a part of me and the forest that had taken his life. Symbolically, while my marriage was in question and the restaurant barely hanging on, the little time I had with Pepper and the forest was all that I looked forward to. While the forest covered thousands of acres, ironically both the boulder from our dog's burial plot and the young boy's rock were only 50 yards apart. Those same hallowed forest grounds we'd gone to escape had somehow now become toxic.

The perversion and remarkable beauty of the preserve is reminiscent of the Aokigahara forest in Japan, also known as the "Suicide Forest." Flanking Mount Fuji, several abandoned cars are regularly found parked at the trailheads each year, belonging to those lost souls who entered the forest, only never to leave. The beauty of Aokigahara, while both breathtaking and overwhelmingly seductive, emits a tranquil lure allowing for one's mind to become distorted and lost. Thousands to date have tragically taken their own lives in the peaceful solitude.

The boys rock in the Forest

One day as we ventured over hills and down ravines looking for our familiar heard of mule deer, we abruptly arrived at an appalling site: acre upon acre of the forest trees we had come to know were mercilessly met with chain saws, reduced to mere stumps. The formerly once thriving green oaks, red maples, ornamental elms, and scentful spruce trees, had all been reduced into mulch, as far as the eye could see. A striking, incomprehensible site stretching beyond the horizon. Imagine being unable to see through a forest filled, countless thousands of beautiful trees of every kind and size, only to one day arrive at the same location to find that same magnificence reduced to nothingness.

The Forest

That was the only time I would call the Forest Preserve County offices. Explained to me was the concept of "controlled culling," when older trees are sacrificed and cut down making way for younger seedlings. I couldn't help but correlate this to animal shelters, where humans decidedly play God by determining the fate of those "less fortunate," and like those trees, are purged in achieving *tolerable* numbers.

Many times, I questioned what had become of our relationship with that very same forest. The same place where Pepper took his first steps while wrestling in the blanketed deep snow, our first hike together, and where we'd come for retreat.

Compelled, I was left to question my faith. I thought of those weakened fish left alone to die in an evaporating, muddy puddle, so shallow they were forced to swim on their sides for survival. The maimed buck, abandoned by the herd he once belonged to his entire life, suddenly left alone to endure a slow and agonizing death. Dogs that were either lost or abandoned, left to wander for days and nights, too unskilled to forage for food, their strength and life slipping away with each passing day. Trees, once towering above the forest bed taking decades to reach maturity, ruthlessly chopped down to make way for those deemed more suited for survival. A young boy's life, not even 16, his life snatched in an instant by a falling tree branch as he innocently played beneath. All this next to an unassuming boulder where a dog was laid to rest, his life cut short by an unfortunate injury that would ultimately give reason for his early death.

Struck by an epiphany, I questioned, how does one maintain faith when their unprotected eyes witness those same virtuous, harmless, oblivious creatures are painfully left to suffer or die alone? Without faith, perhaps it should at least be bestowed upon us the basic harmony allowing us to cope and reason with our shortsightedness, no? How are we, those the ability to utilize logic, to maintain faith whilst unknowing?

On the trail in the forest

CHAPTER FIVE

On The Line

It was supposed to be a typical slow Monday, with only three of us scheduled to work the line that evening, one calling in sick, which ordinarily wouldn't have been an issue. Two of us could certainly manage almost any Monday night alone. Kenny was already gone for the day, and I was doing my usual mise en place on the line, coffee by my side. Stocking coolers, preparing the daily specials, filleting fish and butchering steak portions, reducing sauces, and all the basic preparation that would allow the kitchen to complete each plate before leaving the pass. Most chefs will agree, the most vital task in any successful kitchen is not the execution, but the prep preceding the performance.

Frequently checking the clock, estimating how much time I had before tickets would begin coming in, it occurred to me that my third cook hadn't yet arrived, now over one hour late. In this transient-populated business of low pay, long hours, little appreciation, and tremendous stress, it wasn't unusual to lose a cook once a month.

Countless daydreamers enter the business after graduation with expectations of being the next Cake Boss, Joel Robuchon, Gordon Ramsey, or of having their own TV show after serving only two months on the line. Culinary schools are notorious for churning out wannabe Iron Chefs or Food Network stars popularized on television. Ask almost any apprentice entering the field; naive, most expect to be an executive chef merely with just their graduation papers in hand and absolutely no practical experience.

Any seasoned chef would agree that before enrolling in any formal culinary training, one should postpone school and work the line for at least six months. Slog through those twelve-hour days, torn relationships, late nights, weekends and holidays. All for meager wages, and the experience of being reduced and humiliated by your superiors. If you survive, and through it all still manage to catch the bug, perhaps then you may want to consider a formal education.

Arguably, that same piece of paper, despite its official distinction, means very little when compared to actual line experience. Discussing with Food Network chef and host, Tyler Florence, he agreed: "Grab your knives and go from restaurant to restaurant apprenticing with the best, while at the same time paying your dues."

On The Line

Many prominent chefs interestingly never even graduated from culinary school. Charlie Trotter, controversially one of the most celebrated American chefs, went on to graduate with a degree in Political History. His story famous among peers for dropping out of culinary school only after a couple of semesters. He later immersed himself in countless cookbooks, religiously reading, practicing, and preparing thousands of recipes from those pages. Dining out whenever possible, he would also stage at numerous properties, leaving each after a few months' time once exhausting what each kitchen had to offer.

Grant Achatz, of the iconic Michelin three-star ranked Alinea, located in Chicago, graduated culinary school, however, received most of his experience working under world-renowned chef Thomas Keller at The French Laundry in Napa Valley. Grant personally wrote letter upon letter to Keller, pestering him for an opportunity to stage at the exclusive property. After around his twentieth attempt, Grant got his attention, packed up his knives, and headed to wine country where he'd eventually become the best of friends with his mentor, Keller.

Formal training, while lauded, doesn't secure an executive chef role nor guarantee the stamina required to endure all the bullshit that'll be thrown at you. Even once in the trenches hardly matters; one day, you could have flawlessly pulled off 200 covers, twelve courses each. The next day — and rightfully so — those new patrons in your restaurant couldn't care less about your previous night's accomplishments. Perpetual, each day offers a steady stream of famished customers, never allowing a chef to rest on their laurels.

My third cook a no-show, knowing I was going to be alone; a judgment call would have to be made. Now 5:00pm, the printer was already spitting out tickets as early diners began arriving. Too late to call Kenny for backup, I chose to go it alone. Mondays are always slow, or so I told myself.

Between tickets, I raced setting up the other stations typically manned by three other cooks. Downing another coffee, I meticulously loaded up on sauté — hands-down the most demanding position on the line. The amount of time and detail babysitting each pan, turning, basting, adjusting flames, whisking over twelve burners, two salamanders, and two Vulcan ovens, was enough even for two sous chefs. Fry station? Fuck it! You throw whatever you're cooking down into the basket, giving you two to three minutes before being forced to return, easy! The broilers, charcoal-broiler, and overhead ovens could also be just as easy if there wasn't to many tickets at one time, however, I still had to stock the cooler drawers.

Pissed off, early diners were already demanding my attention, preventing me from thoroughly prepping each station. 6:00pm, and I was now working six tickets. To be clear: six tickets, if all are four tops, is twenty-four bodies. *I've got this.* Just keep your head down, avoid any confrontations with the wait-staff, and eliminate your hold time on each ticket, getting plates out as fast as possible.

A "hold" on a ticket can be for a variety of reasons. Typically, it's when one or several items can be prepared with relative ease, or without very much preparation time involved, and can be saved for last when all foods arrive simultaneously.

Also, when a server puts the order in too early, the kitchen gives the table more time to finish its previous course, thus pacing the diner.

If fired too quickly, diners are then presented with the next course without having finished the one before them; often when the customer becomes irritated having to set one plate aside making room for the next. An amateur mistake and overlooked etiquette rule, it seems today is much more tolerated. Purposely done in many cases for turnover, to subtly encourage you out of your seat making way for the next paying customer. A stunt of this proportion in finer haute establishments, the cook would be openly humiliated amongst his peers or placed back on lowly grunt detail.

Despite my efforts staying out of the weeds, the printer was relentless as it continued to spit out table after table. *How can this be a Monday?* Feeling more like a Saturday night, I sectioned off the broiler with a variety of steaks, including filets, New York's, and a dozen other items. Back on sauté, all the burners were lit, every bluish-white flame hissing and occupied by simmering saucepans or ten-inch fry pans. On fryers, each was bubbling with a combination of batter-dipped haddock, coconut shrimp, chicken, and pommes frites.

The line, some 40-feet in length, forced me to sprint from one end to the other grappling with each station; from fryers to sauté, sauté to broiler, and then back to fryers. Turning and seasoning steaks, raising and lowering items into fryers, babysitting sauté, all the while pulling tickets and placing plates in the window.

With the simple stroke of a slicing knife and drizzle of Au Ju, roast prime rib was the easiest of entrées to prepare. Ironically, both roasts sat idly in a warming box untouched.

Sauté, ever the most formidable, insisted that you repeatedly mess up your fingers with flour and seasonings, leaving the line unattended each time to wash your hands. Next in line, of course, was the fry station. Food trends at the time was anything "batter dipped." Beer batter, pakora batter, tempura batter; at the time it was the envy of everyone's palate wreaking havoc on kitchen fryers across America in every restaurant. The glutinous mixtures caking your hands with each dunk and then into the fryer, each night the grease from the fryers would have to be changed after the batter would destroy the once clear oil.

Eerily silent, the only noise coming from the line for the next two hours was the humming of hood fans, the hissing broiler flames, unabating printers, pans hitting the burners, and the unmistakable tapping sound of my metal tongs opening and closing. With my back facing away from the pass, I'd hear click, click, click, as ticket after ticket spilled out

Counterproductive, there was no yelling, throwing pans, or tantrums. Forced to remain focused, in the back of my mind, I briefly considered a last resort option; that the front of the house not allow any additional customers to be seated, essentially, closing the

On The Line

doors. Unheard of, I shrugged it off. There was no way I'd concede; besides, I was strangely loving every minute.

Each ticket another table, adding more to the total amount of covers, I was confident was the most in my career done alone. Subconsciously, I knew I could've instructed the FOH to call Kenny or another cook, however, I welcomed the opportunity while pushing my limits.

Now 9:00pm, tickets slowing, the hours passed like minutes. The hostess, busboys, servers, and dishwashers, all busy walking through the kitchen, glanced my way in disbelief. So busy that evening, that it required the hostess to work the floor taking orders in addition to the regular wait-staff. I couldn't wait for the end of the shift, not because I wanted it to be over, rather I desperately wanted to calculate the total number of covers I'd prepared. I had to know.

Yes, yes, yes to all the skeptical chefs out there. I did cheat by preparing many of the sauces prior to getting slammed, holding them in the steam table. I had no choice. If I hadn't, that night's service would not have been able to accomplish. The total that evening: 175 covers. The most plated I had ever completed alone off a full menu.

The Bullmarket and all the other shit restaurants before no longer mattered. Plunking down pre-fabbed frozen fish into a fryer, steaks that had been thawed, and tossing frozen chicken wings remain far from any required culinary acumen. I was on top of the world, however, subconsciously knew, that Kenny was going to be pissed.

It's always interesting, humorous even, discussing with acquaintances a dinner party or holiday meal they are planning for;

say, Thanksgiving or Christmas. Listening to them stress about three or even thirty people over for turkey and side dishes, even though many dinner engagements are typically served buffet or potluck. If well organized, should be relatively easy, even for a novice. It's disconcerting, however; the number of people who still insist on rising at 3:00am, in a panic, racing to get the bird in the oven, because, well, Grandma always did it that way. Inevitably everyone always seems surprised, offering the same sentiments year after year: "the turkey seemed a little dry this year." *You think?* If you're eating at 2:00pm and you put the turkey in the oven at 3:00am, the turkey was not only cooked seven hours longer than necessary, but you could have gotten additional sleep as well.

Grandma was wrong, sorry. The next time you prepare a Thanksgiving dinner, remove the legs and wings, cooking them separately. Since they finish cooking long before the breast meat is done, not only will all the meat be moist, but easier to slice, and best of all, you won't have to lose any sleep. Once complete, the breast on a large platter surrounded by its parts and trimmings makes for a beautiful warming table display. Additionally, you won't be subject to any rude comments from your uncle about how dry the turkey was as he nurses his fifth "eggnog."

The service had finally ended for the night, and the line was in remarkably great shape. No flour spilled everywhere, stacks of dirty plates, grease on the floor, or noticeable spills on the stainless counters and cutting boards. I'd been mentored long ago to "clean as you go," each time you finish, you wipe. Finish a plate, you wipe the rim. Spill batter on the fryer, you wipe.

All too often, commercial kitchens employ slobs working the line, spitting out plate after plate but failing to clean as they go. The kitchen viewed as their playground; they are content working in filth for the greater good of feeding the masses. If left unquestioned, the grime begins affecting each successive plate, thus slowing down the line. Ultimately, it has less to do with the plate and more to do with maintaining respect for each station and all you do. I find it excruciating to work with the lazy or those who mistreat the kitchen.

All too many chefs assume that just because they are intently working, hammering out numbers, are not accountable for their environment. A lack of respect for their station, similarly many times they also fail to have a sincere interest in the food they serve. Failure to care for your station and the lack of enthusiasm for each plate fosters a lack of respect for each customer. Always avoid hiring or working with these types like the plague.

It's 9:00am, and the phone rings. Kenny on the other end demanding, "What the fuck happened last night?" For a moment I was silent, and immediately on defense. Rarely did Kenny call me before my shift. My mind raced; *did I leave a fryer on or had I left the prime rib in the holding oven all night?* However, in the back of my mind, I was waiting to get my ass chewed out for not calling any backup the previous night. *"I got hit all at once, so I couldn't leave the line to make the call for backup."* He knew it was bullshit, I could have easily told a waitress or manager to get someone in.

Instead, I put my pride first wanting to test my boundaries, eager to know how far I could push myself. Kenny, having that same determination and drive himself, didn't require much convincing.

Arriving for work that day, I was greeted by long stares, a mixture of disbelief, and handshakes from the owners. In all my career, I would never plate those kinds of numbers alone again. Looking back now, it was a stupid mistake that only fed my ego, risking the reputation of a restaurant that wasn't mine. What would have happened had thirty more covers been added to my total? Would that have been the breaking point? That kind of careless action can conclusively lose future customers and give the restaurant a bad name; but if I had to do it all over again, I wouldn't have changed a thing.

The next time you have five or fifty people over for a dinner party, most importantly remember one thing: mise en place. Without the prep I did that evening, would never have been able to achieve those kinds of numbers. Prior to the arrival of your guests, organization and preparation is the key to pulling off a successful engagement. It's supposed to be fun and engaging, not an event you dread and swear that you'll "never do Christmas again!"

Because I'd proven my worth, Kenny finally decided to take his long-overdue vacation, leaving me in command even though I was still in culinary school. Supervising my first *real* kitchen, I prepared a variety of fresh soup selections, trendier haute dishes, and in good spirit wanted to showcase my abilities in his absence bringing confidence that his kitchen was left in capable hands. I still have the menu card to this day those dishes I had prepared.

Herb-Marinated Lamb with a Dijon Crumb Crust, Dauphinoise Potato & Broccolini Ambrosia, Wild King Salmon Carpaccio aioli, and Grilled Wild Ranch Quail Alla Peperonata with Shell Bean Gratin, and Chanterelles, were but a few offerings that week in his absence.

Feeling as if I were a guest filling in for a late-night talk show host, my genuine goal was to ensure Kenny upon his return I was never out for his job. Not cool, but rampant in the business, usurpers are the primary reason many chefs rarely allow themselves a vacation or sick day. There is always a sous chef or Food and Beverage director ready to burn you, never allowing you immunity.

By this time, I conclusively had the capacity to run my own kitchen but was keenly aware most of my training had come from Kenny. Now my close friend, I never wanted to undermine his role as head chef. Like a virus, politics remain rampant in kitchens; more often it's about who is sleeping with whom, and the special favors that commonly reward the undeserving, regardless of talent or qualifications.

By now, the seed in my mind had been planted; perhaps it was time to run my own kitchen, setting out on my own like a puppy leaving the side of its warm mother's womb. Not long after Kenny returned from a second vacation, the restaurant had changed owners, and office practices with the new management became strikingly reminiscent of my earlier days at the Bullmarket.

A disturbing resemblance; papers and books were strewn everywhere in the office and the disorganization and lack of practical business measures became a troubling reminder of my earlier years. Those warning signs and my need to earn a respectable wage, combined with one sole event would provide me with the urgency to spread my wings before the restaurant eventually became yet another statistic in a landscape of defunct properties.

The office located downstairs in the rear of the building, one had to navigate through a maze of catacomb-like cellars of thick cement walls to reach it. Many times, while the office door was left ajar, management remained unaware for several weeks of money missing from one of the desks. Initially shrugged off, thinking perhaps the cash drawers were settled incorrectly, or for whatever reason, the door was left open again. Bolder even more, the thief would remove $800 in cash.

Arriving for my shift the next day, I couldn't help but notice what I thought were blood stains at several locations on the walls, equipment, and finally all around a prep-sink in the basement kitchen. I was never officially informed, but the police had hidden a dye pack within the cash in the office as a setup. Turns out, one of the night cooks who'd only been employed for a couple of months would hang out at night after I left and take small amounts of cash from the office unnoticed.

Once the dye pack exploded on him, he raced through the maze, frantically touching everything in his path until he reached the sink thinking he could wash it off. Grateful they had caught him; I was beside myself with mixed emotions over not having been informed of the sting or that money had gone missing. I wondered, maybe they'd considered me as one of the potential thieves, even though I was aware for years that the money and office were always left unattended. Perhaps I was overthinking, but it had irked me that my loyalty would ever be in question.

All in all, me and Kenny worked together like a well-oiled machine for six years; it was some of the best chemistry I experienced with a chef who eventually became my friend, and I am forever grateful. With grave disappointment and crushing heartfelt sympathy, I would find out during the writing of this book, Kenny, my dear friend, had passed away before I could express my gratitude for all that he had done for me. *Brother, while I have the memories of what we shared, I will miss you forever.*

My marriage all but over, as a single parent, I questioned, *how was I ever going to continue as a chef and care for my daughter while working in excess of sixty hours a week?* Needing more money, I began pitching feeler resumes, and to my surprise a successful contractor who also happened to own a large hotel would call me for an interview. As it turns out, he was a regular patron of the restaurant who really loved our food. Not only did the hotel operate its own restaurant, but also several banquet rooms, room service, and a lounge with its own menu.

CHAPTER SIX

Holding It Together

Fast forwarding to Peppercorns, if I wasn't at my restaurant any free time I did have was back at the house with Pepper; him by my side as I wrote menus, or in the truck running errands. Many nights after closing the restaurant, I would drive the hour back to the house to pick up "Chub Chubs" or "Pepps," as I'd nicknamed him, only to return to the restaurant with him for a night of painting or miscellaneous repairs during when closed. His company always managing to make those most difficult of times less burdensome.

Recognizing the restaurant and what was waiting for him inside, he would spring out of the truck, pacing as I unlocked the front door. Once inside, he'd race from booth to booth, disappearing under tables, snorting loudly, rummaging for pieces of food perhaps dropped on the floor, missed during cleaning. With vigor and adrenaline, he was excited to be spending time with "dad," out of the house, grateful to be anywhere other than sleeping on a couch for 14 hours straight waiting for my return home.

I found his zealousness to be infectious, energizing me as I climbed ladders to paint trim, repair equipment, or stain booths. Pausing, I'd watch him running down below me, laughing at his antics like a father with his son. Both of us alone, I'd turn up the music, knocking out jobs, often until 3:00 a.m. Hanging out together provided me a sense of reassurance knowing we were doing the best we could at the time, and everything was going to be alright.

Inseparable, the more time we spent together was matched with passing moments of guilt when it was necessary that we be apart. This guilt would often lead me to question the genuine connection we as humans share between pet and us as their guardian. How difficult it must be for them waiting hours on end — the center of their universe — for us to return each time we leave.

All alone, uncertain of our return, surely, they comprehend when we arrive home; through association they anticipate being fed, time to experience companionship, and possibly even go for a walk. But do they comprehend the concept of time, and all those passing hours? How many of us are forced to leave our pets and upon returning home are greeted by their exuberant welcome; the same spirited reception whether hours away, or merely ten minutes.

More fitting, as their guardians and by providing for them, keep them from having to fend for themselves, forage for food, and of

Holding It Together

course overcome inherent survival challenges. However, we should consider: what are those natural instincts we are stifling by allowing them to live in our homes, providing for all their needs? Making most choices for them, are they in fact content with the existence we've provided them? Are they complacent waiting for countless hours, only to be entertained with a 10-minute walk upon our return? Decisions made over not just when they eat, but when they bathe, go outside, experience excitement, share in happiness, fornicate, and almost everything short of breathing.

Arguably, the surroundings of a warm home, comfortable couch, and a bowl of food is far superior an environment versus those dangers on the streets and unpredictable weather, where their lifespans are proven shorter left to fend for themselves. Regardless, how much has human interaction truly domesticated our beloved pets, removing their natural-born tendencies and instincts; and if given a choice, what would they choose?

While most pets have been stripped away from their families at birth in nearly every adoption process, many will never see their siblings again. As we struggle to educate and implement much needed neutering practices to curb excessive overbreeding, I have always been saddened by Pepper's inability to experience that basic, inherent pleasure, and the joy in sharing life with his family, similarly like humans.

And God said, 'Let us make man in our image, after our likeness; and let them have dominion over the fish of the sea, and over the fowl of the air, and over the cattle, and over all the earth, and over every creeping thing that creepeth upon the earth.'
~ Genesis 1:24-26 ~

Taken from the Old Testament, those words while powerful, should give way to pause. How strongly does the passage resonate with those who subscribe to its pretense, and what measures? Specifically, those words: *over* the fish, fowl, and cattle. Is this then suggesting justification for speciesism to the extent that man separate himself from the "creeping," never befriending but rather asserting his superiority? Does our "dominion," warrant us to alter other species? To biotically crossbreed, torture, euthanize, conduct laboratory testing, force-feed, encage for life, chain, and ultimately decide the fate of those *creeping?*

While they can't always express pain or voice their displeasure in a way for us to comprehend, man has decidedly stolen the liberty and basic freedoms gifted to those *creeping* this earth. "Dominion" should perhaps be interchanged with guardian; our superior intellect and agency better suited stewarding for those less fortunate or unable to fend for themselves. It would seem our gift of superior intellect bestowed upon us has fallen short in our lack of empathy and compassion that we fail to exercise.

Holding It Together

Those times spent with animals my whole life, observing, has certainly caused me to question our assumed hierarchy over those we share this earth. Suggesting perhaps we not confuse our superiority with the assumption we must then dominate. At what cost, and to what measure is that rule meant to be taken from Genesis, merely because we can? The right to life has little to do with the survival of the fittest and the ability to protect, but rather what is *ethical and moral*. Once born, each being equally bestowed their right to life, regardless of species, to live, breathe, and experience the gift of existence unprincipled. Our home — their home.

The ethical treatment of animals and animal rights have been debated innumerable times centuries over by diverse and notable authors, scholars, activists, and zealots. Child prodigy and philosopher Jeremy Bentham wrote in 1789, *"The question is not, Can they reason? nor, Can they talk? but, Can they suffer?"* That statement, while incisive, has profound impact its altruism; while we may not fully understand animals, what right do we have as humans to inflict suffering and deciding virtually all of life's decisions for them?

In 1866, Henry Bergh would go on to establish the American Society for the Prevention of Cruelty to Animals. One of the first organizations instituted over the struggle to curb unfair and unethical treatment of animals. He further successfully lobbied for preeminent laws to protect animals from unnecessary and extreme cruelty. These issues affected him deeply after witnessing countless beatings, thrashings, and starvation of horses at the hands of New York City carriage handlers. Many of the horses were often left for dead on the side of the street, discarded like trash to rot once their usefulness was exhausted.

Animals used as commodities, bought and sold, bartered and enslaved on a whim, for the *greater good* of man. Those early efforts, and the selfless work bringing to the forefront cries for compassion, would not be complete without mention of Joy Adamson, the author of Born Free; Richard Martin, the first to introduce animal protection laws to parliament; Peter Singer, author of the landmark book, Animal Liberation; Ingrid Newkirk, founder of PETA; and of course, British conservationist, primatologist, Jane Goodall and her life-work on conservation and animal welfare.

Animals, to this day while recognized as property, a commodity bearing monetary value, warrants at the very least those welcomed into our home the necessity for us to look beyond our self-interest. Through select speciesism however, our prejudice has allowed us to separate those beings we prefer to cuddle, and those allowed for what is on our dinner plate each night. Those we choose to place in cages, and those used for unethical and immoral, painful practices and exploitation.

No animal deserves unwarranted mistreatment or neglect, forced to live in impoverished, unscrupulous conditions when they are under our guardianship. *Guardian*, because we cannot own a life as our property, regardless of what laws may dictate or commerce affords over those sentient beings. Rather, out of the common

Holding It Together

attributes we share and the humane understanding it demands from us, an individual's being and birthright to life regardless of genus.

Our kinship and moral obligation reaches far beyond those dogs and cats we bring into our homes; by estimation, there are some 90-million dogs and 96-million cats in the United States; In comparison, there are an estimated *10-billion* farm animals slaughtered annually in the United States alone. Perhaps trivial to some, such subversive practices account for 97% of all animals used for food production in the United States! As suggested in Genesis, while we may possess dominion, brandishing a larger stick over the subservient, should also hold close the intellect, humane empathy and understanding for those unable to fend for themselves or fail to cry out in our language for us to understand. Perhaps our *dominion* is better suited a welcome burden bequeathed upon us to guide those less fortunate. Regardless of the religion you subscribe, be it science or faith, holds no merit for the infliction animals incur.

Back at the house, I struggled to cram in any sense of normalcy or routine in those few hours we had together each week. Enjoying a warm fire, curling up under a blanket with a book, or watching a movie. I would consciously aim to absorb as many experiences as possible, many times crippled by hesitation knowing in only a few hours I would be back at Peppercorns.

The endless hours at the restaurant, stacks of bills, and the fact I was rarely home was beginning to wear on my marriage. Wavering in my sense of masculinity, every dime earned from the restaurant was placed back in efforts to keep it afloat, most times making it impossible for any restaurant revenue be used for those bills back at the house. Estranged, often the house felt as if it were someone else's home I happened to visit on Monday, just to lay my head for the night. Pushed to experience my entire home life in one compact day, made connecting with my family next to impossible. Each person understandably had their own life, while unobligated to wait for Monday and the possibility I *might* be home.

Early to bed one evening, Pepper, always insistent on laying by my feet every night, had decided to come to the top of the bed. Human-like, he rested his head on my pillow; with the TV volume low, I

Holding It Together

petted him as he stared deeply into my eyes. Guilty from all the hours I was away, I promised never to leave him, and that he shouldn't have any concerns or worries. Although, I may not have conversations with him or expect him to answer back, I've always believed they do understand, in their own way, our idioms. At the time, I never knew those words would soon be challenged.

If not in the forest, animals always seemed to find their way into my life, or perhaps more precise, me into theirs. In one instance, I found an abandoned baby mallard duck wandering alone on our lawn. Before approaching, I'd wait to see if the mother would return, however, once noticing me, with abandoned fear, it immediately darted to my side and followed me around the yard, onto the driveway, and eventually inside the garage.

Along with Pepper, I took the duckling inside the house, tempered water in the kitchen sink, and watched in amazement as he instinctively took to swimming and enjoying his new pond. *Another stray*, I thought; *what have I gotten myself into now? Is it even possible to raise a wild duck?*

That evening of course, after it had been discovered I had brought home yet another animal, realized I would not be able to raise the poor little guy, besides, I was never home anyway. Insistently chirping all night, sleep was impossible that evening. Already feeling a closeness after spending only a few hours with the baby, I had arranged to be late for work so I could search for a local farm sanctuary that might accept him.

Driving up the long gravel road with the duckling in a shoe box by my side, he chirped the entire ride to his new home. The sanctuary assured me it was quite common to find lost ducklings, taking them in regularly. However, my reassurance quickly gave way to skepticism when they placed him in a small fenced in area with four larger birds. Watching anxiously, many times it appeared as if he was going to be trampled to death. Knowing myself and my obsessive nature, I quickly said goodbye and slowly drove away, uncertain over the choice I had made and concerned for his safety.

Unable to leave well enough alone, the next Monday couldn't come soon enough. Hopeful of some noticeable progress in my little buddy, I eagerly drove back to the farm, curious how he was adapting to his new environment. Nowhere to be found, I questioned one of the attendants who informed me that he had survived only a couple days.

Like a punch to the gut, I stood there unflinching, pretending as though it didn't affect me. Instructed it was quite common, many times when alienated from their mother, the young chicks are not able to survive. I refrained from asking, *"is it common that many dies under your watch knowing the likelihood they will be trampled to death?"* Biting my tongue, I became embarrassed that I'd allowed myself to become so emotional.

Looking around at the variety of animals in the small barn, I wondered if they too would meet the same fate. Such innocence... No vengeance, no reason they deserve the pain or death inherent in their struggle to survive. Again, I would question; *how does one find*

Holding It Together

or maintain their faith, witnessing those innocent, forced to endure their fate at the hands of another? Bitter and resentful of my own actions for having brought him to the preserve, suspected I should have just kept and raised the duckling myself. Would he have had a better chance of survival? I needed someone to blame.

My closeness to Pepper it seemed only stemmed my sensibility; those times we spent in the forest clouding my acumen while amplifying my discernment for everything around. Exploring untamed trails, leading even deeper into the sea of foreboding trees, we encountered a dilapidated, abandoned farmstead. Out of sight behind the property was an old, rusty metal spike driven into the ground.

A dirt mound, with the spike at its center, was encircled by a deep trench that must have taken years to wear away, the work of four paws circling aimlessly. I envisioned the poor, tortured soul chained and left alone its entire life, the only escape to indefinitely go around the stake tens of thousands of times. I stared at the spike and trench with a feeling of both anger and disgust; the simple question of why? Plagued my mind.

Those hours while hiking, I would subconsciously be focused on finding anything that would feed my recession. What once provided me with a sense of joy was now a reminder with every step the life I was missing; every encounter with some unfortunate evidence of a poor animal's mistreatment or suffering further deepening my despair. Refusing to use the word "depression," because I always had a thirst and appreciation for life. However, the same hikes that once brought me escape and enjoyment, only now encouraged my hopeless notions.

Slowly, the ride home from the woods would bring me back to reality and the familiar anxiety with thoughts of preparing for the next day at work. Returning home each time became increasingly more difficult as I became drawn to those raw emotions festering inside me. I'd always harbored a sense of guilt; providing Pepper with so much joy on Mondays, however uncertain when we would be together again. Ever loyal, he'd wait.

Back at Peppercorns, it was only a matter of time before I was presented with an opportunity too difficult to pass up. Paying the majority share for the restaurant when I assumed ownership, I'd also left a balance to be reconciled with installments. As anticipated, the previous owner, also a restaurateur, was once again having difficulty keeping his head above water.

Rumor had it that the IRS was knocking at his door, again, leaving him with nowhere else to turn for such a large amount owed in back taxes. Either he paid what was owed, in addition to penalties or be forced into permanently closing. Banks offering little option as they hold an acute disdain for restaurants and their high mortality rates, he would be forced into approaching me for the balance. I embraced the timeliness, always suspecting the opportunity would someday present itself, saving me thousands, knowing his history with the IRS.

Seizing the opportunity, I offered that the note could most certainly be zeroed out; both allowing him to settle his debt with the IRS and for me to pay off my business. *"How does 60% of the balance sound?"* Rebuffing my initial offer but eventually agreeing to terms, the payoff was substantially less. Unscrupulous? Not at all. This was business, but it also helped keep him from becoming another statistic on the restaurant scene. After all, his property was competition, and we shared many of the same clientele. Failing to assist a fellow restaurateur, now that would have been unscrupulous.

In the end it offered little relief; paying down the remainder of the note would still set us back tens of thousands of dollars. Certainly, good business sense reducing liabilities; however, it forced me to ensure the success of the restaurant and return of our investment. The numbers while mediocre after having been open for years, were nowhere near acceptable; it's true, I earned more money employed as an executive chef before taking ownership. However, instilled in me a determination to persevere, refusing to give up, and work even harder than before.

Ever aware of trending restaurants, cooking fads, and what chefs were on the move; my aim was to always set Peppercorns apart from those eateries around me. At the time in the area no one had a website, nor were they using reloadable gift cards as an example. Not only would I be the first in the area implementing both those tools, I also began Facebooking, Tweeting, and using other forms of social media to attract new business. If not in the kitchen **chefing** or greeting guests up front, I'd be sitting in a booth over coffee, my laptop open, emailing and tweaking the website. In no time, I had collected thousands of emails which I entered into a database used to interact with my customers.

Our Frequent Diner Club was next, the first of its kind in the area. The more you dined; the more reward points earned. For Halloween, we held pumpkin decorating classes where parents could drop their children off for hours. We'd then play music, painted pumpkins, and feed a classroom of exuberant kids as a package deal while parents ate lunch or went shopping at a nearby grocery store. While the effort was never to earn an additional revenue stream with a gimmick, my goal rather, was to provide a sense of community and awareness of my product.

As a novelty when Seinfeld was at the height of its popularity, I hired a *Soup Nazi* impersonator who hand-delivered soups and yelled at many of my unsuspecting customers similar to the character on the

Holding It Together

TV show. "No Soup For You!" People loved it so much that it made local papers, and became an annual, week-long event everyone looked forward to.

Around this time, Peppercorns began gathering favorable food reviews with recipes that were often featured in the food section of several papers. Next, I began baking various types of breads from scratch, readily displaying them out front, tantalizing the customers as they entered the restaurant. At its height, we were making 200 zucchini bread loaves a week. Perhaps a coincidence, but other restaurants in the area followed suit.

Business remained cutthroat, particularly when the 2008 recession hit. One of my cooks pointed out that he recognized the owner of another restaurant regularly drive by, peering into my windows. Then my servers notified me that a relative of a different restaurant owner was dining inside the restaurant with regularity, asking questions. My efforts must be working, I thought. When competition attempts to mirror your lead, it's typically a good sign that you must be doing something intuitive. However, I was irritated knowing the ideas I had painstakingly implemented were being stolen each time.

It was then that I decided to kick it up a notch by refusing to close on Thanksgiving Day. This, despite the chagrin from back home, and being unheard of among the restaurants around Peppercorns. Almost as if there was an unwritten rule, or truce for all of us restaurants that Thanksgiving was to be a sanctioned holy day of reprieve, one we would all honor together. The assumption was that everyone would be home with their families, so why bother opening? Well, I was about to break that rule! Besides truly needing the revenue, it also gave me an advantage of capturing any customers displaced by the closure of their regular restaurant. I had to take the chance.

On the home front the decision would cause much strife, however, I was left with little choice. With bills mounting, I went against what everyone claimed would be a wasted effort. Questioned countless times by all the critics: "Who dines in a restaurant on Thanksgiving?" and, "You're wasting your time, selfishly being away from your family!" Many elegant brunches costing upwards of $80 per head on Thanksgiving, I knew my existing clientele would welcome the chance for a warm holiday meal for a fraction of that amount, in a restaurant for that matter.

Unthinkable, I then doubled down in case my theory was wrong. Creating a full course Thanksgiving dinner takeout menu that included all the trimmings, I decided to put my kitchen into overdrive in the likelihood that the restaurant would be slow. Whole roasted turkey, various potato choices, giblet dressing, fresh vegetables, dinner rolls, turkey gravy, cranberry sauce, and even a whole pumpkin pie and one of our zucchini bread loaves for dessert included. When all the menus were ready and the time was right, it hit social media and was plastered on the website. The add read: *"Peppercorns will be open for dining in or Thanksgiving Holiday meal Pickup, allowing us to do the work while you spend time with family."* The message was then delivered.

Holding It Together

As the holiday grew near, order cards were created, including menu choices and a checkbox for each item. Scalloped potatoes, or garlic mashed? Traditional pumpkin pie, or pecan? Three weeks away and the restaurant reservations only trickled in, but I held faith. Then we got our first carryout order for a family of six. Fine, I thought, that's easy, one turkey is more than enough for six people. Then two more carryout orders came in, followed by three more, and so on. Every order fully paid in advance to ensure our final count before the big day; we took orders up until the day before Thanksgiving.

We knocked out 52 home takeout dinners that first year, each dinner capable of feeding six to ten people. This, for all you chefs out there, was performed on the very same line the cooks had to use for the busy restaurant. Without a rotating deck oven, it was accomplished with only two Vulcan ovens and one above the broiler; we cooked 65 turkeys in all. I mustn't forget about the additional 20 turkeys prepared for the restaurant, 80 pies, and endless side accompaniments. How peculiar that the following year, the surrounding restaurants also decided on opening during Thanksgiving. However, no other restaurant dared tackling the beast of catering out full Thanksgiving meals. We owned that one.

Around that same holiday season, a regular customer mentioned in conversation that he had a radio show and asked if I might be interested in calling in for a segment. Having done many interviews in the past, I always felt comfortable when put on the spot discussing food. The call-in was then arranged to take place on a Friday, and the plan was simple, to talk about food, work life, and the demands of owning a business.

What was supposed to be just a three-minute live radio segment turned into a fifteen-minute dissection. In radio-time, fifteen minutes is an eternity; most businesses would kill for the exposure. During the time taking calls from listeners and discussing a variety of topics, myself and Scott, the host of the radio show, immediately clicked, creating a chemistry while hesitating to end the segment.

After the live broadcast and both of us pleased about how effortlessly it had gone, I agreed to come into the studio for an entire show. After covering my role back at the restaurant, I felt relatively confident I could race back after the show well before the lunch crowd arrived. During the show we talked about food, answered calls about cooking, and discussed anything on the listener's mind. The show went over as one of the busiest call-in days in months with the board lit up with listeners wanting to discuss recipes, restaurants, and food in general.

I was then invited back as a regular for a full show once per week. Fridays suddenly became even more frantic, if that was possible. I'd race to the restaurant early in the morning for a few hours, excuse myself to drive to the studio mid-morning, and then rush back to the restaurant where I'd work until closing late in the evening.

As part of my role when on the air, when prompted, I would interject observations or comments about random topics. While initial discussions were food-related, the show slowly morphed into the traditional morning zoo format many stations followed in every

Holding It Together

city. The spin of course, was that I happened to be a chef with many behind-the-scene kitchens anecdotes.

In between calls, I'd have a segment interviewing a local or nationally recognized celebrity chef. During one broadcast, I interviewed TV personality and restaurateur Stephanie Izard. Stephanie gained popularity for being the first female chef ever to win Bravo's Top Chef TV competition. She is now the proprietor of three successful restaurants, a TV personality, and noted cookbook author.

While Stephanie was on hold waiting for her segment, Scott was busy doing one of his bits imitating a stoned hippie when Stephanie was then queued for her introduction. With a slurred voice, the hippie character was debating the quality of weed from the different parts of Columbia, and Stephanie, unfamiliar with our zoo format, responded on live radio, "what the fuck was that?" Followed by a long pause, and then dead air; I then silenced my mic and asked the board op, "*did she just drop the F-bomb on live radio? You did manage to hit the dump button, right?*" I was told there was no dump button nor any seven-second delay. We later found that her words had in fact made live air, one of several words regulated by the FCC which could get the station fined for a misconduct violation or suspension of their license. The hours flew bye at the station, finally providing me a moment to enjoy something outside of the restaurant's cinder block walls, even if only for a couple hours.

Back home more than once, I would remind family members on what days to listen to the radio show until it simply no longer mattered. Met with disdain when I landed the radio gig, knowing it would only place more demand on my time or somehow encourage the restaurant even more. Preferring the restaurant fail and just be done with, those around me were eager to abandon the business long before acquiring the radio gig. Regardless, I refused to cave. While they never heard the radio show, or simply didn't care, it only encouraged our disconnect, wounding me deeply.

Not to worry, the show only lasted seven months, when the radio station was bought out and the format changed. Radio legend and personality Steve Dahl was brought in during our time slot and just as quickly we were no more. There was a discussion of moving to another station or doing a podcast, but it never materialized. I reminded myself of my priorities, most importantly my obligation to Peppercorns. Operating a restaurant was no part-time job, while hosting a subscription-based podcast as opposed to live air seemed to be for those desperate or washed up.

Little was I aware that while the restaurant seemed to be holding its own, it was headed for the most challenging times ever experienced. Initially shrugging off the 2008 recession out of ignorance, I refused to believe it would hurt business and those strong enough would survive. Reasoning that if a sound business offered an exceptional product for a fair price, the hardest working would persevere unscathed, regardless of economic conditions. Charging onward, I watched costs, offered specials, and micromanaged every decision by questioning how each would ultimately affect the bottom line.

Holding It Together

No less than six months later, a restaurant that had been a staple in the community for decades, unannounced closed during the night. Initially brushing it off, my reasoning was that the place was spent and stale from years of sameness, until when a couple months later a town favorite steak joint would also suffer the same fate. During the night, with the doors locked by the property owner, the restaurant manager was arrested inside the building while attempting to remove the equipment. It was a stupid mistake; even if successful removing those items; the greasy, damaged and aged equipment typically only fetches pennies on the dollar. Why risk it?

Closures suddenly became common, until it was a matter of who could hang on the longest or at least until the recession ended. Either this, or who had the deepest pockets to help them float their business; everyone oblivious that the economic downturn would last years. One fanatical operator decidedly chose to open a new location during the bloodbath of 2009. For this, you've got to give him credit for having the biggest balls, or perhaps for being the naivest. At the time, the assumption was that they must undoubtedly know what they're doing, since they already had two additional locations under the same name. This new location, on a busier street than Peppercorns and almost twice the size, ended up closing in less than one year. Sobering, their bravado would also cause the downfall of all three their locations successively.

Shuttered, they placed a 20-yard dumpster at the back of the abandoned restaurant, filling it with its contents. Everything reduced to junk after they spent $100k remodeling before opening. Those properties that remain open longest while solvent, is not always a matter of who has the darker cherry wood or best stemware. Food quality should always take precedence over ambiance. Countless times I've had the unforeseen fortune of dining in shitholes, however, amazed with the quality of food.

One late evening after closing, curious, I went to investigate. The dumpster picked through by scavengers like roaches in the night, most of the items were either junk or full of grease. I didn't go there for chairs or fixtures but was in search of something even more valuable. Perhaps a filing cabinet containing the office invoices and dailies, which I happened to find sitting directly on top the heap of debris. By dailies, I mean receipts, credit card transactions, and tickets accounting for what the restaurant was taking in when it was operating. To me, this was much more valuable than any piece of furniture.

The invoices and receipts offered no intrinsic value, but I could easily calculate their gross take, allowing me to compare to Peppercorns. This was golden since everyone's books are manipulated or rarely disclose any factuality; *yes, most restaurants have two sets of books.* To throw this haphazardly into a dumpster was not only foolish, but it demonstrated the efficacy, or lack thereof, causing them to fail in the first place. Pouring over the documents, the failed restaurant experienced remarkable numbers upon its initial opening, however days leading up to its closure experienced an astounding 80% drop in revenue, less than a year later.

Holding It Together

Credit cards transactions, which are near impossible to manipulate, totaled more than $80,000 for each month. Their last month of operation totaled less than $7,000, not including the take on cash. The monthly lease alone was $12,000, triple net. On top of that, food cost, labor, utilities, insurance, and taxes, must all be factored in when estimating your chance for survival. Although I never sampled the food at that particular property, if they ran the restaurant like how they capriciously discarded their books, it's amazing they even lasted for a year. Credit card receipts don't lie, and cash is king in the restaurant business. While he could get away with fudging his cash receipts, the massive drop in plastic eventually crushed him.

Carefully watching my numbers, I began noticing Peppercorns experiencing the same drop in business those around me were suffering from similarly. Down the street, a Vietnamese restaurant closed, where someone else reopened it only to close again in less than two years. Further down, a breakfast house and two chain restaurants would meet the same fate. I soon began to doubt myself as the numbers gradually dropped, and I shamefully I started cutting staff to make my numbers. The sense of desperation felt among the employees. *What am I doing wrong?* Ignorantly refusing to believe I was anything like the others.

Within months, Peppercorns was dealt a devastating blow much closer to home. The anchor tenant behind the restaurant, long rumored to be suffering, announced its closure effective immediately. Just like that, the supermarket was now dark inside, and its parking lot empty other than moving trucks loading any salvageable food inventory. A local favorite, the supermarket brought overflow traffic into my restaurant daily, while its closure caught everyone by surprise.

Peppercorns was now the largest footprint location on the lot, with the anchor tenant now vacant behind it. Not only did this affect the foot traffic into Peppercorns, but the large, vacant store became an eyesore that created a decrepit view of the entire lot. All eyes were now on the restaurant, intently watching for when it would be next to close.

Some of the Gang at Peppercorns

Things only got progressively worse, and for the first time ever, I was unable to make the lease payment. While I had the money, however, refused to dip into our savings any longer. Not only had we absorb the opening costs, but we still had to pay ourselves back the advance used to pay down the restaurant deal I had made before.

Holding It Together

The deal while a great move at the time — saving us thousands— in hindsight that same money surely could have been put to better use. Satisfied at the time for my assumed keen business sense, I carried the burden for my miscalculation and the magnitude of how serious the recession would be felt.

The goal, rather than about turning a profit, became more focused instead on remaining solvent, holding on, and riding out the recession. Rule number one: vendors had to be paid first. Without food, there would be no customers. Even though I'd missed my first lease payment, I knew time was on my side since the supermarket had closed. The property owner would have no choice but to wait for the rent, or else he'd risk losing Peppercorns as his largest tenant.

By month's end, with little revenue left, the summer's brutal heat would spike my electricity bill after running both rooftop HVAC units nonstop. Sweaty in my dress clothes, I'd regularly scale a ladder behind the building, pulling a hose behind me. Once I got rooftop, I positioned a sprinkler from the hose, hitting all the coils of both units with cool water struggling to keep the inside temperature comfortable. If you ever see a hose running up to a roof, you'll know why. I couldn't afford a new HVAC, nor was the landlord going to pick up the cost during these crippling economic times.

Having already cut labor and squeezed pennies from every other area, we continued to make 30-day net terms with each vendor, while most other restaurants that managed to remain open were now required to pay cash on delivery. I would order from one vendor, wait 30 days until the invoice was due, and then order from a separate vendor; each time I was granted another month before they required payment, thus never being placed on COD. This was done indefinitely while riding out the recession. Again, without food there would be no restaurant.

The building owner, ever understanding and never threatening, remained content being paid whenever business levels recovered. His suggestion that I remodel to attract more business, however, was laughable. Amidst struggling to remain solvent, did he really believe I was going to pump $100k into *his* building? One afternoon, he ventured inside the restaurant, both checking on how I was doing and eager to pick up his check. However, I was not in the mood. With only a handful of tables in the restaurant, I opened the cash register, took out the drawer, and handed him the tray full of cash. *"Here, take it,"* I begged. *"What more can I do?"*

"Sell, sell, sell!" Was pleaded to me back at home. I countered, *"Who is going to buy a restaurant in this economy? Restaurants are free everywhere!"* You needn't pay me a dime for my business when you can go down the street and get a fucking steak house turn-key! Besides, many of those closed restaurants were completely operational with all the equipment still left inside. You could literally get a license, turn the key, and open a restaurant, that easy. I refused however, letting go of Peppercorns, never in my life have I *let go* of anything, nor was I about to. Restaurants are notorious for closing even during prosperous economies, like hell was I going to be one of them, regardless of the economic climate.

Holding It Together

Encouragement or support from anyone would come at a premium, and the decision weighed on me constantly. Losing control of the restaurant, my troubled marriage, insistent bill collectors, and meeting payroll; the pressure became brutally relentless. Constantly around people, yet I never could have felt more isolated. At home, at least with Pepper I was able to keep my sanity whenever we could grab time alone. Fighting for survival, I needed the support of Pepper that he provided more than ever.

CHAPTER SEVEN

Head Chef

Nervous about the head chef interview at their corporate office, I intentionally left a 5 o'clock shadow thinking it would to mask my youth. Fortunately, there would be no second post-interview or tasting, reasonably certain I'd landed the job. Tastings, or many times mystery baskets are supplied, often requiring the potential candidate for a leading chef role, to prepare one or several courses. These are then presented to an individual or committee for review. I have always found tastings to be somewhat imperiously pretentious. How is it that one meal prepared in a foreign kitchen can be used to account for years of experience? More often, chefs, when parting ways with a current employer, will many times demonstrate their abilities in the very same restaurant they are leaving under the guise that the table eating is a group of "acquaintances." In all truth, line skills and plate presentation are but only a few of the responsibilities that a chef assumes.

A common misconception is that the head chef is toiling away all day on the line, supervising each plate leaving the pass. It must be said that almost all Michelin-rated or four-star property executive chefs never even see your plate. More likely, it was prepared by a line cook, sous chef, or maybe if you're lucky, the chef de partie. This, if you happen to be even dining in a restaurant with a defined kitchen brigade hierarchy.

Chosen for my new role based on the conclusive dining experiences my new employer had while dining at the restaurant I would be leaving; I was offered the position the very next day. A respectable hotel with impressive kitchen space, I'd land my first leading chef role years before the age of 30. Those days of toiling away in abysmal conditions, flipping frozen burgers, dropping pre-cut, pre-breaded, pre-fabbed frozen resemblances of something mildly edible into week-old fryer grease, were now behind me. Despite the demands of being a single father, I knew I couldn't turn down the role of head Chef at the hotel.

By far, the new position would demand the most accountability from me to date of every kitchen that I had worked before. In addition to heading multiple food outlets, it was also my duty to balance labor costs, menu development, staffing, training, food costs, sanitation, supervise the restaurant, bar menu, room service, and all banquet execution.

There would be no rationale for accepting the position other than that I finally wanted to run my own kitchen and needed the money. Not necessarily in that order. Ungodly hours on a crap salary made

Head Chef

little sense anymore despite those fondest of memories working with Kenny. While I admire those chefs, who sacrifice their lives immersing themselves in their *craft* for meager wages, I, however, had bills to pay. My first marriage all but over, I'd been given temporary custody of my daughter, however, after accepting a head chef role as a young single father, I had serious reservations about how I would pull it off.

Currently the best of friends with the mother of my daughter, I think she would agree; the only good thing that came out of our marriage was our beautiful daughter Amy. That, and our union was never given a fair chance. Although married, however, I had always been selfishly immersed in working, trying to earn a buck and searching for direction. Divorce commonplace among most chefs, we ignored all those early indications warning us to be more cautious before we got married.

On the first day that I was to begin my new role, I drove to the rear of the hotel a full hour before scheduled to start. Tentatively slouching in my car with the visor down, I spent the next thirty minutes surveying the back-door exit. Sure enough, the door swung open and a middle-aged man wearing chef whites shuffled out, carrying a box to his car. Presumably, the just-terminated executive chef, he once again went back inside, returning with a second box. Sitting in my car paralyzed, my heart sank into my stomach, disgusted for having taken this man's position away from him.

"John," I later learned, was discharged literally minutes before I started that day. Knowing nothing of this man, I envisioned him with a wife and children at home, a mortgage, and now he was without a job. Aggrieved with my new boss for his callous actions before I had even started my new position, I questioned, *what am I getting myself into?* Reminded once again how cruel and dispensable we are in this business. I'd now have to go inside and face a brigade of cooks, sous chefs, servers, the general manager, food and beverage director, sales team, and banquet staff that had all worked closely with this man for years. *No pressure, right?*

With no acquaintances at the property, I went in totally cold without backup support or anyone that could offer me the slightest bit of comfort. Introduced to my staff, and all front house management, certain, I was referred to as the *"asshole new guy who got John fired!"* Later, I would find out that John, was in fact friends with many of the staff. My office, which was adjacent to the head of maintenance, forced me to endure his cold disposition lasting for weeks. Months later, I learned that they used to share coffee every morning before starting each day. They happened to be best of friends, even while off the property.

Eventually it was decided in court that my daughter, Amy, would be with me during the week, and with her mother on weekends. Between mom helping pick up Amy after school, and weekends being the busiest time at the hotel with banquets and the demanding restaurant, it worked out perfectly. As we grew, our family of two, the days were intense to say the least. Each morning I was forced to wake Amy at 4:00 a.m., getting her to daycare before heading to the hotel for work. A 45-minute commute typically meant I walked in

Head Chef

the door 15 minutes before opening. Ovens, fryers, and flattops would all be cold, and many of the staff were already there.

To say it was nerve-racking would be an understatement. *What if the daycare staff failed to open on time? What if I got a flat tire? What if Amy got sick?* Countless times I would question my motives for having ever accepted the position.

In a matter of months, I managed to settle into a groove and eventually arranged for one of my cooks to assume morning openings. Weekends would consist of 14-hour days, with both a busy restaurant and a multitude of banquets. Content that Amy was taken care of when with her mother, admittedly, for years I questioned whether I had made the right decision in wanting my daughter to live with me. *What kind of life is this for her to be living?* Shuffled back and forth from home to home, forced to awaken her at ridiculous hours. Those thoughts and the guilt would haunt me to this very day.

My immediate task in my new role was to organize the entire kitchen. I first implemented prep lists that I found were nonexistent or perhaps destroyed by the previous chef. Common in the business, one of several tactics used to sabotage anyone assuming their role if ever terminated. To destroy any documentation or work practice procedures that could make the newbies job any easier. That, or taking three whole fresh salmon and then placing them above the kitchen ceiling tiles, left to rot, only to be discovered later after the rancid smell fills the kitchen. Yes, that has happened.

I would later find out that under the previous kitchen management, that functions were always late and rarely went smoothly. Many wedding parties would complain, uncomfortably being forced to wait for food, and when it finally arrived was cold or not the dish they had expected. Without prep lists for each function, it'd be utter chaos in the kitchen, each employee having no clear definition of their role or specific job detail.

With four banquet rooms came four different menus, parties ranging from 20 to 500 guests, many times only minutes between each function. I then made it imperative that we incorporate BEO sheets, or Banquet Event Order templates, used to outline every party and their expectations, stressing specific details for each task and every client request. Who the florist was, the headcount, the party's time of arrival, estimated time they wanted to be served, and how many people at the head table. Every detail noted would help to streamline operations eliminating any questions. Only then could the chef, sales team, cooks, food and beverage, banquet captain, and servers, all be on the same page with unequivocal objectives for each function.

Next, a deep cleaning and sanitation of the entire kitchen was completed. I had inherited a freezer that was stacked from floor to ceiling with unlabeled previous function leftovers, all freezer-burnt and unrecognizable as to the content. Ice crystals so thick on top of each item, it would take having to thaw the product if I ever wanted to find out what it was. Most of the finished product in the freezer that had been purchased were items that should have easily been

Head Chef

prepared from scratch, rather than cooked from a frozen state. Everything was discarded.

The kitchen equipment coated in grease and in disrepair, it became clear why the previous chef had been fired. Grease so thick on the sides and under much of the equipment that it would require a putty knife to scrape it off. Slowly pushing the knife, yellowish grime and grease with food particles attached would roll off the knife. Next, the layout of the line was modified; every gas line was disconnected, and each piece of equipment relocated, eliminating unwarranted steps and wasteful motion at each station. Chefs would no longer crisscross or bump into one another, making it impossible to achieve a fluid rhythm. Finally, recipes; virtually nonexistent, were then developed for those staple items to ensure their consistency.

Volume-cooking came easy. Basically, preparing the same food, however, on a larger scale, it provided me an opportunity to play with larger toys. Tilt kettles, steam-jacketed roasting pans, alto-shams, huge mixing wands, or "sticks," and revolving deck ovens; allowed us to serve hundreds at a time with minimal effort.

In the first couple years, we recorded the highest hotel occupancy rate and largest gross revenue capture in both banquets and the restaurant. More importantly, the restaurant was turning a profit. For decades, hotel restaurants were considered a mere amenity to each hotel property — a loss-leader — like those cheap crappy continental breakfasts served every day in hotels across the country. In exchange for your stay, you are given a hearty choice of frozen Danish, stale toast, sugar juice, and weak coffee. Rarely, when a restaurant was located inside a hotel, was it able to stand on its own without kickbacks from the room revenue. The restaurant would essentially compliment the hotel, management grateful when paying guests would choose dining in.

Weekends became so hectic, I'd grab a room at the hotel rather than drive the 45 minutes back home, only forced to return a few hours later for another frantic day. Keeping the same room for the following night, I developed a habit of hiding my personal items and a change of clothes in the same room. Standing on the bed, I'd pop a ceiling tile just wide enough to slip in my belongings. On one occasion, as I struggled to reach into the opening, a large dildo rolled out and landed on the bed. I couldn't help but wonder what other items might be hidden in these rooms?

On other occasions, if the kitchen staff was on schedule, I'd grab a few guys, many of my close Hispanic staff, and we'd watch TV in my room before the evening service. My Spanish becoming fluent after having worked in numerous kitchens with my Hispanic cohorts, I coveted the comradery we shared. All in all, everything seemed to be going well, while managing to maintain a respectable 30% food cost, it seemed everyone was content.

Over time the hotel and my responsibilities quickly became routine. Each day new guests would arrive, never allowing you to rest on your laurels. With three shifts of food service combined with business meetings during the week and a variety of banquets each weekend, the hotel which was once a side business venture for the proprietor was now a consequential money stream. Every Sunday

Head Chef

night, Kool and the Gang's, wedding song, "Celebration," or the occasional "Chicken Dance" music, combined with loud laughter reaching inside the kitchen from the ballroom would signal another successful end to a long week.

After five years — an eternity in the food business — with trends changing and the demands to remain relevant, pressured, the owner began a complete remodel of the entire hotel. The undertaking would require months of work, endless dust, agitation, and constant strain on behalf of all the department heads and employees at the hotel. The owner, with whom I had developed a comfortable rapport, was suddenly firing Food and Beverage directors every three months. Then without notice, the executive housekeeper was let go, and finally the general manager terminated. Tensions remained high, everyone uncertain if they would be next.

One after the other, it became a revolving door of managers and employees unable to endure the constant scrutiny. During this interim, one of the *three-month* Food and Beverage directors had developed a poor habit of issuing indecipherable banquet event order contracts. One party in particular — the guests being vegetarian — had requested broccoli gratin asiago as one of their courses. At a modest count of 250 guests, required we use one of the large tilt-kettles for the soup, making it easier to accommodate hundreds if necessary. However, any indication that they were vegetarian was nowhere to be found on the BEO.

In most scenarios if there is no indication otherwise, chicken stock was the go-to base for most soups. So, well, you guessed it.

The entire party, which had requested a vegetarian menu, had just been served chicken broccoli au gratin. My sous chefs knew it, I knew it, and all the cooks knew it. After service both the General Manager and Food and Beverage Director, came into the kitchen offering rave reviews of the party, however, swore, after tasting the soup that it had been prepared with chicken. Welcoming the positive feedback, all the cooks glanced at each other, shrugged in unison, and confidently asserted they had no idea what management was talking about. All 250 guests, oblivious of the chicken broccoli cheese soup they had been served.

The hotel would continue with its cutbacks due to an occupancy drop, this after a new Radisson property had completed construction only a couple of blocks away. On numerous occasions, I'd work as both the chef and the Food and Beverage director after one of the owner's tirades having fired and vacated the F&B position, again. Ordering liquor, making sure the bars were set up, scheduling service staff, and supervising the banquet captains, my workdays became even longer.

One day I'd supervise banquet room setups, order linens, and make limousine arrangements for the bride and groom, while other days I was back inside the kitchen prepping a steamship round for a buffet. I welcomed the challenge allowing me to gain invaluable experience, however, I knew the hotel had become dysfunctional. Food and Beverage, while easy, made me realize I lacked the temperament to babysit and rely on others after delegating tasks; I

Head Chef

much preferred to be hands-on in my kitchen environment rather than simply barking out orders.

After one round of firings, the owner hired yet another F&B Director, combining the position with that of head sales manager. This new position was filled by none other than his girlfriend; the beginning of my end at the hotel. With no F&B manager to train her, she began her career at entry level with zero experience. Now in charge of two departments, her new role completely foreign to her, I was to provide her only training.

The *training,* however, would never materialize. In my fifth year, outlasting the tenure of any previous head chef, general manager, or any other department head, I found her work ethic pitiful at best. Throughout my career, I'd always made a point of keeping my head down and remaining focused avoiding the politics, preferring my work speak for itself. But I soon found it to be impossible.

Unable to grasp the timing for party execution, no understanding of banquet event orders, how to inventory liquor, set up a function, or any comprehension of industry terminology, the "Princess" in a matter of no time had become overwhelmed. Open bar, family-style, risers, eight-round, Queen Mary, plated, 86, banquet captain, scheduling, and who performs what duties — all industry reference jargon that was completely alien to her.

It wasn't long before I began resenting having saved her ass multiple times, the oblivious owner assuming all was well under her guise. Months into her new job, she never once would stay late into the evening to close out a function nor would she ever supervise the setting up of an event. All part of her job description. Banquet contracts became nonexistent, and many times instructions were simply handed to me on sticky notes. Any responsible individual in this business is completely aware of her type and their defining character traits. Strolling in at 9 a.m. and leaving at 3 p.m., evening functions were essentially left to their own devices, many times unraveling into anarchy.

On many occasions, wearing my filthy chef whites in full display, I was embarrassingly forced into the ballroom, troubleshooting banquet maladies. My whites blood-stained or smeared with various foods, I only imagined what the bride and groom were thinking. It became common for me to frequent as many as four ceremonies in one evening. A master of disguises, I quickly learned to keep handy a sportscoat in my office or clean chef jacket readily available for any occasion.

Only a matter of time before everything would come to a head, during a hectic lunch, the line, while caught in the weeds, was down some 15 tickets. It all played out in minutes. Strolling into the kitchen, the unmistakable sound of her high heels clicked on the kitchen quarry tiles as she made her grand appearance. Oblivious that the kitchen was struggling, she calls my name from across the pass, and then again two more times, clearly visible how busy the line was. "Paul, Paul?" Like nails on a chalkboard, I despised the sound of my name escaping from her lips. Instinctively I knew what she wanted. Ritualistic, the Prima-donna had arrived late for work and

Head Chef

was now famished only two hours into her shift, demanding that her hunger be satisfied.

If you're not in the business, understand this: The Golden Rule during the heat of any rush is that no employees are to order food. Period. It further stresses the line, while paying customers always take priority. If the line happened to be slow during any particular moment, one of our chefs would assuredly prepare you a meal. God forbid, Princess eat the already-prepared food selections in the employee cafeteria and be forced to mingle with the peasants.

An addendum to the Golden Rule: No verbal Instructions! Always, always remember this rule. The chef can't give a rat's ass that you like your sandwich lightly toasted, without swiss cheese because your stomach disagrees, and that you prefer provolone, while you fancy your baguette to be cut on a bias rather than in half like mom used to do. Just type it into the POS for the love of god or write it down! If we're 15 tickets deep, you're now asking us to stop the line, and then listen to your diatribe pontificating your instructions, expecting us to recall every minute detail from memory.

Back on the line, now capturing my full attention, Princess immediately violates the addendum to rule number one. Not in the mood, I bend down to look at her between the stacked plates, face to face through the pass. She began, "Paul, can you make me—" I interrupted. *"Do you not see how busy we are on the line? Your meal is going to have to wait until we knock these tickets out."* Never once did I yell or unprofessionally bring any of the staff's attention to our minor altercation. Regardless, she abruptly spins around in her fucking high heels and storms out of the kitchen, click, click, clicking away. I then struggled to regain my focus on the line both pissed at her and myself for having remained in control. I so wanted to unload on her but held my restraint. After five years of stellar numbers, delivering lower than expected food costs, excellent labor reports, and always coming in under budget, I knew my job was now in jeopardy over a fucking tuna sandwich.

Decades later, I still question why most properties can never solely be about cooking and customer satisfaction as the priority. Politics proliferating most properties, wind up suffocating many kitchens and their creative ability. Was it because I oversaw my own kitchen, or had I finally become the stereotypical temperamental chef? Hidden in the back, away from the front offices and political posturing, at one time the kitchen had always provided me a sense of comfort. Similar to being on an island all alone, impervious to the daily drama unfolding in the other departments.

Soon I began longing for those days when all I had to do was show up for my shift and rock the food, my coffee nearby on a shelf. Looking back, it all seemed so much simpler. Now there were reports, menu development, meetings, an immense staff, and countless personalities forced to navigate. I quickly discovered that rules don't always apply to everybody.

From day one, chefs are grounded and conditioned with the predominant aphorism: The customer is always right. How dare she march into *my* kitchen, expecting to be catered above the needs of a paying customer! That the kitchen line be forced to come to a halt,

Head Chef

and the head chef personally prepares her meal, finishing it specially decorated with a sprig of parsley.

Things were never the same after the incident, and the writing was on the wall. Sales started to noticeably slip, along with service. Resentful and harboring a sense of betrayal for having doubled for months as both Food and Beverage Director and head chef, I resorted to primarily focusing solely on the kitchen and my direct staff. Perhaps then, she would be exposed if everything were left in ruins other than the kitchen. Strange, by putting the customer first, I had become the "unapproachable Prima-donna star chef."

Making matters worse, a third hotel was being built less than a quarter mile away. The desperation became apparent when ownership chose to franchise the property to gain additional exposure. Occupancy continued to languish, and no longer was the hotel a unique boutique property, having become synonymous and dated.

Having grown tiresome of the drama, once again I was reminded of the instability of my profession and after five years, needed a mental and physical break. Unable to afford a sabbatical and preferring not to be the next chef walking out the back door with his box, I had to be selective in my next chef gig — one that would also allow me time to spend with my daughter.

Rarely during job interviews would I discuss being a single father. Acknowledging your family or any interests outside of the profession is many times a common amateur slip among chefs when looking for a job. Considered taboo to have secondary interests, let alone the demands and distractions of a family. While workplace discrimination protection has found its platform mainstream in the corporate world, it seems that same affinity has yet to find its way inside most kitchens.

Known by most in the restaurant circle, several hospitality groups in Chicago are notorious for seeking out young, unsuspecting chef talent. Not necessarily for their skills, but rather for their stamina, no distracting secondary interests, no immediate family, and a willingness to work for meager wages. These same properties are infamous among young chefs for burning them out with 16-hour days. However, many of those very same restaurants are on the edge of haute cuisine, are Michelin rated, and promise that one could work with the best and freshest of ingredients, side by side with an acclaimed chef — Michelin, Forbes, James Beard, Food and Wine Magazine, acclaimed chefs. Common that while these chefs work depraved hours, many times earn somewhere between only $15-$29k in salary. Barely enough to survive on, and the sad fact when divided hourly, the pay is far less than minimum wage.

Finding a head chef position while ensuring I would work no more than 50 hours a week would prove impossible, forcing me to assume a lesser role. Fortunately, it would allow me to avoid the politics, cancerous scheming, and endless pasteurized meetings. The money decent, I could also work during the day and be home with Amy most nights. On weekends between Friday and Sunday, the restaurant's busiest time, when Amy wasn't home, I'd cram 40 hours into three days.

Head Chef

Microbreweries, while not only popular with beer enthusiasts, but to a growing number of discriminating foodies as well. I became fascinated by cooking with artesian varietal beers and their pairing of foods. At the free-standing restaurant, I was no longer forced to deal with banquets or the other frenetic demands, making my new position a cakewalk. A welcome change where I could perform my job unscathed and simply go home after my shift, or so I thought.

Crises, while a prerequisite in the business, I made every attempt to avoid the pitfalls attached with management or anyone else at my new gig, either with the head chef himself, the restaurant staff, or the owner. I remained vigilant to my adage of keeping my head down while avoiding confrontation. The head chef, while undoubtedly talented, remained in constant turmoil with the owner-operator. His menu creations, many of which were derived from having staged at Le Titi de Paris, a favorite haute French restaurant outside of Chicago, struggled to gain footing with the microbrew crowd.

When envisioning a Microbrewery, think countless beer taps, prominently displayed large brass brew kettles, German steins, and dusty deep-cherry wood furnishings. Brew Masters with beards in plaid shirts experimenting with different hops, and various ingredients like that of a winemaker. The clientele was not interested in foie gras, blanquette de veau, or French gastronomy. Why not expand on the German ancestry instead? Hell, the owner himself was German! Would it not be better suited to exploit on that same theme?

Paul Barthel

Why not offer a charcuterie of homemade sausages, favorites like shepherd's pie, Irish boxty, and Wiener schnitzel? Detached and refusing to interfere, I watched the chef struggle, remaining true to the dated cuisine classique traditional French methods, and his identity, rather than complementing the restaurant's congruity. All too common defiant chefs — however driven — many times stubbornly remain paralyzed in their comfort zone, oblivious to the customer's palate and what the demographics may dictate.

Despite the restaurant's clear lack of direction, business remained steady, enough that rumors of a second location began circulating. Despite having the time to knock out a couple more culinary classes and spend time with my daughter, I found the money as a sous chef mediocre at best. Intrigued, the possibility of getting transferred to the new restaurant was on my mind, and at the same time breaking into the city market at what would be the largest microbrewery in Chicago.

Predictably, the chef and owner's arguments became loud and careless, many times in the presence of staff. Yelling, arms waving dramatically, fists slamming on the stainless-steel tables, and ultimately, threats. After having staged while the chef took a vacation, I felt ready if called upon, but I refused to conspire against him during his absence. To this day, I refrain from burning anyone by plotting against them, it's just not cool. Since I'd been there myself, I knew all too well what the chef was going through. At the same time, I was also uncertain I wanted anymore punishment by assuming his position under such turbulent ownership.

Head Chef

Arriving for work one day, eerily silent among the staff, there was no official announcement that the head chef had left, and I simply slipped into his role. It would be an entire week before the owner even acknowledged the chef's departure, and that I would be taking command of the kitchen. Grateful, however hesitant, I found myself once again disgusted with the unprofessionalism that permeated the business, and all the broken lives left in its wake. If anything, I was content to not have been the antagonist for his departure, but beside myself for how it had gone down.

I first attacked the menu and specials offered daily. Beer pairings, expanding on the German fare, and homestyle comfort food offerings, with a balance of lighter selections to accommodate a variety of palates became the theme. With little notice, I acted on an idea I'd had for months and arranged for a live, limited grill offering in the thriving outdoor beer garden, using a separate portable kitchen stand-alone. Menu selections would be prepared directly in front of a captive audience while dining al fresco. This idea was the first cut of my teeth as head chef and strongly contested by the general manager's wishes. Regardless, I did it anyways. Let the politics begin!

Cleaning up an old commercial grill, I filled two propane tanks, rolled out a micro-fridge, stocked it with mise en place, set up a stainless-steel table, and in no time, I was ready to put on a show. Convinced it would work and that there was nothing to lose. With live German music playing outside, a picturesque sunset, summer breeze, and strung-up Italian lights lit everywhere, the setting was perfect.

In the beginning, prior to the outdoor kitchen, were table upon table of random beer drinkers, all without food in front of them. Money was simply being left on the table, I thought. This was about to change. Despite the general manager's chagrin over being forced to staff the garden and count more money after closing, the live cooking station was a smash.

You know his type, someone who'll do most anything to avoid additional work, despite any beneficial results — the glass is half empty mentality — all suggestions met with reservation. More likely, because it wasn't his idea. The smell of ribs and sausages permeated the entire outdoor area finding its way onto the parking lot as cars arrived. So busy at times, that the main dining room in the restaurant slowed as people waited to dine in the celebration.

Initially, I personally worked the station to ensure its success creating a food spectacle of sorts. Flames would shoot up over the grill, exchanging laughter with customers and encouraging any interaction that would draw them to the food so they would open their wallets. Not only did it provide me a chance to get out from behind the line in the kitchen and greet my customers, but it also allowed me to generally piss off the general manager.

The microbrewery's kitchen was miserably small compared to that of the spacious hotel I had grown accustomed to, and it was in serious need of a paint job. Now that I was in control of the kitchen and the new menus complete, I next decided to paint the entire

Head Chef

kitchen myself on what would have been my day off. Repeatedly I asked for monies to purchase the paint supplies, but it never happened. Patience never a strong virtue of mine, I went out and purchased the paint materials myself.

On the line, chefs are accustomed to quick results: A customer looks at the menu, the ticket hits, we cook the food, and bam, it's done. Next! *So, what's the holdup with the paint?* The surroundings in any work environment are reflective of the end-product, and I found it unacceptable working in an unkempt kitchen. Spending $150 on paint and supplies, it took one day for the project, which encouraged an entirely new feel in the kitchen. Most of the staff questioned why a head chef would bother to paint someone else's kitchen, on his day off, no less. Strangely, it made no difference to me, suggesting, *"do you not feel more inclined to serve a better product from a kitchen that is now presentable?"*

Not surprising, when it came time to submit the paint receipt to get my money back, the general manager with exaggerated skepticism let me know of his disapproval for failing to gain his permission. Once again, he felt a sense of betrayal for having been left out of the decision, despite zero labor costs and a kitchen that now looked incredible. Days later, without having yet seen the kitchen, reminiscent of his strained relationship with the previous chef, the owner proceeded to scold me for purchasing the paint without asking.

Fairly certain the general manager had ratted me out; he could have just as easily paid the receipt and filed it. All this over $150, or the equivalent of a party of four diners. It was no secret the general manager and former chef were close friends, remaining in contact even after his departure. In the general managers eyes, I could never fill the previous chefs shoes, and despite any of my successes, even those contributing to the bottom line, were met with skepticism or a lack of enthusiasm from the "strawman," as I referred to him.

The whole kitchen-painting episode left me humbled, reminding me once again how essential it is to never let your guard down. If you're going to stab me in the back, I'd much prefer you use a knife rather than a spoon. Garnering several favorable press reviews, my position remained secure despite the painting debacle. Later it was announced that I would be getting the transfer and heading to Chicago to open the new location. Not surprising, however, *strawman*, was never considered for the position as general manager of the new location, he would be left behind.

Taken aback, my first time walking into what was a shell of the future microbrewery, was easily four times the size of the one I would be leaving. A monstrosity to say the least. From the very beginning, it was apparent after the behemoth real estate purchase, that the owner may have overleveraged. Remember the precept: six out of ten new restaurants fail within the first year, while 90% of those are due to undercapitalization.

The assistant general manager, I, and a few select others from the previous location were all chosen to open the new property. As part of the agreement, we'd have to work during the buildout. Working the line the previous day, I was now sweating side by side with the

Head Chef

AGM sanding and staining columns, painting woodwork, and hauling materials from floor to floor. Suddenly, I had become a carpenter. My new executive sous chef, whom I had hired to represent the new restaurant when it opened, walked out on day one after handing him a paintbrush. For me, the tasks were a welcome break off the line; for a short while, I escaped the air-borne grease that would stick in my hair, stifling heat, and intense pressures of the kitchen. Not only was I adding a large-scale opening to my resume but was essentially given a blank check to design and layout my future kitchen.

Any experienced chef would agree that before you design a kitchen, you must first come up with a menu or a general idea of what foods will be prepared. Despite assuming my new role over a new kitchen, reluctantly, the menu was highly dictated by the owner. Coming full circle, I found myself in similar shoes to those of the previous chef at the first location. Not only was the menu confusing but was overly assertive, failing to consider the labor required and amount of prep it would take for each dish.

Left with little choice other than I go along, I resorted to focusing my efforts on designing the kitchen and selecting the equipment, frugally spending money as if it were my own. There was no need for steam-jacketed kettles, rotating alto-shams, or any unnecessary equipment that might strain the budget. The kitchen was designed to be functional while emphasizing station-fluidity, thorough refrigeration, and plenty of line space for each chef. It had all the necessary tools, and a few toys to boot.

The gut work and eventual buildout would take months, our work commencing with a mere shell of a former brick and mortar three-story factory. For those with the imaginativeness to endure, the work was not without its rewards. Often, we would sample the variety of craft beers once the brewery became functional. Pale Ale, Oktoberfest, Railroad Stout, Belgium Stout, Lagers, Ambers, and Wheats. We then hit the streets of Chicago dining out at a host of restaurants sampling and *borrowing* ideas in preparation for our own menu.

Each day afforded those who stuck around a sense of belonging, and each passing day, one day closer to opening. Pranking each other during the buildout became commonplace. Because parking in Chicago came at a premium, we regularly took parking tickets off other vehicles and placed them on each other's cars watching the reaction from a distance. On other occasions, one of us might find their car missing completely if the keys were left unattended; we'd be left to wander the surrounding blocks, setting off the car alarm, searching for our car.

The worst – or perhaps best – prank was when all the bathrooms were being constructed on the second floor. One brave soul became ruthless with their continued use of the men's bathroom farthest stall, relieving himself regularly without flushing. Each use causing the level of human waste to rise mere inches from the toilet lid. Left behind to ferment for some unsuspecting victim, it was eventually discovered by none other than the owner. With the toilet clogged, and no one coming forward, wearing an elbow-length latex glove, the

Head Chef

owner was forced to scoop the shit out himself. Stumbling out of the bathroom with his face beet red, coughing, and in tears from vomiting, it took total restraint on all our parts to remain straight-faced whilst protecting our jobs.

After months of hard work, the buildout was finally completed. The result leaving beautifully exposed rustic-factory brickwork adorning each floor on all the walls, and stained hardwood distressed flooring on all three levels. Each floorboard meticulously sanded after years of taking a beating when a factory. The grains, now visible, and wood integrity, completely restored. Each cavernous, vaulted ceiling in the various rooms was over twenty feet high, with massive overhead railroad tie beams, accented with salient behemoth cherry wood-stained columns and ironwork-crafted sconces. The kitchen would require all new plumbing, gas lines, and duct work that had to be vented three stories up to the roof.

The main floor's dining room was designed with a mixture of carpeted, raised step-up booths, deep stained oak tables, and a full wrap-around bar with dozens of tap lines offering a variety of signature craft beers on each side of the bar, complemented by hanging stemware. The tap lines were brilliantly run through the floor into a massive refrigeration enclosure located in the basement so no kegs would be visible on the main floor. Gone were the days of being forced to physically swap out the unsightly kegs in front of customers.

The floor-to-ceiling windows directly facing the street were consumed by towering, brilliant shiny brass and stainless-steel brew-

towers. Cars driving by less than fifteen feet away, and pedestrians couldn't help but notice as they passed. The other two floors were converted into party spaces, fully equipped with their own bar, banquet area, and private room sporting a cigar, martini, and cognac lounge. The views were breathtaking; just outside many of the windows stood the iconic Chicago skyline and much of its architecture. Everywhere you looked there was money spent in the tens of thousands. We were ready for the opening. Or were we?

It was no secret my desire was for a soft opening, preferring to offer a combination of sample portions from our menu combined with hors-d'oeuvres, served either passed or stationed on islands, allowing guests a chance to mingle. Despite my pleas since this was not my first rodeo and having been in this situation before, my request would fall on deaf ears.

Instead, I was instructed to hit up as many vendors as possible for *"free stuff."* Free stuff, meaning frozen appetizers or anything easily sheet-panned, baked, or deep fried. *Are you fucking kidding me?* Rumors were circulating that the owner had financially invested well over a million dollars into the building, and he now wanted me to serve frozen sawdust meatballs on opening day.

Vendors, eager for our business in trade for future orders, proved easy to secure all the free crap we would need. However, we were about to open as a major player in a metropolitan city entrenched in its food culture and culinary astuteness. And the avail of critics who reached thousands of followers and those living near the restaurant, in addition to people I knew who were coming to sample my menu. Money was tight, but no one knew just how tight.

Even before the doors would open, I held strong reservations as phones were left unanswered or when unopened mail would accumulate in the office. Further adding to my suspicion was when the installation of the kitchen floor quarry tile was scrapped at the last minute, leaving a cement finish covered with an epoxy. I remember questioning how it could have ever passed a health inspection.

Food particles wound up getting trapped in the uneven cement textured surface, and when mopping, the strings of fabric from the mop would tear off and get caught in the rough jagged flooring. Looking across the surface was a sea of broken blue strings, all ripped off from the mop head. The kitchen became an embarrassment when on displayed walkthroughs with visiting customers or associates.

For the grand opening, I hit up Sysco, Reinhart, U.S. Foods, and any other vendor I could for the "free stuff." The evening finally arrived, each of us ambivalent about what was to unfold. However, serving frozen resemblances of food by-products off sheet pans left me concerned. As the opening hour neared, a line of people formed outside, wrapping around the building. Looking out the windows, even more people were waiting in their cars until the doors were unlocked.

Once the doors opened, the crowd was massive and immediately uncontrollable, unlike anything I had ever seen. The hostess station eventually abandoned, left the masses to flood inside, ungreeted.

Paul Barthel

Like a flash mob assaulting a department store or a rave, the hordes of people was relentless. At any moment I expected to witness someone bodysurfing over the crowd. Had the fire marshal been there, we would have quickly been shut down for maximum occupancy code violations. Like a packed concert, people became sardines next to each other while unable to turn, much less make their way among the throngs. Appetizers left the kitchen at a feverish pace. Frozen rumakis, pigs in a blanket, sawdust meatballs — all those frozen crap appetizers people are accustomed to at cheap cookie-cutter banquet hall weddings or local dive bars.

Reminiscent of those unadorned days back at the Bullmarket, we were serving dioxin byproducts laced with MSG, shaped, microwaved and manufactured, bearing little resemblance of something mildly edible. It became as easy as spreading the shit out on sheet pans and placing them in the oven, or merely immersing the product in a deep fryer for three minutes. Hell, the kitchen crew from the Bullmarket would have been proud. Case after case, we served the chemically processed synthetic pieces by the thousands to the masses. Meanwhile, confident the kitchen could keep up, I changed into some clean whites, allowing me to circulate the rooms, welcoming guests, reluctantly representing the grub being served.

Making my way through the mob of suits and short skirts, was only made easier by sticking out in my stark chef whites. Shaking hands and greeting each encounter, I convinced myself that perhaps they were too inebriated on the free beer and wouldn't remember the frozen pizza puff they had just washed down. Mortified, I then ran

Head Chef

into a chef friend sitting at a high-top with restaurant cohorts, his expression obvious. Pulling me close, he flatly offered, "what the fuck is this?"

Moving on, my mind wandered as I greeted face after face. Should I have threatened to quit, forced into preparing this, this lesser than cafeteria quality sustenance? It was now suddenly apparent that I had failed in making my case clear, what a colossal blunder it would be, but for now I was fully immersed and would have to get through the night.

The elevator full, I ran up the staircase to the second floor. Thanks to my chef whites, I managed to push through the crowd, making it to one of the bars. The bartenders buried; patrons were waiting four-deep surrounding the bar while the taps were pouring non-stop foam. Empty glasses were being held upwards everywhere as people were becoming increasingly agitated. Nowhere to be found, the owner was lost in the sea of bodies, and servers trapped in the masses, unable to move, or hiding out of humiliation. With an idea, I squeezed my way back through the mob and headed towards the basement.

Surrounded by kegs and tap lines running in all directions in the massive walk-in coolers, I grabbed several sleeves of plastic beer cups. Leading three servers inside with me, I told them, *"fuck the glasses at the bar!"* I then tapped directly from each by-pass spout in several of the beer lines, filling cup after cup and placing them on trays. *"Take these up to the second floor, give them out with a smile and brief description, and then head back down here for more."* Struggling to keep up, one after the other, servers returned with their trays empty. Confident the kitchen was experiencing no issues serving the frozen sawdust byproducts, I continued pouring.

On my knees, with one hand holding a cup and the other tapping from a spout, I looked up for more servers only to be confronted by the owner staring down at me. His mouth gaping wide open, demanding, "what the hell are you doing?" Responding, *"—Uh, none of the bartenders can keep up, people are pissed off, and on top of that, the beer coming out at the bars is foam! How the hell do you think the beer has been getting out so fast?"* Flabbergasted and out of breath, he ran off, muttering incoherently. Adrenaline coursing through his veins, he reminded me of someone watching their house burn down with only mere seconds deciding what to save. By placing something in the hands of the guests, certainly avoided what could have easily gotten ugly, perhaps sinking into a riot.

Hors-d'oeuvres depleted and cut off around 11 p.m., I wouldn't arrive home until 4 a.m., only to return a few short hours later for our first official day off the real menu. Not nearly enough caffeine in my system, it would have been more fitting had a catheter of coffee been strapped to my waist and an IV run into my arm. I couldn't help but wonder, if yesterday was that busy, how insane will our first operational day be? The microbrewery so large that I had concerns how servers could effectively navigate each room, return to the kitchen, and then get back to their tables with food still warm. These challenges would plague the property indefinitely.

Head Chef

The capacious space turned out to be a nightmare from day one; frustrated cooks watched their plates bake under heat lamps, and sales of appetizers and desserts became nonexistent when servers figured out it would save a trip to the kitchen by not offering at all. This significantly reduced check averages, and ultimately the bottom line. All the craft brews would require a description for any new customers, demanding the servers spend *even more* time at each table, thus neglecting the food. To provide better service, station sizes were then reduced, and servers outraged as they watched their tips plummet. Tensions flared between the back of the house and the front until food runners were then brought in, reducing trips servers would be forced to make back into the kitchen. Payroll then became exacerbated crippling any returns on profit.

Over time the restaurant subconsciously succumbed to dysfunctional acceptance. We managed to post impressive numbers on several occasions, but nowhere near a consistent level that could afford the massive buildout costs, mortgage, taxes, electric and other fixed costs. The mediocre numbers were then met with micromanaging, followed by cuts in labor and then finally, food quality; the kryptonite responsible for most restaurant closures.

There were nights we'd unexpectedly get slammed with only three servers on the floor and no hostess. The food would come out late, guests would wait forever to be seated, and diners idled at their table while waiting for their check, waving their arms to grab anyone's attention. The desperation eventually made its way into the kitchen, and the preparation of food remained in constant flux. The house staple menu item — stout batter dipped haddock — became a question of, should we end with beer batter then fryer, or batter, flour, fryer? It seemed everyone was suddenly now a chef with a recipe in their hand that was going to save the restaurant.

Tastings became embarrassing, while the owner regularly changed menu items on the fly. Plates would be under constant scrutiny looking different each time they left the pass, and the main menu was redesigned less than two months after opening. Unwavering in his misjudgment, the owner insisted on substituting our once-popular haddock with the poor-quality pollock to save money. No comparison, it's the very same fish slapped between a bun at most fast food restaurants. Not only is it a distinct taste disadvantage, but it's impossible to work with. The pollock, was not only to greasy, but would shred due to the weight of the batter, breaking apart each time it was pulled from the fryer. Each fillet would have to be patted down to absorb the grease, becoming a nightmare to serve.

The newest menu, or *menu of the month*, as it was referred, created out of desperation, attempted to mirror a host of restaurants. A potpourri of German, American, Irish, French, and Cajun confusion. Wiener schnitzel was suddenly listed next to Jambalaya, and filet carpaccio next to mozzarella sticks. Yes, those same mozzarella sticks you can find in most sports bars. A menu purposefully designed to appease every palate, and every ethnicity. A *global* menu, if you will, page after page, the menu was likened to a small novel making it impossible for the kitchen. Reminiscent of those menus found in many dive Greek breakfast houses. The only thing we were missing were breakfast options.

In less than a year after opening we'd gone through a whole service staff, all original bartenders, two salespeople, and three general managers. My foot was already out the door, sensing it was time to get out, when the inevitable happened.

Coming from a food critic, who managed to slip in and out unnoticed, however, unlike small local print reviews, this was in a major Chicago newspaper. My only bad review in over 30 years chefing. While the microbrewery was behemoth, and the largest in the city of Chicago, it demanded that it be critiqued eventually. I knew that it was only a matter of time, but I'd hoped to abandon ship before it would take place under my watch, thus avoiding my name being attached to the doomed Titanic.

Unfortunately, the critic delivered his review when the kitchen was in one of its several menu transitions and lacking any clear direction. The critique while scathing, however, was littered with bits of promise. "Where are the sausages, or German food?" it questioned. It went on, describing the structure as being too large, suffering from an "edifice problem," overtly desperate for attention, and uncharacteristically large for a microbrewery. There were positive bits, while most was written suggesting how the issues could be corrected. Regardless, I felt as if I'd been punched in the stomach.

Pissed at myself for not having left sooner, I would own the review. Like a quarterback losing in the Super Bowl despite being a team effort, or infamous French chef Bernard Loiseau of La Côte d'Or refusing to blame anyone but himself for losing a Michelin star. Unlike Loiseau, who would later go on to commit suicide for losing that star, reviews are only good until reviewed again. I would survive.

As it turns out, the review boosted business, suggesting that any publicity is good publicity. But it was too little too late. One evening in the office as I was going over bills, reviewing profit and loss statements, and discussing operations with the owner, I witnessed something I'd never seen before, in all my years. Always stoic and resigned, the owner began shedding tears, deducing the restaurant's dire circumstances. The Chicago location had cost over a million dollars for its purchase and buildout alone. This was not including the current operational expenditures, labor, taxes, nor food and beverage costs. In addition, the other location was also experiencing its own drop in numbers. Suddenly, I felt the urge to hug him, but I also believed that many of his own decisions were to cause.

Should I stay until the end until the doors locked, and IRS sticker slapped on the door? Would I eventually be fired anyway? I weighed the options, finally choosing to leave, accepting a new position after five years with the microbrewery. By leaving, I had hoped that perhaps new management could resuscitate the business, however, less than a year later, even under new direction, the microbrewery would close its doors for good. To this day, I am unaware if it was seized by the IRS or forced into closure and liquidated. A short time later, not so coincidentally, the first location mysteriously suffered a catastrophic fire, closing it down permanently as well. German lightning perhaps?

Autumn and the beautiful leaves

CHAPTER EIGHT

In The Eyes

It was to be our last day on the resort grounds. Accessible only by boat or seaplane, we were vacationing on a remote island in northern Minnesota, the entire week had already slipped away. Back at the cabin, mom was straightening up, while my dad, I, and my two brothers were on the dock preparing for one last fishing excursion before heading back home. The smell of fresh lake water and pine trees still offer me pause, bringing back fond innocent memories from those times we spent together as a family. At the time, consumed with boyhood, I would assume like most, was disregardful of those precious moments as they played out before me, never to happen twice.

Indifferent to fishing, I merely enjoyed the company. The four of us together, on the open water, the gurgling of the outboard motor, the smell of gasoline from the engine, and the wind in our faces as we made our way. As a young boy, my dad had always amazed me. He instinctively knew how to start and steer the boat, or where to settle in for the best fishing. It seemed at that time like he was capable of anything and could do no wrong.

Bouncing on the waves, the outboard motor would block our voices, forcing us to yell while exploring on the lake, settling in one spot and then another. Trolling for what felt like a couple of hours with no prize to show, finally, dad decided on a marshy area he was confident was stocked with dinner.

Not long after, perhaps ten minutes of idling, I watched my red and white bobber being pulled under. Probably nine years old at the time, my older brother Nick had to guide me, showing me how to loosen up on the line, giving the fish some slack, then slowing, eventually reeling it in. As I held the reel, we all watched the fish floundering at the end of my line, my dad lifting it from the water to reveal a two-foot walleye. I immediately recall not wanting it.

Simply wanting to go for a ride in the boat with the guys, I hadn't given much thought to what would happen had I actually caught a fish. Hell, it was my brother Jim who threaded my hook with the poor, innocent worm. The walleye floundered and bounced around feverishly in the boat after my dad pulled the hook from its bloody mouth. Marveling, I remember watching its shiny, scaly, silver-green body at the bottom of the boat curving as it sprang up each time,

In The Eyes

struggling for oxygen. For its life. Congratulated for making the first catch, everyone eventually resumed fishing. However, my eyes never left my friend as its movement and his spring slowed, and eventually stopped, while lying near my feet. His unblinking eyes seemingly staring up at me, gills once searching for breath, were now still.

I desperately wanted to throw him back into the water. *What would my dad have thought? What would my brothers have to say?* At nine years old, I felt compelled to *man* up to the fact that despite being the youngest, I'd made the first catch that day. I should, of course, be proud. Right? As it turns out, I recall that was the only fish we caught on that outing, yet it had been my fish, and the life I had taken on that day I remember most. To this day, decades later, I have never fished again.

1966 with my two brothers. Sarge somewhere near.

Experimenting with life in Wyoming for a few short years, on one excursion, us four men gathered up a couple rifles and proceeded to hit the foothills for rabbit or whatever else we could scrounge up. Using a .22 or .308, us boys would take turns with the .22 while dad commanded the larger rifle. Hiking for what felt like miles, open range land awash with sagebrush, rock, and sand, we spooked out a variety of game hiding in the brush. Never did I argue for my turn, however, when my time did come, I much preferred shooting the rifle while using an old can or stick as my target. Deliberately brief, my time passed with either an intentional miss or I'd simply profess to having grown tired from carrying the rifle, willingly handing it off to one of my brothers.

In Wyoming, our plot of land was adjacent to the working farmlands and the foothills of Washakie County, a stone's throw away from the Big Horn Mountains, where hunting, trapping and raising cattle was a way of life. The same farmstead where our first dog, Sarge, lost his life after being shot and paralyzed by a farmer. Walking into the garage, it wasn't uncommon to find two or three freshly skinned game pelts hanging from the rafters, left to dry after my brother Jim trapped and skinned the prey. Fox, beaver, or raccoon, Jim, ever resourceful even while in high school, had begun making side money by trapping the animals and then selling the fur.

I could not help but imagine the animals trapped while still alive, sometimes days before the traps were checked. I questioned, how were they to meet their deaths? Shooting; a quicker, kindlier demise, unfortunately also leaves a hole in the valuable pelt. The animals forced to suffer; other methods would be utilized in protecting the valuable fur from damage. While I admired my brother's ingenuity, I couldn't help feeling saddened and helpless for the poor animals. Remorseful for the ill-fated creatures, I would pacify my grief by conveniently convincing myself that it was common practice; however, those images would be burned on my ceiling.

Almost all homes in the area had a second deep-freezer for game meat, or else they rented a cold storage locker for all the excess that was to be processed or waiting to be butchered. Venison chili, venison steak, venison tips; all the same meat, however, prepared different. The distinctive, gamey flavor masked by either a sauce or heavy hand using a variety of spices. It was virtually impossible to drive down the road during hunting season and not see a deer either over the hood or in the rear of a pickup bed, its legs, head, or antlers protruding over the side.

Chicago born and bred, then moving to Wyoming, my parents would become farmers overnight, suddenly deciding they wanted to raise chickens. To my astonishment, the baby chicks were shipped in the mail, two dozen fur-creatures arriving in a flat box, with tiny air holes cut into the sides. Looking through the holes, you could watch them running around and staring back at you. Upon opening the box, were these adorable, yellow fuzzy creatures, all chirping in unison. It wasn't long before we had over 200 chickens running around the yard. I was at least grateful for their being allowed to roam free, rather than factory-confined in two-foot square battery cages for life.

Over time, I would adopt an ornery pet rooster that followed me everywhere, however, the guard rooster he was, like a dog, he would attack others whenever they turned their backs on him. When mom wasn't home, I'd bring my pet rooster in the house and let him walk around and nest on the couch next to me while I watched cartoons. More than once I was forced to clean his shit off the carpet before mom returned. I always suspected she knew anyways but also knew how much I loved my bird and so, she would say nothing.

Looking back now, other than the occasional egg money we received from locals, the hens must have cost more than their worth, and quickly we had too many. One day, I watched in disbelief as one by one, mom placed their heads between two rusty nails driven into an old tree stump, bringing down an ax onto their necks. Gruesome while true, chickens do in fact run around with their heads cut off. Their bodies would flail violently, and wings would flap while their heads lay still on the log. Watching this once but never wanting to see it again, I refused in helping.

Instructed that I must pitch in; the chickens still had to be prepped before butchering. A basin was then filled with warm water, while their still-warm, lifeless bodies were submerged making the feathers easier to remove. The stench of death, bloody water, and wet feathers was unbearable. Working in the pool of floating, bloody feathers; the chickens eyes many times still open, seemed as if they were staring back at me. Purposely, I performed my job as imperfectly as possible, complaining all the while; elated when I was removed from plucking duty. After their feathers were removed, the chickens were then butchered and frozen, serving as our dinner for months.

After growing accustomed to our new way of life, alone and bored out in the country, many times I would go out shooting at random objects to simply pass the time. Looking around for my next target using a .22, I spotted a bird perched on a tree limb some 80 yards away. Far off and at a disadvantage having to aim upwards, I knew there was no chance I would hit the bird. Even if I did fire, at my age and inexperience with a rifle, the accuracy from such a distance would be impossible. Or, so I thought.

Adjusting the sight line by raising the barrel slightly over the target to account for range, I then paused. Exhaling on the squeeze, I lightly feathered the trigger. Just as quickly, the bird dropped straight down, never having a chance. Killed instantly. Surprised, I stared across the distance at the ground where the bird lay. I Immediately felt a sense of remorse and juvenile in my actions. No larger than an apple, the bird died instantly as the result of my selfish boredom. Kneeling, I gazed at the lifeless bird, angry at myself and melancholy for having taken its innocent life.

To this day, I struggle discerning those who track and kill innocent creatures, suggesting it's an acquired skill. Consider, the minimalist of effort it requires to end a defenseless, assailable life. To shoot a stationary target with a high-caliber munition, its velocity over 3,500 feet per second, the prey oblivious of the hunter's intentions. Hence, a virtual "sitting target." A sport? Hardly.

Certainly, the trek and arduous chore of having to stalk the prey can be laborious, however, the impassive gesture when taking an innocent life, bearing the same right to subsistence, I find both reckless and totally lacking empathy. While I fully support our Second Amendment right for protection, defense against tyranny, and for target sport shooting, nonetheless, blood-sport killing is hardly a sport, rather a useless disregard for life or desire for carnage.

After executing the innocent bird, I placed the .22 back inside the house and buried him next to the very tree it last perched upon. Years would pass until I picked up a gun, never again taking aim at an animal. Mindful that millions of birds live and die each year, and one bird bears no significance in the grand scheme of life, but for me to have made that choice, only to satisfy my curiosity, I would never forget. Decades later, that day and the bird are still fresh in my mind as if it were yesterday.

Strange, how we as humans are compelled, deciding what's best for those non-human sentient beings we share our only earth. The lack of compassion and empathy we fail to summon for those unable to fend for themselves, while we ironically lay claim to bearing a higher intellect. Should it not be part of our responsibility, then, to advance our conjectural superior intellect into cognitively applied actions that benefit all species? For the most part, our understanding and clemency extends to only our brethren, but how can we allow ourselves to about-face, abandoning the fortitude non-humans are owed, in addition, own in their birth-right, the same as humans?

In The Eyes

Closer to home, arguably, canines remain our dearest of non-human friends, and as close to multicultural domestication kinship among species that we are fortunate enough to share. Are they on the favorable side of speciesism while treated a larger equal and with more reverence simply because we have molded them into our likeness? Is it then our similar traits that bonds us, rather than say that of a goat?

Once a predator that was highly avoided, pure-bred grey wolves and the eventual bond we now share with them would take thousands of years before they would be welcomed into our homes. Other species, while ostensibly lacking the reasoning, are decidedly placed in cages as a commodity or held captive for other purposes, undoubtedly ignorant of their own capture or their eventual demise. But are they?

While if fortunate enough to be afforded any space, most, however, are bound to a life pacing back and forth in zoos from adjacent walls or imprisoned in battery cages and stockyard pens, force fed for optimal yield, unwillingly raped in gestation crates for mass reproduction, or waiting for their eventual slaughter. One must ask, are you willing to exchange your life for three square meals a day, held captive, exploited as entertainment or a commodity? We as humans typically define that as a prison.

To this day, we perform innumerable biological experiments on them with the sole intention of furthering our own species' preferment. Callously executed or probed are those chosen souls, many times without anesthesia, sadistically leaving them both injured and suffering. Those *fortunate* enough to survive endless testing, the victim is left to endure months or years of suffering, while the *newest* drug or treatment efficacy is analyzed.

Out of sight, out of mind, we impetuously assume the laws we have created certainly must not be allowing such horrors as described. While others, ill-conceived, hide behind such claims, finding comfort in what the living world has created; rabbits are hunted by hawks, tigers eat gazelles, and dogs chase cats. The strongest allowed to survive. However, it should be eminently noted that this is decided by the course of nature rather than for sport, cage, exploitation, commodity or experimentation.

During the mid-seventies, Yellowstone would witness the almost complete extinction of the brown bear, native to the protected park system. Listed as a threatened species under the Endangered Species Act in 1975, through wildlife preservation, cleaning our own garbage left at campsites and a conscious effort, at last count there were nearly a thousand grizzlies roaming in and around the National Park.

On the other hand, while we encourage hiking, camping, and other outdoor activities in Yellowstone, regretfully every couple of years someone sadly gets mauled to death by one of those very same protected brown bears. Search parties are then formed, which then track and kill the grizzly. Slaughtered for being a bear. *This is what bears do*; protecting their young or their environment! While we applaud and marvel at the bear, it seems we are now asking the bear to stop being a bear and be more like us humans. Our encroachment

In The Eyes

as a species appears relentless to mold or domesticate what we cannot understand or accept. Shame on the bear for being a bear.

After losing my dog Pepper, and while doing research for this book, I was inherently exposed to a whole new world unto itself. That, of course, would be the animal rights movement. The countless organizations and efforts bringing light to those animals with a plethora of causes; The American Society for the Prevention of Cruelty to Animals, Animal Legal Defense Fund, The Humanitarian League, the Captive Animals Protection Society, Farm Animal Rights Movement, and of course PETA, to name a few. There's even a Lobster Liberation Front Organization!

Yulin Dogs at Market

This does not include the hundreds of chapters, shelters, and localized grassroots efforts by individuals vying for welfare, representation, and liberation efforts for our dearest of friends. Despite these promising fronts, nothing could have prepared me for what I was exposed to in preparation for both this book and my eventual struggle to be reunited with Pepper. I would receive countless emails after my story broke about the heartache others were also similarly experiencing in their own lives. While comforting knowing I was not alone, it also demonstrated the lack of resources protecting their best interests.

Exploring my course of direction and viable means to reunite with Pepper would germinate a seed that had been planted decades earlier inside me; my love for animals that I have always felt. Naive and unprepared, I was consumed studying similar heartbreaking stories and the gravity of wrenching data and instances of pervasive animal abuse that was conveniently being filtered from wary eyes. The gruesome images and videos I would happen upon leaving me mortified, and at the same time paralyzed with inaction.

For example, the unforgivable slaughter of the majestic Greyhounds. Used in racing, once they become too slow, injured, or the racing track loses its popularity and closes, their displacement often leads to their being euthanized. Their entertainment value exhausted, they are then discarded since they no longer provide any intrinsic value to the business.

Photographs became the worst. I would stumble on strategically placed images, either to get your donation or to push an agenda.

In The Eyes

Photos of dogs mauled to death, victims of the underground Pitbull dog fighting circuit, where each dog is trained to fight to the death. And then there was the infamous hurricane Katrina. In New Orleans, thousands of domesticated dogs left abandoned, starving in flooded waters or in locked cages, forced to swim as the water rose until they grew too exhausted and flood waters consumed them.

Conveniently hidden kill shelters, inhumane laboratory testing practices, vivisection performed without anesthesia, appalling and insufferable livestock living conditions, and of course Yulin and Boknal. Bombarded with a world foreign to me, I was left reeling and feeling totally helpless and immobilized. The abysmal statistics, data, and the barbarous, indifferent world of animal abuse eventually becoming my torch.

An interesting exchange I once had with an acquaintance from the Guangxi Province of China about Yulin and the annual Lychee Dog Meat Festival; in his defense, he submitted that not everyone in Yulin participates in the yearly Lychee solstice festival. The "festival," a ten-day celebration typically held during the month of June, upwards of 15,000 dogs are killed and consumed over three weeks.

He reminded me that dogs are eaten there in much the same regard as Americans slaughter and consume millions of turkeys each year during Thanksgiving. How can we then ridicule their culture without being hypocritical? I suggested that he had an excellent point, while the best defense I could muster was, *"turkeys, however, for the most part have not been selectively domesticated where they live in our homes or sleep in our beds!"* I knew my argument wouldn't stand though, because many of the dogs in the Guangxi Province are raised similarly to how we raise and treat turkeys for slaughter here in the States. Besides, by using select speciesism, I had failed while conjecturing that a dog's life somehow is supremacist that over the turkey.

Yulin. Notice the cramped space.

What I was unprepared for, however, was coming to terms with the practices employed when massacring those poor, defenseless dogs, both during and before the event. Many of the dogs are slaughtered in ritualistic ways they believe preserve and keep the meat tender. Numerous are burned alive by propane torch or fire while forcibly being held down, boiled alive in large vats of water, or their throats slit, left to bleed out and die a slow, agonizing death. These gruesome images would haunt me; my mind fixated, mentally crippling me for days trying to make sense of it all.

These same dogs are kept in cages to mature for years, barely able to turn from being so cramped, stacked upon each other in rusted crates. The bones in their legs many times growing deformed and rigged with fibrous dysplasia from not moving and being unable to fully stand. Of no concern, since there is hardly any meat on their legs for consumption.

Today, there are numerous campaigns and petitions demanding that the Yulin Festival be discontinued, many of which I subscribe and support. However, many people fail to realize that Yulin is only one of many celebrations similarly found in other countries as well. The Boknal celebration in South Korea, and in addition to Nigeria, Vietnam, and Thailand are only a few places where it doesn't necessarily have to be a festival or holiday finding dog meat with regularity.

While America has come a long way in support of animal rights, it has taken centuries of questioning and challenging the stigma associated with the fair and ethical treatment of those non-humans. It wasn't until 1866, under the guidance of Henry Bergh – founder of the American Society for the Prevention of Cruelty to Animals – when the New York legislature adopted animal protection and policing powers for mistreated animals. Horses, which were used for transportation among other practices, were essentially dispensable once their resourcefulness had been depleted. Bergh himself witnessed the merciless beatings and punishment they suffered at the hands of carriage drivers on New York city streets. The malnourished horses, once exhausted and unable to pull the carriage any further, they were left to die on those very same city streets.

What first began as a merciful anti-cruelty effort to curb abuse, furthered into establishing measures for the ethical treatment of animals, utilizing *compassionate* empathetic practices during slaughter, and later, anti-vivisection petitioning and eventual laws governing the practices and experimentation of helpless animals.

Those early efforts and the individuals who risked outcast from society, who fought the dogma with what were considered absurd demands at the time, resulted in many of the laws we now have today protecting those creatures unable to speak for themselves. While the consumption of dog meat is considered taboo here in the States, it is unfortunately considered acceptable in many other countries. Those cultures and their practices remain entrenched in religious beliefs and traditions, like those of us who consume turkey or ham on holidays. While turkeys nor pigs live in our homes, we choose to hold dear and spare the lives of those animals closest to us through select speciesism.

These efforts prompt the question: where should the line be drawn for allowing activism, petitioning, or the creation of new laws, when it's an accepted way of life in other cultures? Whenever in New Orleans, I find myself paying homage, making a pilgrimage to visit the poor horses on Decatur Street. Lined up in the sweltering heat, they pull load after load of carriages, filled with unassuming tourists. I cannot help but be reminded of the countless horses who

In The Eyes

were destined to live their life until only death would provide them peace from pulling those carriages decades earlier on the streets of New York City.

As a child, I enjoyed the occasional zoo outing, however, I now view zoos as nothing more than docile constraints. Chosen animals removed from their natural habitats while placed on display for our amusement. Where do we draw the line, and when is it considered mistreatment of those animals without encroaching on the norms and ideology of those indifferent societies and even our own culture?

With travel being a large part of my work, driving past semis on the interstate, knowingly, I will turn my head the other way when passing those filled with livestock being transported for slaughter. On one occasion while filling up for gas in Iowa, I ended up directly next to an eighteen-wheeler full of live turkeys. I could not help but look into the thousands of eyes peering out of metal holes, seemingly out of desperation. Their poor expressionless faces were silently asking for anyone to do something, anything. Hopeless, the vision was engraved in my mind, haunting me as I drove hundreds of miles across I-80 to my destination in silence.

The cramped, inhumane conditions combined with unbearable heat in a metal coffin, with no water, traveling hundreds of miles to their ultimate deaths. Their lives having been created with one sole purpose; bred, fed and raised for consumption, however, they have as much right to humane treatment as your canine companion that greets you every day when you come home from work.

Paul Barthel

While protesting and petitioning can often lead to promising laws and encouraging results, the ultimate mechanism of seeking reform or outcome can typically be achieved through financial resources, or more commonly; the bottom line. By abstaining from frequenting zoos, the likes of Sea World, dangerous rodeos, circuses where animals are exploited, or roadside attractions where they are used as mere entertainment. Refusing to purchase cosmetic products where their research was founded based on animal testing. Abstaining from commodities manufactured using animal byproducts or when animal welfare is placed in jeopardy. As a tourist in Spain, I refused to witness the still-legal traditional bullfighting massacre that takes place across arenas every day. Defenseless, the bull is methodically stabbed to death as one spear at a time is delivered by the Matador.

It has been corroborated that the refusal to partake and spend resources, thus suffering low attendance or decreased consumption, is the most effective approach in curbing animal oppression. One most notable example is the demise of the Ringling Brothers Circus. Initially, it was the exploitation and apparent neglect of *all* those animals in question, while ultimately it was the elephant that saved his brethren. Through countless petitions, picketing, and reduced attendance, until finally, the conceding removal of elephants led to their closure after 146 years of operation. Enough people had finally spoken.

SeaWorld, while currently under protest as I write this, their killer whale shows having been suspended, are under increasing public pressure following mysterious marine deaths and ongoing trainer

In The Eyes

injuries. Greyhound tracks continue closing one by one across the country as they experience dwindling attendance numbers. The word getting out about the unnecessary breeding practices, living conditions, and slaughter of those older greyhound dogs unable to race any longer.

It wasn't until 2016 while under protest, that the FBI recognized animal abuse as what they labeled as a *"crime against society."* Those who abuse animals will be held equally accountable as someone who abuses a human. According to the FBI, this is the official definition of animal cruelty:

"Intentionally, knowingly, or recklessly taking an action that mistreats or kills any animal without just cause, such as torturing, tormenting, mutilation, maiming, poisoning, or abandonment. Included are instances of duty to provide care, e.g., shelter, food, water, care if sick or injured; transporting or confining an animal in a manner likely to cause injury or death; causing an animal to fight with another; inflicting excessive or repeated unnecessary pain or suffering, e.g., uses objects to beat or injure an animal. This definition does not include proper maintenance of animals for show or sport; use of animals for food, lawful hunting, fishing or trapping."

Paul Barthel

The FBI, partnering with the National Sheriffs' Association and the Animal Welfare Institute finally agreed that animal abuse, neglect, or torture can be early behavioral indicators for those who will commit future violent crimes in society. While it is a crime for humans to commit domestic violence against one another, and therefore, the logic should also apply to those sentient creatures as well living among us.

CHAPTER NINE

Losing Pepper

In the years following 2008 during the recession, Peppercorns, while managing to hang on, however, was not left unscathed. In all honesty, I too questioned many times whether it would've been wiser succumbing during those most grueling years. My selfish efforts, while forcing me to immerse myself in the fight for its survival, would not come without its cost. Exhausted both physically and mentally, I engrossed myself, determined keeping our covers up. If not for my regular patrons whom I was indebted, Peppercorns would have certainly had to pack it in on more than one occasion. Humbling, I survived as other restaurants and store fronts around sat ghostly dark and vacant, while Peppercorns had almost become a memory as well.

During the most difficult of days, I intuitively knew that keeping my vendors current was essential, followed by meeting payroll. Third, would be to keep the lights and gas on. I would suffer the humiliation of having a utility shut off only once. Embarrassing to say the least, I was however grateful it had not occurred on the weekend during our busiest hours. Without a warning or knock on the door, my chef signaled me into the kitchen when the stoves wouldn't fire. I immediately knew that what I had become resourceful at avoiding for months, had finally happened. Walking out the back door was a bright pink SHUT OFF tag attached to the gas meter.

Forced to dip even further into personal funds, I was told it would be 72 hours before the gas would be switched back on, almost as if they were insistent on teaching me a lesson. Under no circumstances was I willing to lose three additional days of revenue waiting for a truck to merely flip a switch. Forced to post the ambiguous notice on the front door, "closed for repairs," anyone in the business knew it was simply code for "bills not paid." Thankfully, it had taken place on a slow Monday. I then informed the staff, sent everyone home, and proceeded to order a pizza for me and three of my regulars who happened to be inside the restaurant at the time.

How strange it must have been for the pizza driver. The four of us in this dark, cavernous restaurant, all alone, waiting for a pizza. I made every effort to make light of the dire circumstances, however, with the sour economy and the striking display of vacant storefronts, I didn't have much to explain. After considerable begging and a

Losing Pepper

reactivation fee, the gas was turned back on by the next morning. Regardless, my ego would forever be bruised, clear that Peppercorns, was in fact mortal.

While never actively listing the restaurant for sale, there was always inquiries about whether Peppercorns was on the market or if I would be willing to entertain an offer. Perhaps because it had survived during the harsh climate, the consensus was that the restaurant must certainly hold value. One party would seemingly be interested one moment, then would disappear for months, a promising sign that the recession was weakening. Each time, I would grapple with my feelings of letting my baby go, a bittersweet sense of betrayal after having made it through those trying years following the recession.

The fleeting interest from window shoppers became typical, eventually bordering on irritating. An endless stream of armchair entrepreneurs, weekend chefs, self-proclaimed *consultants*, or experts desperate to give their business sense, *after* the recession, nonetheless. Countless times I would be forced to endure the long account of someone who had "the perfect lasagna recipe." Everyone was decidedly a chef and were going to open a restaurant with their own perfect lasagna, pizza, or custom burger. Most were either employed as an unappreciated accountant, bored at home, driving a steel coffin to work every day, or failed, having missed their calling as a chef. Each with their own aspirations, set out to make millions with their *lasagna recipe*.

Without prejudice, it goes without saying, these are typically the quickest and surest of restaurants to close their doors after opening, if not in a couple years, in a matter of months. Being a *good cook* at home with your lasagna has virtually nothing to do with running a successful restaurant. Characters who dabble in cooking or who come in undercapitalized are traditionally first to exit. While it depends on what source you're referencing, six out of ten restaurants are gone in the first couple of years, while a staggering eight out of ten close within the first five years. Operating a restaurant is by far the most volatile of businesses, with closures rampant even during prosperous economic climates.

Months passed until the prospect would surface again visiting Peppercorns. As it turned out, he had a friend *secretly* staking out the restaurant once a week, nursing a cup of coffee for hours. He'd watch me at the cash register, making notes of how many customers were inside the restaurant, and basic everyday operations, passing hours sitting in a booth.

I always made an extra effort to play along, exchanging obscure restaurant small talk allowing him to bend my ear. With as much convincing sincerity I could muster, I would listen to his advice about what I should be doing differently, or where I was failing. Apparently, I was still green after three decades in the business, including eight years of operating Peppercorns. All this during the crippling recession of 2008, yet my doors were still open.

Four years after one of the worst recessions in history, while I was able to survive when businesses were folding everywhere, I

Losing Pepper

questioned, wouldn't things only get better now that the economy was in recovery? Maybe I could add the bar I'd always wanted, or perhaps do a complete gut rejuvenation that was badly needed? I'd always wanted to extend the outdoor patio into al fresco dining. After almost nine years of toiling away, it was clear that I didn't want to abandon my baby.

After endless negotiations over countless cups of coffee, the offer of a partnership was thrown on the table by the potential buyer. Knowing very little about this man, his work ethic, or financial stability, I wondered why I'd want to have a partner if I was already making it on my own. However, I was intrigued by our discussion of a potential second and even third Peppercorns. His influx of cash combined with my experience made the offer extremely tempting.

Feeling pressure at home to sell with no desire for any partnership, or any involvement with any type of restaurant for that matter, I reluctantly returned to him with a price. As expected, while the offer was rejected and despite our breakdown in negotiations; there he was again, the next Sunday morning waiting in line for a table.

The restaurant was bustling, full of diners as he looked on, and I could tell he was bitten by the bug. Cocky, I countered his rejection by *raising* the price an additional $10,000, defiant against taking any less. Subconsciously, I knew this would keep me in my restaurant, confident he would renounce any further discussion and walk away.

Despite the insistence back home that I sell, business was recovering, and I would keep my restaurant after all. Certainly, after arrogantly raising the price. My heart sank when he surprisingly agreed to my raised offer. Apparently, after having witnessed a packed restaurant with a line out the door, left him feeling both bullish and hungry. Yet another fledgling restaurateur eager to market his secret *homemade lasagna.*

I recall the panic sweeping over me, knowing I had been out of commission for almost a decade. Ten years older now, and ten years independently self-employed, I found truth in the adage: "there's nothing like being your own boss." Returning to the market as an executive chef, knew I had limited patience for 20-year-old Food and Beverage directors fresh out of hospitality school convinced they were going to revolutionize the food industry. Recollections of cooks not showing up, corrupt unions, Prima-donna sales directors, and 70 hours a week of working for someone else scared the shit out of me. I was reminded of some lyrics that played over in my head, faced when selling my restaurant and losing my identity.

Too many hands on my time, Too many feelings, Too many things on my mind. When I leave, I don't know What I'm hoping to find, When I leave, I don't know What I'm leaving behind.

~ Neil Peart ~

Back at the house, it was argued that there would be no more opening of any business again, leaving me with a feeling as though my one shot had been used up. While grateful to have been one of

Losing Pepper

the few fortunate to have survived those difficult years and sold the business, I found little comfort in losing the restaurant which I had spilled my blood.

Friction in my marriage became constant. The mere suggestion that we sell eventually devolved into demands that we close altogether when there weren't any interested buyers. *Over my dead body!* Selfishly, I refused to cave, reminding everyone what had been discussed years ago, that it would not be easy. Not only had I sacrificed my life, but looking back, I failed to sympathize and realize the sacrifices everyone around me had also made.

The announcement of the offer of course met with excitement, only further fueling my resentment. Bittersweet, the prospect of returning to my life, however, I knew it was only a matter of time before I'd be punching a timeclock again, dealing with all the bullshit and politics. More than once, I almost sabotaged the sale, but as it turned out, I would have to let Peppercorns go, my marriage now in question.

No longer speculation, we sat in a booth for hours discussing numbers, staff strengths, food costs, vendors, expenditures, and basic overall operations. Despite successfully having sold the restaurant, I felt as if I had failed on so many fronts. Leaving the restaurant that I bled for, I couldn't help but feel I was turning my back on those customers I had grown so close to. I came to know their schedules, where they lived, their professions and families. In many ways, it was like abandoning a close family member.

Only the papers were needing to be signed, and as a condition, I agreed to stay on at the restaurant as a consultant during the transition. Forced into hiding my discomfort working with the new owner, side by side, I stood with my former employees and soon to be ex-customers. Not only out of obligation, but as a courtesy and gesture of goodwill, in the hopes without prejudice that the new owner would thrive and do even better than I had.

Explicit in my instructions, I suggested to the new proprietor that he discern my current operations and consider anything I could have improved upon, thus learning from my mistakes and increasing his chances of survival. Did I offer too many menu items, maybe not enough cooks on the line, was my décor dated? I welcomed any response as informative and non-judgmental. Dumbfounded, his only response would be questioning why I had chosen to have hanging plants inside the restaurant. *"What!? Hanging plants? Are you serious?"* After days pouring over business procedures, his success apparently was hinging on whether the plants were to remain or be taken down.

The nonsensical observation that he found the plants most striking, I then asked, *"So, is that your plan in the grand scheme, to remove the plants?"* Once again, I was reminded of the plentitude of armchair chefs wanting to open a restaurant because their *uncle Ralph* had told them they make a good lasagna. It was then that I knew he was in trouble, even before his first day.

Driving home the importance that he absorbs everything that I had learned in my eight years' operating the restaurant, I could not

Losing Pepper

have been more urgent. *"Dude, you're going to have bleed in order to survive here! Day and night, it will require your undivided attention and determination. Changing the fucking plants won't do shit!"* With only a modest background in the food business, he'd never held position of general manager, chef, or owned his own restaurant. While he had somewhat of an adequate beverage background; Peppercorns however, had no bar.

Keeping my promise for that first week after the completion of the sale, I arrived first thing every morning to help operate what was now his restaurant. Introducing him to the staff and customers, going over the POS system, working with the cooks, and so on. In a matter of only a few days during that first week, I found myself alone while he was out *running errands*, or *touching base at home*. Since I held part of the business note, it was in my best interest that this guy makes it. His failing could potentially mean I'd have to litigate the balance if he were to ever go belly up. I couldn't help but feel a sense doom.

Eventually, I slowly slipped away for good, never stepping back inside again. In only a matter of a couple of months, I would be blamed for ghosting him. I was forced to remind him that I am not his employee, but if he ever needed my help, I would certainly assist. In all fairness, when I took over, the keys were literally tossed to me, and on day one, I was alone. There was no introduction to all the employees, no tours, nor any return visits from the former owner to ensure I was successful. I knew that he simply wanted me to babysit his restaurant and bend my ear while complaining. Too painful for me to return, I couldn't endure both the good and bad memories created there. Besides, my work was done after fulfilling our agreement.

It wasn't long after, I learned he was coming in late, often absent during lunch hours, and basically neglecting the restaurant, leaving it up for grabs essentially. I of course was to blame for his abysmal numbers and according to him, my books were a lie, and now the sale price was too high for the asking, and he'd been ripped off. While I respected the new owner, I couldn't have been more insistent the demands of the business and not to be taken lightly. Not for the faint of heart, as an owner, you basically must forget about having a life outside those walls, while apparently my message had not resonated.

In the entirety of his ownership, he continued to struggle for less than two years until eventually dumping it. The next owner, or victim, supposedly also made a great lasagna; she would last only six months. It was then handed it over to someone else surviving for only three months. All three owners collectively surviving for less than three years in total. As it turns out, it takes more than a good lasagna recipe, as they all had learned.

Sadder still to watch it die than never to have known it. I recall the rumors of Trotter sitting alone in his restaurant after his twenty-five-year infamous run after having served the last diner. All the chairs empty and kitchen eerily silent. Ironically, the sale of the restaurant came too late and only further estranged my marriage. In a funk state of mind after selling the restaurant, I felt both isolated and

Losing Pepper

lacking direction for the first time in my life. However, I was finally able to spend more time with Pepper, and once again he provided the necessary companionship that held me together.

Sulking in the plenitude of my own pity, I began reassessing the choices I'd made after 30 years of working with food. The intense pressure, the quick problem-solving skills it required, and the theatre of it all that coursed through my veins; I lived for it. But at the same time, I wanted my life back, and the time to find out who I was again. Uncharted and uncertain, I decided I would take a break from food for the first time in over 30 years — placing my knifes to the side — welcoming an opportunity that piloted me in an entirely new direction.

Requiring frequent air travel as part of my new career, I often found myself many times choosing to drive instead, allowing time for reflection. Removed from phones, contention, and the uncertainty awaiting back home, the open road became therapeutic, while more likely a means to avoid my problems. I devoured any travel they would give me. New York, Philly, Boston, Detroit, St. Louis — I took it all. I'd be gone for a week and then come back to an unfamiliar cold house, no longer a home and no one to greet me. Family photos were removed from the walls, and with a chill in the air, silent, we slept in separate rooms behind locked doors, only the murmur of a TV on the other side of each door, living in avoidance of one another until conditions became unbearable.

Preparing to leave for yet another week of travel, something didn't feel right. On a whim, I grabbed Pepper's collar, his food, and at the very last minute decided to take him with me. Despite my apprehension and being entirely unprepared, we had a blast. He'd stick his head out the window, cheeks flapping in the wind, and stopping at truck stops and rest stations. I became an expert at sneaking him in and out of hotels by first checking in and then discreetly bringing him in through side doors. At first, I'd request two queens, thinking he'd like his own bed, however, in typical Chub Chub fashion, he preferred sleeping with dad. As customary, he would hog the bed each night, the empty queen bed next to us, used for luggage.

At some hotel, "Chubs" hogging the bed

Losing Pepper

While Labs are notorious for shedding, I'd bring a lint roller and go over the sheets, carpet, and bathroom floor collecting dog hair, ripping each sticky tape off one after the other. Meticulous in my cleaning of each room, never once was I forced to pay the $250 hotel fee once caught with a dog. Taking pictures of all the places we had gone together, at last count placed him in having visited over thirty states.

Each city visited had its own food culture and landmark restaurants that would beckon me. Chophouses, microbreweries, taquerias, delicatessens. Faneuil Hall in Boston, Quincy market in Philadelphia, Katz's in New York City, food was all around, from one city to the next. No longer grounded in the food scene, I still found myself yearning to hit every grotto or marketplace. Having a job to do, I'd leave each city behind for the next, restaurants unvisited and food never sampled.

Strange, while I now had plentiful opportunities and a multitude of restaurants to visit, ironically, I avoided each chance. Peppercorns still a vivid memory and wounds still fresh, I avoided TV shows centered on food, familiar restaurants, and many chef acquaintances. Le Bernardin or Masa in New York, Zahav in Philadelphia, Mistral in Boston, or Marcel's in Washington, I'd simply forge on to the next city, my job at hand, leaving each restaurant behind, and each experience. Besides, if Pepper was with me, we had much more fun at the end of a workday, just hanging out at the hotel, eating microwaved chili.

After a long day on the road

Returning home was always the most difficult part of each jaunt. Every outing and my eventual return ushered in harsh realities. I'd count down each passing mile, arriving closer to what was once my home, now merely a place to rest my head. With the papers filed and divorce proceedings initiated, on one trip, I had mistakenly chosen to leave Pepper back at the house. This error in misjudgment would set the stage over the course of the next three years to be reunited with my best friend. Arriving back at the house to an eerie silence, for the first time in years, there was no barking, no tail wagging, nor my best friend to greet me at the door. In addition to many of my personal items being stacked into a pile, more importantly, Pepper was gone.

Losing Pepper

Purposefully hidden, it became apparent that my largest mistake was allowing for my attachment to Pepper to be openly displayed. This slip would haunt me for the duration of my efforts if I were to ever see him again. I knew where he was, however, removing him would've gotten ugly. Trusting, I naively assumed due to our work schedules that we could remain civil during the divorce and ultimately share custody of Pepper. Cleverly premeditated, however, it became apparent that Pepper was to be used as a tool. Being on the road could not have come at a better time for my sanity, yet I foolishly allowed myself to abandon the gravity of each decision, almost as if it were a chess match.

It was during that time it was suggested that I remain extremely cautious; common, for an estranged spouse to instigate conflict further seeking a false Order of Protection to sway the judge while discredited the defendant. Since the house was no longer a home, living conditions jeopardized, and Pepper gone, it became time for me to leave. I was not about to be placed in a situation that allowed for any false accusations or coercion. The cards had finally been dealt.

Procrastinating the arduous process of choosing a lawyer, suddenly became a priority. Anyone going through a divorce understands the depressing and humbling experience of having to select representation when your life is suspended. Each attorney, one more than the last, found it peculiar, the urgency I placed upon the return of a pet over the house and other marital assets. After several consultations, I obtained representation, someone who seemingly recognized the importance of Pepper and my longing for him that he be returned.

Telling me everything I wanted to hear, my newfound counsel assured me Pepper would be coming home. Investments, property, the 401k, cars, and the house became secondary, while I stressed from day one that Pepper was my primary motivation. Lawyers are notorious for promising the world meticulously racking up hours, and systematically breaking you down. Gradually, you let go of those things you once found imperative, to prevent further bleeding, imploring that you regain some semblance of your life. Physical properties that were once cherished, become outweighed by legal fees, no longer practical contending over. However, there was no dollar amount I would place on Pepper.

Mere weeks into legal proceedings, I began questioning my choice of representation. Unanswered calls, dangling questions, no reassurance, and no motions filed. Innumerable times I requested that an Order for Visitation be submitted, or split custody resolution be proposed for Pepper. Nothing, and no explanation. Months later, and only after pleading, a court order was finally granted, allowing me to retrieve a few belongings from the house. Pepper of course deliberately absent, concealed from me once again.

Months would drag offering no details about Pepper before I would happen to discover on my own that no such laws existed for pet visitation. In almost every case, the party vacating the property essentially sacrifices any visitation fairness. Essentially, there was nothing to petition or motion! Unfortunately, animals under state

Losing Pepper

law are considered basic normative marital property. Thus, falling under the same jurisdiction as those physical marital items in question during the divorce proceedings. Such as a table, lamp, TV or other similar inert object. Never once explained to me from my counsel, suddenly, it seemed as if I was left with little recourse, despite the reassurance from my strawman representation.

"Legal relations in our law exist only between persons."
The Institution of Private Property —
Charles Reinold Noyes.

Things only got progressively worse. Through my own research, I had stumbled on a devastating realization — while in most litigated pet cases, the party having possession of the pet is essentially awarded the animal upon final promulgation. It became ever clearer that Pepper's removal was not by coincidence, rather because the longer Pepper was held, the likelier it would appear in the eyes of the court that he was content, prospering, and appeased in his current living arrangement. Perhaps suggesting under false pretense that I willfully abandoned him. Possession clearly became a calculated advantage for the claimant.

Around that same time, I became acquainted with an existing subculture, almost a whole society unto itself. Not only would it supply me with a clearer perspective offering me guidance, but also stir my deepest of sentiments — the struggle of those involved in the world of Animal Rights and Welfare. The liberation, right to life movement, and ethical treatment of not just those pets dear to us, but also those animals in the wild, held captive, on farms, exploited for the sake of experimentation, commodity or those neglected.

I began pouring over previous cases and seeking out individuals who endured similar circumstances, assured I was not alone. One landmark case involved a bitter divorce lasting four years, costing the petitioner over $90,000 in legal fees. Four whole years, I thought, all this while taking into consideration the relatively short life of the animal to begin with. Amazing, the love and relentless determination they truly must have felt for their pet, never giving up.

Another example left the petitioner horrified upon the sudden and mysterious death of their dog. The death occurring *after* it was decreed the defendant would lose the pet in the final divorce settlement. Case after case, I began reading about court practice procedures, animal rights, and welfare; the thought of losing Pepper only fueling my compulsion.

The same as a coffee table, lamp or chair, our pets are subject to being used as pawns while treated as objects. Like a child, who is unable to speak and defend themselves or seek adequate representation. Certainly, there should be a law ensuring the best interest of the animal, no? Is it not prudent for at least those animals we choose to bring into our lives, that they be treated ethically and humanely in all fairness that their needs are met? Who cared for and fed the pet most? Who walked the pet? Who spent most time with them?

Losing Pepper

Once I had prepared myself with this information, I then took several case references examples back to my attorney, only to be met with tetchiness and amused observation. Suddenly, I had become a budding armchair lawyer in his eyes, his repugnance growing intolerant the more I refused in letting Pepper go. It became a contest of time and money to wear each litigant down, and the question of how soon do you want your life back and what you are willing to sacrifice in exchange? Time became my enemy. I detested the obligatory trips to the courthouse, ushered in like cattle being led to slaughter. The "divorce floor," as it was aptly referred too, hallways filled with tearful casualties, each protesting and squabbling for what was once theirs, that the pie being divided was somehow unjustly unfair.

In the adjacent courtrooms, each waited for their sentencing and admonishment from the judge for having gotten married in the first place. Arms waving, fists pumping, and the occasional outburst or verbal threat was commonplace. It became heart-wrenching waiting for *your turn*, listening to each stranger plead their case before you. Money, money, and more money being the primary anxiety, and of course, the innocent children caught in the middle. I could be there for only one hour before walking out, emotionally spent and depleted.

Wandering the halls in the *divorce* building, by chance one day I had gotten off on the wrong floor, stumbling upon the law library and its volumes of knowledge readily available. Quiet enough to hear a pin drop, it provided private cubicles to work, copier machines, and free Wi-Fi. Between the law library and Starbucks, I spent hours reading landmark cases similar to mine, and learning how to prepare my case. My attorney, whose advice came sparingly, provided me little guidance while my case status was continually in question. It was then that I slowly began to build my own legal cognizance, skeptical of the longevity of my attorney and me as his client.

Each motion or hearing was followed by another thirty – sometimes ninety – days of waiting, due to backlog or additional case preparation allotment. Life became suspended as I painstakingly waited for any notice for when the next court date would be. Months lingering into years without Pepper were undoubtedly the most heartbreaking I would experience. Congruent to managing a line in the kitchen, my case preparedness consumed all my free time, affording me ample courage to endure those unsparing moments without him.

On occasion, I'd hit the road again, only to find myself reminiscing over those times with Pepper and the reassuring company he once provided. I began to fly to each location rather than forced to look at the empty passenger car seat next to me. Oddly, I would long for those nights he caused me to lose sleep while he hogged the bed next to me. With no desire to return home, I found it much easier to keep working, moving, and occupying my time as a diversion. If left indolent, my mind would be left to wander. *Am I failing him? What more can I be doing?*

As time dragged on, I increasingly held serious doubts about whether I had chosen the most competent of representation.

Losing Pepper

Although a skilled attorney, yet after decades of practicing law, he appeared burnt out and lacking the necessary passion my case would require. Concerned, I became distracted by minute nuances, like the torn carpeting in the offices when I visited, the rack cut of his cheap J.C. Penny suit, or the mounds of paperwork unfiled, left on floors and strewn across desks. Sadly, it became reminiscent of those restaurants I had worked, weeks away from closing. I could not help but feel the correlation with a sense of anguish.

Animal rights efforts and the struggle for their liberation has been highly contested for as long as magistrates have existed. Compassionate animal welfare zealots, relentless in their steadfast efforts offering a voice for those silent creatures. Most agri-farmers, ranchers, scientists, packing plants, and hunters would argue that animals lack the necessary rationale, understanding, and cognitive thinking to warrant such nonsensical actions. Thus, they remain vigilant against those prerogative liberties in policy — even for man's best friend. No surprise their loyalty remains steadfast protecting the bottom line and shareholders.

If preferential treatment is then granted for dogs, perhaps the courts would next be whimsically arguing cases over pet turtles or hamsters. Risking opening Pandora's Box — offering no clear authoritative end — has paralyzed each effort in most cases to the extent of inaction. Will cows eventually have a choice about how they will be slaughtered? Will hunting be banned indefinitely? Certainly, the NRA and their lobbyists think differently. Lobbyists and special interest groups have been opposing the advancement of such policies for decades. Rather than grant prerogatives to those that have become domesticated and welcomed into our homes, it's safer to lump all animals together and forgo any forbearance for a select few. Unless of course, it was to somehow benefit humans.

Supported by heavy constituent protest and relentless humanitarian efforts, many states have begun to waver under pressure. Regardless of whether empathy plays a role or warranted intimidation, new laws implemented only within the last twenty years, are now overshadowing what took a century to achieve. While slow on the side of rights recognition, anti-cruelty resolutions seemingly would outpace the latter, perhaps only because more visible to the public with the advent of the internet and relentless efforts of welfare organizations.

Those very efforts bringing to the forefront the squalor conditions and gross overcrowding at what are known as factory farms. Chickens crammed into metal battery cages for the duration of their lives, never to walk on grass or feed from the ground, in many cases compressed so tightly they are unable to turn their bodies. These enclosures while less than half the size of the average household oven, are shared by four to six hens.

Toxic ammonia so pervasive from the fecal waste and urine, that large fans are used to push the air. In the stifling heat of the aluminum sheds, many holding tens of thousands of birds, in many cases the fecal waste becoming in each cage that it reaches inside the unit causing the birds to walk on their own excrement. Cages stacked upon each other so that the bottom dwellers are often darker in their

Losing Pepper

plume from the fecal waste that falls down on them. Through what is now considered *animal science,* the birds are fattened, while their bodies become grossly overweight and limbs distorted, and their breasts enlarged to double the size of what should be considered normal. This, to reach market weight before being slaughtered by the time they are only seven to nine weeks old. On average in the U.S. alone, over one million chickens are killed every single hour and 9 billion every year. Consider in comparison, during the writing of this book, the U.S. human population is around 330 million.

Livestock transport trucks moving confined herds, drive for hours in metal coffins with little or no water provided in the suffocating heat, agribusinesses failing or blatantly ignoring their basic necessities. Once arriving, they are electronically shocked while dangerously forced to navigate narrow metal truck ramps on their way to slaughter. Held in holding pens — the smell of blood pervasive — they are eventually herded through a chute one by one, while efforts to keep them calm are employed to prevent undesirable darkened meat if killed while anxious or in a state of panic.

Once reaching the kill floor, the animal is then restrained and stunned before the use of a steel rod cap-bolt gun is instantly driven into the forehead killing the animal instantly. Using constructed concealed confinement to prevent cows from witnessing what awaits them — many times unsuccessful — cows are sometimes killed in plain view of those waiting in line while looking on.

In the grand scheme of what has become referred to as "meat science," where scientific measures are now commonplace to genetically modify each commodity — cows have a much better life than their farm friend, the pig. Breeding sows for example — singularly remain in gestation pens so confined for the duration of their lives, unable to turn or barely enough room to lie down on the cold *cement* floor. Once giving birth, she is then separated from her piglets only to be forcefully impregnated again. This cycle will typically last six to nine times, and once she is unable to bear any additional offspring, she is then ruthlessly slaughtered with the remainder of hogs. While the estimated hog population is around 70 million — roughly 8 million of them sows — they are destined to a life of proven psychological and physiological torment.

Through animal husbandry practices animals are treated as production units rather than the sentient individual beings they are. Commodities whose environments are so manipulated and engineered that the majority will never experience the basic joys of life. Those occasional cows, or perhaps a pig or chicken, you may drive past when in the countryside, openly grazing, are but a mere fraction of those living in impoverished, torturous, unsanitary conditions that you will never lay eyes upon. Those that are unable to spread their wings, graze in open pastures, experience what it's like to walk on grass, or even sleep while lying down.

In appalling conditions, it is estimated over 12 billion farm animals, including sheep, cows, chickens, pigs, ducks, and goats are bred, raised, and slaughtered annually for consumption. This in the United States alone, while this figure doesn't even account for marine animals, which is estimated at over 50 billion every year. 25 million animals are used for fur, and over 100 million are used for vivisection experimentation, where animals are mercilessly cut open, dismembered, or fatal chemical concoctions administered while testing the efficacy. These numbers fail to account for those animals that are hunted for sport, killed while in shelters, or mistreated and left to die under various circumstances.

Arduously, laws are being proposed, one by one, and perceptions changing only after awareness of maltreatment has been administered, decades later, and billions upon billions of animals inhumanely abused, psychologically tortured, and carelessly executed. While promising, funding and lack of viable resources to ensure compliance and enforcement of fair and ethical practices remain a constant struggle.

Countless times from animal rights enthusiasts, I was reminded to refrain from using the word "liberation" when discussing basic animal welfare. Welfare encouraging moral principles encompassing fair and ethical treatment, while liberation on the other hand is indicative of affording and bestowing their basic freedoms and right to life.

On more than one occasion, a farmer set me straight with a clearer understanding of the difference between animal rights and animal welfare. Each right granted potentially costs billions of dollars whenever new laws dictate advanced farming machinery, larger living quarters, or conditional oversight. No surprise why the Animal Rights movement, like no other, has taken centuries to gain traction. Any measure of representation or voice for those living beings protesting for the least bit of comfort or care, can cripple those very same farms and company boardroom, cutting into their bottom line. *However, one must question, what is right, if not moral?*

On the lighter side and on a more promising note, for those creatures habituated into our homes, recently in the year 2019, California, became one of the first states to ban the resale of dogs, cats, and rabbits from mills. This is a considerable step aimed at curtailing overpopulation by only allowing the resale of rescues. Further, California Assembly Bill 2274, previously recognizing pets in divorce as community property, now encourages judges to consider factors like care, medical attention, safety, and feeding in determining custodial rights. Like children custody laws, divorcing pet owners can now petition for sole, joint, or shared custody of their pet. As California is clearly in the forefront on many warranted rights issues, it's laws like these that offer a template, while many additional states are aggressively beginning to follow suit or take measures even further.

Finally, there is a sweeping change in many states; petitioners are ever closer to setting standards for enacting newer confinement laws for many farm animals. For example: That egg-laying hens be allowed to roam cage-free. That gestation crates for sows and veal crates be banned, egg sales be stricken from those hens housed in battery cages, and that concentrated feeding mechanisms be reexamined that can cause many animals to starve or become trampled to death. While refreshing that compassionate agribusiness laws are being adopted to account for their health and welfare,

Losing Pepper

continuing and melding efforts must allow for the flexibility of changing scientific developments and accepted animal husbandry practices.

Humans from their origin have been inherently obstinate on relinquishing any normalcy or right to life those beings we share on this earth. What *is* normal for them when their life is manipulated and massaged from birth? While we struggle to define their roles in a human world, it remains painstakingly difficult to understand why it has taken so long. At the very least, why even for those companion animals domesticated and welcomed into our homes? No discredit to cows!

Dogs have remained vigilantly by our sides for thousands of years, used in our military, police departments, schools, prisons, and for special needs. They wait for us to come home each day, learn about us, and then mirror our habits. It is proven that they even share empathy with us and would ultimately place our lives before their own. Remaining ever loyal, each night they climb the staircase by our sides, one step at a time, welcomed into our beds, providing us with warmth and the reassuring comfort each night. Unconditionally, they worship you for the five minutes you play with them at the end of your day and are willing to wait yet another 24 hours to do it all over again.

A dog is the only thing on earth that loves you more than you love yourself.
~ Josh Billings ~

The gift I am sending you is called a dog and is in fact the most precious and valuable possession of mankind.
~ Theodorus Gaza ~

How is it we allow ourselves to be confused the difference and defining moral obligations between their basic rights and welfare? Chiefly, after all they have done and provided for us. Is it not basic welfare that they have rights as well, guided by humanity as their guardian in good conscience?

CHAPTER TEN

Growing A Backbone

Little could have prepared me for the struggle to reclaim Pepper more than those years on the line. Not just at Peppercorns, but also the countless hours toiling away in the bowels of some of the most derelict of kitchen conditions. After ten years of running larger kitchens, I'd decided it was time to explore other opportunities, while Amy, now a young lady, had grown accustomed to her father as a chef and the unpredictable work hours. After the microbrewery, I decided to step back, accepting a more relaxed position running a kitchen allowing me to be home most nights with my daughter for a change.

A welcomed role as head chef of a small catering company in Chicago; my days would begin at 4:00 a.m. and end around 3:00 p.m. The kitchen embarrassingly small compared to what I had grown accustomed, however, provided a homey feel without the political posturing. A pleasant opportunity, our primary focus was catering to early-morning breakfast accounts, corporate lunches, office parties, and the occasional family celebration. The pace was feverish, however mindless, assembling tray after tray of fruit platters, continental breakfasts, or hundreds of boxed lunches and hot meal buffets to be transported across the city. At best, operations were adequate, while antiquated. The kitchen operations took place in essentially what used to be a garage exiting into a typical Chicago alley.

Operated by a rope, we rolled open and closed the garage door and loaded each truck before leaving. Exhaust fumes from idling vehicles would bellow into the kitchen filling the room each time with carbon monoxide. Every day was a challenge, while entertaining in its own way, uncertain whether each day would be our last. At the time I didn't care, so long that I was home with my daughter at night, could avoid any politics, and my check didn't bounce.

Before long, the novelty eventually wore off, and my complacency was replaced with aggravation from pounding out thousands of mindless cookie cutter platters, and it wasn't long before I felt stifled and my skills underutilized. My exacerbation only grew when the owner insisted each platter when finished, be complemented with a sprig of parsley or borage blossom. As if that final provision proffered perfection in its own nonsensical way. It seemed I would never escape parsley.

Weary from sameness, I longed to modernize our operations by offering tastings in the storefront and revamping the choices on our

Growing A Backbone

hot menu selection. Restless and not thinking clearly, I questioned aloud, *"why are we not catering dinner parties?"* The words slipped off my tongue, forgetful Amy was at home evenings, and I had just volunteered myself for even more hours. Strange, my preference for troubled businesses; in some masochistic way, they made me feel needed, and able to contribute to their growth.

Determined not be confined to indefinitely fanning sliced fruit on platters, I began setting weekly goals. We commenced by offering new menus, evening cocktail receptions, personalized chef stations, and the occasional tasting that would take place on the premises. The formal tasting allowing each prospective client a chance to sample our food and service, thus giving us a chance to showcase our product.

We would set a table, the kitchen would prepare the menu choices, and I would then make an appearance in my chef whites, describing each dish. Next, I then worked with sales by answering inquiries, continuing to push that we become a respectable premier Chicago caterer. It wasn't long before our new aggressive — about-face — began taking hold when the owner burst into the kitchen asking me to field a call from Disney. Yes, that Disney! As it turns out, they were farming out invitations for bids, mandatory they procure three quotes.

The request was for 300 custom movie-themed boxed lunches, delivered to a select movie-plex for a new Disney animation. My mind raced. I could prepare a fun food theme package, prominently featuring the cartoon character in the movie. Included inside each box would be a matching caricature napkin, a baguette sandwich, side of fresh fruit, and a fun dessert. All placed in a matching movie popup box wrapped with a cinematic projector bow.

Within an hour, I quickly made the calculations of what our cost would be and then added a respectable return profit. In less than a week, we were notified that we had won the project due to our theme boxed proposition and ingenuity. I was personally asked to accompany the entire lot of lunches to the movie theatre to set up myself. It wasn't long before the fresh and aggressive business-oriented attitude became infectious, delivering the company its best fiscal year in revenue since having become incorporated.

With any upward growth curve in business, there is even more added responsibility to maintain its consistency and focus, this many times more difficult than the actual climb itself. While it's exciting when growing any business, are the increased demands placed on the daily operations and those efforts in maintaining sustainability. Predictably, this would be short-lived.

In less than a few months, a recurring trend had been allowed to fester where the drivers were coming in late. Imperative that they leave out the doors for the first run by 6:30 a.m., blasting me and the entire kitchen with our morning dose of toxic gasoline vapors. In his efforts to save money, the owner would take the commuter train instead of fighting traffic each day, thus conveniently allowing himself to stroll in after 9:00 a.m., hours after all morning runs were to leave. By this time, I had already burned through five hours of my day.

Growing A Backbone

Frustrated, I silently questioned how someone could demand their workers be on time, while foolishly leaving the business up for grabs during those crucial early-morning hours? Food was now being delivered late, orders were becoming less frequent, and staff resentment had begun to spread. Unprepared for such a rapid growth in business, drivers continued using their own vehicles as part of their agreement when hired. Essentially, if you had no drivers report, there would be no delivery. I had never been assigned the role as General Manager, nor was I once instructed that the drivers were my responsibility. It was only a matter of time before perfect storm would hit.

Happening on a busy Friday, all the food had been prepared, carefully wrapped and sealed, cambro after cambro stacked and labeled with each account name, and speed-racks ready for delivery. However, there were no drivers, and no owner, despite some 30 accounts waiting to be delivered across the city. Realizing this day was inescapable, I instinctively made a habit of hiding my truck two blocks away and out of view. At 7:30 a.m., forced to take an earlier train, the owner bursts into the kitchen. Steadfast, there was no way he was going to use my truck canvassing the city, in Chicago traffic, mind you! Understand, these vehicles took a beating; racing through city streets, dodging traffic, parking, idling, potholes large enough to swallow a Fiat. It was all too common for drivers to return after getting keyed, sideswiped, bent rim, or stranded somewhere with a flat tire.

Yelling as he stood at the kitchen door entrance, "Fuck, what's the problem now?" Answering, *"I'm not sure, but all the food's ready to go."* And then, what I had anticipated: "Paul, we're going to have to use your truck!" To say I was pissed would be an understatement. By choosing to take the train every day, leaving his car at home knowing we have driver issues; he's now surprised? *Seriously?* As it turns out, he always knew I was hiding my vehicle, allowing him a sense of comfort knowing this day would eventually happen and Paul would assuredly cave.

Having witnessed his driving, I relented under one condition; that I go along, however, drive my own vehicle. We sat uncomfortably side by side, awkwardly making small talk as I drove from each stop to the next, fuming as we hit pothole after pothole, cambro units bouncing around, certain that the foods had now become salad. Arriving at each office, I would leave the vehicle while dressed in my blood stained and food splattered chef whites, riding corporate elevators, setting up in boardrooms in the presence of dozens of suits. Lawyers, accountants, and a conglomerate of professionals — embarrassing to say the least.

Drivers were reprimanded, fired, and then the pattern would repeat itself. Anyone who has subjected themselves to rising every morning at 3:30 a.m. understands it requires a special breed. Transients, druggies, and temporaries were the norm; we would go through dozens of candidates until ultimately finding one who would adapt to the ungodly hours, if only for a couple of months. Each day, I continued diligently hiding my truck further and further away,

Growing A Backbone

denying its whereabouts, and at the same time the owner kept insisting on risking the train.

Our exchanges over time became rigid, many days not speaking at all. Ever more stressful, at the height of operations, business growth helped to acquire evening accounts for the very first time. Requiring that a chef supervise the various functions each night, many of the chefs developed the same habits as the drivers. With no chef, the drivers would be forced to deliver the food and then fake it by donning a chef jacket, never having so much as scrambled an egg in their life. In a matter of no time, business began to decline just as quickly as it had increased, and customers that had ordered for years were no longer answering their phones.

A catalyst for my exit, would leave me disgusted having little to do with the business mismanagement. Arriving each morning, on occasion the garage door would accidentally be left raised inches off the cement floor from the previous evening allowing for air circulation. Mind you, this door is facing an alley in the city of Chicago. With the door slightly raised, even an inch, one could count on critters finding their way inside.

First to arrive, I would turn on the lights, surprising the occasional rat frantically running over canned food goods, rice, or flour. Despite the magnitude of the rat population in the city, this type of infraction, unless you had the proper connections, even in Chicago, would immediately get shut you down by the health department. The rat sightings would turn into somewhat of a joke, until one day a driver decided to set out glue boards without telling me. Arriving the next morning and turning on the lights, I was immediately greeted by this indescribable inhumane shrieking. Two alley rats trapped on the same glue board, desperately fighting for their lives and to peel themselves away. Humiliated, I took the stick part of a broom handle, opened the garage door, and slid them outside where I wouldn't have to hear or endure witnessing their slow death.

Rescuing them off the pad was impossible; their legs and bodies contorted, they likely had suffered broken bones in their efforts to escape the thick glue. No living being should be forced to endure the suffering they were experiencing, despite our association

Arriving later and pleased with his efforts, the driver who had set out the glue boards the night before took a cinder block, and with one fell swoop did his business. For days, I had recurring thoughts about what I'd witnessed. *What's become of my career?* Disgusted with myself for having taken this job. At the same time, I was finding it difficult to understand that while the owner was hitting his best numbers since incorporating, he was letting business go to shit. I had experienced enough.

Weeks later, I landed the Executive Sous Chef role on Chicago's Navy Pier. Chicago's city treasure, and most infamous tourist trap, similar to Times Square in New York, or Fisherman's Wharf in San Francisco. A monstrous Ferris wheel that overlooks the city on Lake Michigan, botanical gardens, a concert venue, overpriced restaurants, convention space, and countless trinket shops, populate the quarter mile strip, jetting out onto the lake. We were responsible for two on-pier restaurants, the massive grand ballroom, festival hall conventions, and dozens of meeting rooms that flanked the property. Common for us to host upwards of 2,000 people regularly with either plated options, buffets, or cocktail receptions with an array of menu choices suited for any palate.

Pressure was intense, and at the same time would throw me back into the scheming politics, however, it came with its perks. A city contract property, Navy Pier was awarded to the owners of the Chicago Blackhawks, while run by its food service division. With that came not only tickets to both the Chicago Blackhawks and Chicago Bulls during the Michael Jordan reign, but tickets to concerts as well. The Stones, Genesis, U2, all the names you could imagine, however hardly had anytime to attend. In addition, once a year, managers would be invited to owner Bill Wirtz's house. As part of his appreciation, they were driven out in luxury coach buses to his beautiful estate for a day of managerial workshops and team sports, and each year, the corporate Christmas party would be held at the United Center, where both professional sports teams played.

During one Christmas party the United Center had no scheduled events, both professional sports teams were out of town, no concerts, and no traveling circus was in town, leaving the UC dormant. Excusing myself from the festivities, I wandered the cavernous venue in the hallways below where the Bulls and Blackhawks' locker rooms were. Eventually I made my way onto the hallowed wooden main floor that Michael Jordan owned. Dimly lit and strangely silent, surrounded by 18,000 seats, I couldn't help but feel overwhelmed staring up into the multitude of empty seats and skyboxes.

Paul Barthel

While I have the utmost respect for the Blackhawks organization, "Rocky," Peter Wirtz, and the Wirtz family, however, politics in the food service division on the pier was unlike anything I'd experienced. Turnover rampant, not at any time was performance based on a chef's culinary acumen, rather on who you knew or were in favor. Steering clear of the politics, naively assumed I would be able to simply cook, and then be allowed to go home, or so I thought.

Common, was it to prepare all day and then serve 2,000 people that same evening; functions that often pulled in hundreds of dollars per plate. The union kitchen staff was so large that rather than cooking, my days were spent babysitting. Rooms, stairwells, and alcoves were abundant everywhere on the massive pier, providing the *children* an unlimited playground and places to hide while dodging work.

One cook who presumed he'd gone unnoticed would punch in and then mysteriously disappear the entire day until it was time to punch out. I later managed to track him wandering the various shops, however when confronted, he claimed to have been "running food." A union property, there was no such thing as an immediate termination; each position was coveted and carefully protected by union bylaws and unscrupulous union stewards. Finally, after several infractions and successive warnings, I drew up the necessary paperwork to have him terminated, and only a short time later came to find he had been reassigned per the directive of the executive chef.

I attacked my job like no other, admitting that despite rats on glue boards and serving Mrs. Paul's Frozen fish, I had never witnessed in all my career such gross mismanagement of any culinary department, despite the magnitude of operations and size of the kitchen.

Freezers and walk-in coolers remained jammed solid with food item leftovers and gross over-ordering miscalculations from previous functions. Tens of thousands of dollars of product were left stacked from floor to ceiling with idle inventory. Getting inside the main walk-in freezer required you to climb on top of food cases, laying your entire body horizontally, until you could find a place to shimmy down and look for a specific item. If fortunate enough to find the item, it would be near impossible removing it. There existed no inventory system nor accounting of where each product was, whereby every item and its location would have to be from memory.

During the busiest times despite ample walk-in coolers, we would rent a refrigerated semi-tractor trailer (reefer truck), parking it on the loading dock, per the directive of the executive chef. This too was completely stocked from floor to ceiling. The purchasing department, a complete ignominy, would randomly place each new delivery, tens of thousands of dollars of various products, wherever space would allow, haphazardly and un-inventoried. Cooks were sent on expeditions to find product, returning hours later with the items. Nothing organized or labeled, and total disregard for any systematic inventory system.

Food cost calculations and eventual month end inventory numbers submitted to corporate were a farce. To arrive at an accurate inventory count, each item every 30 days would have to be counted and priced when auditing. Dumbfounded by the extreme waste and impossibility to accurately account for each item, numbers were manipulated to arrive at an acceptable month-end entry. Each day became less and less about cooking, and more about watching your back.

Meeting with the Executive Chef who rarely left his office, I was asked if I knew anything about the tape recorder found amongst books in his office. He then produced the recorder that someone had discreetly hidden. No idea what he was talking about, it became apparent that I was way in over my head with all the drama and cut-throat politics taking place behind the scenes.

During my efforts to adapt to the machine, we were assigned yet another restaurant on the pier. This particular footprint location was directly in front of the pier itself, where all the tourists initially arrived when visiting the landmark destination. The previous restaurant, having failed only two days before, the location now sat empty. A blemish on the entire pier itself, senior pier officials sought to quickly occupy the vacant space. A beautiful restaurant with an elaborate mahogany bar, once owned by the late actor-comedian John Candy, was mere feet away from the beautiful waters of Lake Michigan. On those same waters only a short distance away, was comedian Jackie Gleason's, former antique wooden sailboat on display.

Like the TV show Restaurant Impossible where failing properties are transformed overnight, under pressure to open the restaurant as quickly as possible, within days we redesigned the menu, staffed the restaurant, and stocked the kitchen. It became a race to open,

Growing A Backbone

preventing any further embarrassment on behalf of pier management by avoiding any vacant storefronts.

There would be no soft opening, on the very first day with entirely new management, a mostly scratch menu, green staff, rotisserie display, and a beautiful summer day on the shores of Lake Michigan, we got slammed by never-ending hordes of tourists, and the curious wanting to dine at the *new* restaurant. Twelve hours open to the public, twelve hours of madness — each table emptying while immediately another group was seated in its place.

The executive chef, I, and a brigade of cooks worked the line feverishly to hold down the kitchen. Every couple of hours we would radio the main kitchen at the other end of the pier, a quarter mile away, to *find* more product, bringing it down ASAP. Having to navigate through the crowds, an hour later a golf cart would pull up with an assortment of vegetables, steaks, seafood, or whatever else they could substitute. At the onset, I watched the chef flounder as he struggled to call out tickets, clear it had been years since he'd done time on the line. Delegating from his office chair had taken a toll on his skills, however, we were now in my backyard; I lived for this shit!

Instinctively, I knew we were going down glancing at what must have been 30 tickets on the speed rail, with even more dangling from the printer. Reminiscent of the old days with my coffee nearby, I hovered over two stations, relieving the chef from calling out tickets. Louder and distinct, I barked out each order, and side by side in the trenches we began pounding out food, refusing that the last slot on the speed rail ever be occupied again by a ticket. Plates began leaving as fast as the servers could pick them up from across the pass, while on the line, we developed an immediate camaraderie only a cook could understand.

Hours escaped as the restaurant repeatedly filled and then emptied like nothing I'd ever seen. The bright summer sun dancing off the waves only a short time ago was now replaced with a cityscape of lit skyscrapers. Embarrassed and his absence unnoticed, the head chef silently withdrew back inside the safety of his office. Mistakenly, I had demonstrated with relative ease how I found working the line, an error on my behalf that would haunt me soon enough.

Serving conventions, elaborate weddings, and corporate gatherings a quarter mile away from the restaurant, at the opposite end of the pier; was where most of the revenue was generated. One evening could be a corporate event with hired talent like Bill Cosby, and the next evening a political fundraiser with the President of Mexico in attendance. However, the recently acquired restaurant had no head chef and was basically winging it each day with a band of misfits.

Within less than two weeks, the restaurant manager notified culinary that the kitchen was rarely able to keep up and always besieged in turmoil. As it turns out, the same cook I had previously terminated had mysteriously been placed in command of the very same kitchen. Instructed that I was to solve the restaurants issues, I then realized that my skills demonstrated that first day on the line had worked against me. Suddenly, I had become an overpaid glorified line-cook, once again, sent back out to babysit the children. Over the

Growing A Backbone

next couple of months, riding golf carts from one end of the pier to the other, I would alternate between both the restaurant and main pier functions. Arriving on weekends at 4:00 in the morning, I wouldn't leave until past midnight, only to return in a few hours.

Even then I recall in the midst of it all, surrounded by people, plates clattering, the noise from the crowded restaurant; my head would be bent down focusing and working the line, my thoughts however trailing off thinking about mom, the missed birthdays, and family gatherings. My father's passing; he was hurriedly placed into the ground, and dispassionately within hours I was back on the line. Work, it seemed had always taken precedence, allowing for avoidance or reason to be somewhere else. One of my brothers had recently been hospitalized, while my other brother, I had failed to make his wedding. Never intentionally absent, a chef simply *does*. By always *doing*, may implore selfishness, yet the business of a chef takes no prisoners. Anything less, and one is not suited for the role. Years earlier, while I admired and wanted all of what my mentor, Kenny, was experiencing, I was now knee deep.

Back in the central kitchen preparing for the day's events, one of the walk-in cooler light bulbs went out, making it impossible to find anything in the dark. Secretly, I had stashed away a package of bulbs in my desk for this very occasion, replacing the bulb as quickly as possible. Being a Chicago city union property, required that you call an electrician, even for such a simple task as changing a light bulb. Once again, politics rampant, if a union electrician were to show up, we would then be expected to feed them, while gracious for their services, and the light bulb. A quarter mile long pier with countless venues, the lightbulb was not a priority, However, failure to play the game could mean hours with a flashlight picking through food boxes in the dark. I was determined not to play along, and like hell was I going to prepare anyone a meal for changing a damn light bulb!

Union or no union, I feverishly unscrewed the cage and plastic cover, took out the old light bulb, replacing it with a new one. Catching the eye of another coworker, I was eventually brought up and instructed to follow protocol. Once again, I was reminded that it was never about your job performance, rather in this instance, those acquaintances you nourished. This also explains why Chicago continues to lose countless major conventions and revenue, as corporations, in effort to save money are fleeing to Atlanta, Orlando or Las Vegas for their convention needs.

A sweltering August evening, things became increasingly antagonistic when we were executing a function in the grand ballroom for 900 guests. As part of the diners' intermezzo, they were to be served a sorbet trio decorated by a mint leaf. While the central kitchen freezers and the scooped sorbet were notably some 500 yards away, it required runners to navigate through hallways and two sets of stairs when delivering to the main ballroom.

The head chef, sensing the moment had arrived, radioed for the intermezzo to be brought down and readied for serving. I recall the feeling and sense of relief that it the wasn't me who had made that ill-fated call — heard by everyone in food and beverage, on all radio receivers. Dozens of tables not yet cleared of the previous course;

the sorbet glasses would wait. During the dog days of summer, and the brutal humidity Chicago is known for, the sorbet was forced to be served even before clearing the previous course. The champagne sorbet, by the time it had reached most of the guests, had reduced to slush and the three separate flavors indecipherable topped with a floating mint leaf. Mind you, this was a $150 per plate black-tie event; no plates sprinkled with parsley were to be found here.

The Banquet manager, captain, and F&B director all cognizant of what was being served. Immediately, a horde of cooks was then ushered back to the main kitchen and instructed to *find* some product, any product, offering a semblance of what was being served. Racing back to the main kitchen, desperate, we balanced our bodies on top of the towering stacks of boxes in the freezer looking for anything. *"Do we even have that much product left to serve 900, and in three different flavors? Do we have 900 additional champagne glasses merely lying around?*

Locating some dated, freezer-burnt anomaly that was once edible, we frantically assembled a team of scoopers on a make-shift assembly line. Custodians, the general manager, and anyone else with two hands were given a spoon and some mint leaves we had left over. When one tray was finished it was then raced down, and once again by the time it had made it, was served as a slush. There was no beating the August heat and the stifling Chicago humidity, the kitchen was simply too far from the grand ballroom.

The next day a cloud hung over the food and beverage department and culinary team. All team members were doing anything they could to cover their own asses despite it being the head chef who had created the menu and then ordered the product down, certain I had nothing to worry about. Regardless, while he was the executive chef, my position was that of executive sous chef. Technically, I still held responsibility in the traditional kitchen hierarchy. Fair?

Time would ease the sorbet scandal, while the general manager who'd hired me and with whom I had a great relationship, eventually left his position, opening a B&B in Key West. Still friends, I would later visit his charming property in the Keys. After his departure from the pier, food costs repeatedly came into question from corporate, service began to suffer, and eventually the decline in conventions took its toll. A city property out for bid, the company lost their contract to a more experienced national operator infamous for operating stadiums across the country. Most people went on to lose their jobs, replaced by those within the new organization.

The insistence over who would become the fall guy over the sorbet scandal became only one of many blunders in the ladder of corporate malcontents. A cancerous culture of guarded egos, faltering restaurants, uncertainty of who was sleeping with whom, and having to keep watch for the eventual knife in your back became unbearable. While I am grateful for the chance to have worked for the generous Wirtz family, feeding thousands from the immaculate, spacious kitchens, with an abundance of the newest kitchen gadgets, and plentiful staff, I decided against becoming another statistic and began circulating resumes.

Growing A Backbone

Hooked on the challenges of volume food production and the addictive tendencies it provided from feeding hundreds or thousands at a time, I searched for a similar venue that would allow me to continue utilizing those skills. Putting out fires as it were, enslaved by overwhelming numbers, and the pressures of meeting a deadline each evening. After a brief search, I not only found a larger property, but one that would take me out of the city, thus avoiding the insufferable commute each day.

Volume cooking while daunting to many chefs, my fascination had always been with those Avant-Garde haute restaurants, sometimes as small as 60 seats or less. Operated by revolutionary chefs, the likes of Thomas Keller, Joël Robuchon, Grant Achatz and of course, the late Charlie Trotter. Each night serving degustation menus, many times comprising upwards of twenty courses for each guest. The intricacy and meticulous detail placed on each portion and the gustatory senses as it were, dinners often lasting over four hours.

Not uncommon, for many of the chefs to begin their workday at 9:00 a.m., not finishing well after 1:00 a.m. Many of the chefs on salary, when their take-home pay is divided over the number of hours worked, in many instances is far below minimum wage. Low pay, however, most grateful for the opportunity.

Earning even one Michelin star demanding nothing short of brilliance and the attention to detail unparalleled. Equal importance placed on the china selected, decor, mood lighting, employee uniforms, and training. Early in his career, a chef friend of mine accepted a line cook position at Trotters. The first week, he never even so much as boiled water. While he held a culinary degree, instead, he was placed on cleaning detail that included polishing the chrome piping under each sink. Humiliated, he quit after one week, never even having held a knife.

The goal of perfection, even if for only sixty covers at a Michelin level, can be daunting. Much more pressure than the 1,000 I would feed out of large stock kettle troughs. While one can certainly demand perfection of themselves, instilling that same tenacity amongst your entire staff is near impossible. Trotter, ever the perfectionist, penned a book dedicated exclusively to the pursuit of excellence, and wrote:

"I have always looked at it this way: If you strive like crazy for perfection – an all-out assault on total perfection – at the very least you will hit a high level of excellence, and then you might be able to sleep at night. To accomplish something truly significant, excellence has to become a life plan." – Charlie Trotter.

As executive chef of my new position, I'd be responsible for the 300-seat dining room, concession stands, an open site grill, eight skybox suites and several additional on-track food pop-ups. One of the largest harness racing tracks in the country, capable of seating thousands, it would be my last role as an executive chef before I would open Peppercorns and Pepper entering my life.

Growing A Backbone

Day one began with no introduction to my staff, no knowledge of who my purveyors were, nor any briefing on the existing kitchen operations. Dressed in my whites, I walked into a completely empty kitchen mere hours before the first evening's race and before the throngs of customers would arrive. I came to know my staff, each one by one as they arrived for work. Previously coming from a property where employees were discriminately protected, I was determined not to fall prey to favoritism or intimidation.

In the main dining room, it was much easier to offer a buffet, in addition to a smaller full menu to choose from. Off the buffet, I immediately set out offering fresher foods and chef-manned stations. Customers were then able to choose from a variety of sauté or carved items custom ordered, with a flair of showmanship as each chef was able to engage the diner. Not only did it become an attraction, but it also cut down on waste since each chef prepared just enough for each guest.

We prepared whole steamship rounds, horseradish-crusted beef tenderloin, roast pig, a variety of fresh pasta dishes, and a live dessert station including scooped ice cream. An immediate success, that provided a spectacle that not only livened up the buffet, but instilled new life into the dreary, dated menu offerings served previously. Next, I then addressed the logistics of the main kitchen. Located on the second floor and the dining room on the third, it sometimes took as long as 10 minutes for entrees to leave the pass. I then Revamped the menu by lessening its choices, and cutting line labor, thus forcing more patrons to dine off the buffet, which in return delivered a higher check average.

Next, I then eliminated the frozen appetizers, frozen pastries, precut fruits, and precut crudité that had been a staple at the track for years. Painstakingly, my next task was to create typewritten recipes for everything off the buffet that we prepared to ensure each items consistency. Photos were then taken and cataloged for each item and how it should be presented on the buffet and in skyboxes. I then tackled the line set up. Like a Three Stooges episode, each night cooks would bump into one another frantically running from one station to the next. The line was then rearranged, moving each piece of equipment allowing each chef to remain stationary, eliminating wasteful steps and cross-over.

Convinced theft was rampant on our open-site grill, I instituted that each food item be portion controlled and inventoried at the beginning and end of every shift. Countless times, I watched the cashier leaving the cash register open, or concession workers concealing their own sleeve of candy bars and reselling them for three-times markup, pocketing the difference. In all my years at the track, theft was the one persistent problem that remained a thorn in my side. I eventually conceded that no one could be trusted.

In the kitchen, I watched John dispassionately cutting cubes of cheese on Thursday, in preparation for our live race night on Friday. Talking aloud with the other cooks, at the completion of each sentence, he waved the French knife in the air, asserting his point. Cubing a variety of cheeses for what seemed like hours, meanwhile,

Growing A Backbone

his friend Craig – who easily topped the scale at 400 pounds – *worked* at another table arranging a charcuterie on a four-by-four mirror, managing to make the work last a third of his shift. It seemed like I had walked into a Good Ol' Boys Club once again. Everyone knew everyone, and once again, a union property, were taking all the time necessary to ensure they racked up their 40 hours each week with as little effort as possible. I remained vigilant that this too would soon change.

Set out to embarrass John, I grabbed a separate chef knife and cut up the remaining variety of cheese blocks in mere minutes. The schedule was then rewritten so that much of the prep would be done on the same day, eliminating countless hours of unnecessary labor. I personally came in alone the day before, knocking out most of the prep myself, anything to prevent the malcontents from collecting additional hours. As head chef in management, I was not part of the union, requiring extreme caution when cutting hourly union labor. Having learned this from the pier, I eventually found it easy to filter the dregs out of my kitchen in other creative ways.

It wouldn't take long discovering who was milking hours, had no skills, or lacked ambition — much less care about their job. Just give someone a French knife and watch them perform. The way they hold the knife, maneuver it, and how they use it to chop or slice is often a complete giveaway. Having little experience is by no means a reason for termination, however, those having no desire or willingness to learn were a waste of my time and resources.

More often, I discovered it's much preferred taking a novice under your wing rather than deal with those corrupt and jaded personas. It was apparent I had a band of misfits draining the clock — all self-proclaimed, *"victims"* in life. If you asked them, how it was possible to achieve more work, the question was usually met by either suggesting more hours or additional people, (friends) that should be added to the payroll.

John was the first to go. Expecting to cube cheese as his menial task for the duration of a live race day, I would have the fromage board already finished. Only now it included soft camembert, Pecorino Filiano Cheese, hand crafted Gouda, olive paté, crackers, flatbreads and a variety of fresh grapes. In the center was a wedge of French Brie. I then did the same with the crudité, charcuterie, and pastries that were on the buffet. All were carefully decorated, garnished and shrink-wrapped, ready for service. Suddenly, their shifts became awkward, forced into making up work, to appear busy.

Carefully checking the union bylaws, I found no mention of how their hours must be spent while inside the kitchen. So, we cleaned and cleaned, and then cleaned some more. Once the kitchen became spotless, we cleaned even more. Most cooks, holding a deep contempt for cleaning detail, I decided taking it to the next level. Next, we hand scraped the baked-on black carbon off each sauté pan, layers built up after years of use. We polished kettles, and then dismantled, and after cleaning, reassembled each convection oven. The Vulcan ovens and Salamanders were next. Forced to work on

Growing A Backbone

your knees, reaching deep inside each oven, scrubbing years of baked on burnt grease. After service, we did it again.

By this time in my career, I had amassed many contacts with quality chef's, ready at a moment's notice should mutiny strike. Never intentionally setting out to fire anyone, my only request was that each employee put in a fair day's work. Humiliated from cleaning, John was first to file his grievance with the union. The union then contacted the F&B director, who then reminded the union steward that John was technically still getting his hours, so no violations could be warranted.

As the kitchen became increasingly hostile, John warned everyone that if "things didn't change," he would walk. A complete disgrace to the kitchen, culinary arts, and chefs alike, John held no desire to grow or further his culinary astuteness. As anticipated, he did an Oscar worthy, "fuck you," storming out on a live race night.

Over a relatively short period I grew into my new job and started enjoying my work. Diners who once gorged themselves on hot dogs off the grill, were now comfortable venturing into the dining room for our elaborate full-service buffet. Food and labor costs were now in line, the buffet was thriving, and, I had managed to completely turn over the entire kitchen staff, bringing in new, vibrant blood. More importantly the press was on our side, providing the track with several favorable reviews and generously printing a couple of our recipes.

Every Christmas, I would take a few hours each night assembling twelve feet of pressboard covered with hills of meringue to look like snow. Over the course of a week, a small gingerbread village would meticulously come together. I'd create a racecourse with stables, various sized buildings, a water tower, and a moving train that circled the entire town. Other than the train, every ingredient was edible and prepared in-house, made with gingerbread, assorted candies, chocolates, and pounds and pounds of meringue to simulate snow. I'd finally found my own sanctuary that allowed me to focus on food, free of politics. Culinary became its own private respected entity, left alone, almost as if we were an island centered on this huge track. But only for a time.

Without giving it much thought, I applied for a temporary corporate chef position for the 2003 U.S. Open, during the track's off-season. *If the track is going to be dark for a couple of weeks, why not add something to my resume?* The position was mine after only a couple interviews. While I had plenty of volume experience under my belt, I had never experienced the numbers we would eventually put out during those weeks. An entirely new level of cooking; was only made possible by a small army of head chefs, sous chefs, cooks, and prep cooks who were responsible for upwards of 30,000 patrons daily. Corporate tents, media tents, VIP tents, the Players Area and of course those customers on the links. Each day we'd arrive at 3:00 a.m., not leaving until 11:00 p.m. While the money was mediocre, I could have cared less and would have done it for free.

As the tournament entered the final round, I recall bending over while working, and when rising, was greeted by two suits from

Growing A Backbone

Corporate, inquiring if I would be interested in a position for its primary account at FedEx Field in Landover, Maryland and the Washington Redskins; requiring that I relocate. Never officially turning down the position, I simply didn't follow up. I couldn't. My life with my daughter was planted here.

2003 U. S. Open. A fraction of the team.

Back at the track, on a roll and continuing to put out good numbers, I began pushing for more changes. The kitchen, with its low ceilings, had no space for the compressors on top of each walk-in cooler. Someone had made the decision years ago mounting them directly on a wall inside the kitchen. This not only made the kitchen unbearably hot but required us to yell as we spoke over the constant drone and vibration coming from the motors. Venturing off my safe kitchen island that I'd created, I was now forced to reach out to facilities with a maintenance request. Now vulnerable, I loathed filling out the paperwork request and the fact that I needed assistance from another department.

Making a strong case, I suggested a new compressor line be piped to the adjacent storeroom where they could run all day, bothering no one. Judging by the response from maintenance, you would have thought I was asking them to work until 3:01 p.m. Over the following weeks, a flurry of emails was exchanged as I made my case, which they resisted until the day of the move.

The assistant to the head of maintenance had spent thirty years at the track, and he had seen it all. Characteristically walking with a limp, grey shirt unbuttoned three buttons down, exposing a fortitude of protruding white chest hairs, and large circular gut that hid his belt. To him, I was the arrogant and young prick chef set on changing the culinary world, and he, unwillingly, was at my disposal. Even while running the new copper line, he continued under heavy verbal protest. "What's the goddamn point of moving these when five years ago, I was the one who installed them here?" Taking the bait, I responded, *"When the fuck in all my time here have, I ever asked for anything from maintenance?"* Further, I then pressed on. *"Ah, so you're the one who put the compressors up on the wall. What the hell were you thinking?"* Experiencing an influx of new blood, the track was alienating many of the old timers, resistant to change, and he was the last of the dinosaurs. In the end, I got what I

Growing A Backbone

wanted, never calling on maintenance again, resorting back to my safe island.

In all my time at the track, witnessing the blatant and rampant theft would be my Achilles' heel. If you have ever gone to a stadium or ballpark and wondered why all they have is potato chips, pretzels, and individually packaged items, it's most likely due to theft and ease of inventorying. For every item that leaves commissary, a representative dollar figure must be returned. Even the beer man at the park issued 20 beers, if sold for $10.00 each, must return to commissary with $200 in their bank before being sent out again with another 20 beers. Candy, easy to conceal, can be placed in a purse or pocket and then sold for ten times the cost. Portion control always remained a challenge to thwart the con artists who were always one step ahead.

Though my relationship with the Food and Beverage director was workable, I always had my reservations. While his skills dwarfed mine in his canniness for political posturing, most times employee infractions or evidence of theft was merely brushed aside, never a reprimand or termination. Perhaps because of close friendships, too much paperwork to file with the union, or most likely his sheer laziness.

Finally, with hard evidence, I had determined that two concession workers had been stealing from the Grill. When they denied stealing, I slammed my fist on the desk; despite my proof, only a simple warning was handed down. Suddenly, it became my life's mission to make their hours at the track a living hell.

I began by cutting hours, scheduling mindless cleaning detail, and then separating them from each other and placing them on the worst shifts. In the end, I wouldn't be forced to terminate anyone, because they would be willingly running out of my department on their own. Both girls finally eliminated from my staff, until during our busiest day of the year while doing my rounds, I noticed them working together at the farthest end of the track, away from the main kitchen. At a concession stand I had no control over, my hands were tied since they were no longer under my supervision. I could only imagine the revenue pocketed that day in the stand.

Over time it became common that I would be forced to look the other way. One night after the kitchen wrapped up, I poked my head into the outdoor beer garden. Picture a large bar, beautiful summer weather, live music, and throngs of people singing and dancing. Needing to touch base with the F&B director before leaving, behind the bar, he exuberantly pulls me to the side, smiling from ear to ear.

Reaching into his pocket, he proceeded to pull out and show me rolled bundles of cash. Suspecting where the money came from, I immediately looked at the bar; sure enough, kegs. Kegs, while portable, can also be untraceable revenue streams, making it easier to manipulate the numbers. "Oh, the revenue fell short because four of the kegs foamed," an explanation often used. But why would you have thousands in your pocket? I wanted to ask. I recall walking to my car disgusted and demoralized, working so hard to create something, and knowing others were pissing it away.

Growing A Backbone

While the track was experiencing its best numbers in decades, however, my bonus was tied to the food and beverage performance for the *entire* track. This included liquor and concessions, over which I had little control. I stumbled upon learning this only after completion of one my annual reviews; while my kitchen had a stellar year, when mixed with the overall payroll, insidious mismanagement and theft; all F&B numbers were inherently affected. Pissed off, I surmised that perhaps everyone else at the track had it right with the notion of *"getting yours while you can and fuck the next guy."*

Ever resourceful, fraud eventually found its way into my kitchen. When receiving shipments one day, I noticed several extra boxes of tomatoes, four cases of potatoes, and a variety of other food items I had never ordered. Once again, the next week, several more cases would show up. Not only had I not ordered those items, but the prices were strangely higher than normal. Determined to get to the bottom, I called my sales rep who suggested that I check with F&B, since it was, *they* who ordered the items. As it turns out, the previous month was the annual food vendor show, and for every item you ordered at the show, each attendee would receive a cold hard cash kickback in return given out on the day of the event. As it turns out, the F&B director was going to the show and pocketing the kickbacks.

I never ordered those items, nor did I have any use for them. Not only were those items screwing my inventory costs, the product would spoil if left unused. Each week I refused the items, forcing them back on the truck, not knowing if the cash would have to be returned, waiting for a confrontation from F&B, although it never happened. I wondered what else was going on that was crushing my food costs, preventing my bonus, and ultimately jeopardizing my job. Track corruption seemed unavoidable, even on my island.

The track continued its roller coaster; year after year, while it employed hundreds of people, was on pins and needles when the Illinois Racing Board was required to split the allotment of racing dates equally between all the area tracks. Tracks were either forced to go dark for months or in many cases were granted three measly race days a week as part of the agreement. The less racing, while less hours, equaled more job cuts.

Harness racing was facing a slow death that would never recapture those glorious days decades earlier when the stands would be filled with 30,000 rabid horse racing fans. A more discerning clientele, millennials have no patience waiting twenty minutes between races, especially when the actual race itself only lasts a couple minutes. Despite aggressive and costly marketing, it had become an old man's sport.

Enter casinos. As gaming expanded across the country, not only harness racing, but thoroughbred track revenue handles suffered as well. Many tracks shuttering altogether or became what's known as Racinos; a combination of both casino and horse racing. While the expansion of more casino licenses was protested from the tracks, the State of Illinois eventually mandated that the tracks be entitled to a percentage of revenue from the newer casinos, after determining they

Growing A Backbone

were strangling the already wavering livelihood of each track. This, in the sum of tens of millions of dollars.

Politics remained pivotal in continuing to ensure those percentages and the survival of each track. Without it, the tracks would surely fold; either that, or the Illinois Gambling Board allow slots in all the area racetracks. This, of course, was in turn fought by the casinos. Every employee, from hamburger flipper to stable hand, would be watching closely every year, what went on in the downstate Capital of Springfield with the politicians.

Concern over race day allotments, combined with how long the tracks would be allowed to milk the casinos continued to plague the track year after year. Each year, rumors would circulate that the track was about to lose its cut from those casinos, obvious to everyone that the tracks could no longer survive without it, with thousands of jobs on the line. While the tracks numbers were respectable, it would require massive, marketing campaigns and costly giveaways in attracting the passive younger audience.

Back inside the kitchen, things seemed to be unraveling for reasons having nothing to do with food costs or my performance. Our new F&B director, whose ink on his hospitality degree had not yet dried, decided implementing policies on all labor without checking union codes or bylaws. Under the new rules, no employees were to wear jewelry and makeup, and would be scrutinized while on the clock. Many refused to acquiesce, ultimately leading to a walkout leaving me with a skeleton crew in my kitchen. Months later, I was required to appear at a union hearing with owner's, all the department heads and union officials in attendance. The fired employees were not only fighting for their jobs back, but also back pay for all those weeks missed.

There I was, once again, *not* cooking and wrapped up in someone else's bullshit; either I betray my own staff who I had grown close or protect my career siding with the track. Fortunately, the F&B manager suffered his own fate, lasting only a couple months in what became a revolving door of mismanagement. This, after those union employees were granted complete vindication that included all monies owed in the rears. If it wasn't a union problem, stress over race dates or the new Food and Beverage director du jour, it became a string of other issues that left me deflated and longing for the early days with my bucket of parsley and hanging out at the Bullmarket.

Five years at the track, it was discovered yet another kickback was taking place. This time in the dining room, where servers were found skimming dollars off the top of every buffet, in addition to their tip percentage. Their argument was that the buffet had become overtly popular while no one was ordering off the menu any longer; thus, cutting into their tips. I never knew my real food cost because it seemed everyone had their hand in the pot.

One busy Saturday night while making my rounds, I passed an employee bathroom just as the door was opening. Two servers were exiting at the same time followed by a plume of smoke, the distinctive smell of marijuana following them. Since most of the dining room patrons chose to order off the buffet, left plenty of play time for many of the staff. Ever the babysitter, I could have said nothing, but it would scream my approval if I were to simply let it go unnoticed.

When confronted, they countered that they were not under my department rule and that I, could essentially do nothing. They got me on that one; since servers reported directly to the F&B director and knowing he would do nothing, left me looking like a fool. The blatant disregard and lack of work ethics on my watch shook me to the core like no other. Making matters worse, I was unprepared when I found that one of the servers was protected all the way to the top. Unbeknownst to me at the time, the married general manager of the entire track and one of the very same servers were often spotted in her car after closing.

Exhausted by mismanagement and having to go along to get along, after almost six years at the track, the writing was on the wall and it became time for me to leave. Deflated, not only with the track, but the derelict properties plaguing the business, that will chew you up and spit you out, I found a restaurant that I would take over as chef-owner entrepreneur. Peppercorns.

The racetrack was now over a hundred years old and millions of people having frequented the grounds. I'll always hold the grand old lady dear to my heart, allowed to have taken part in her history. Leaving on my own terms, never having caved to the temptations. My years at the track allowed me to witness countless smiles on those customers' faces, feeding tens of thousands of people with food that I'd prepared only hours earlier. And of course, the comradery I enjoyed in the kitchen with those true professionals that I would like to think I helped mentor on their own paths.

My leaving would have impeccable timing. Harness racing continued to struggle, and the purses continued to diminish, while fighting for race dates remained a constant battle. Layoffs ensued, followed by them closing entire sections of the track off from the public and combining positions in effort to save money.

Only a few years later, it all came crashing down when Illinois Governor Rod Blagojevich and his Chief of Staff, John Harris, were arrested on Federal Corruption charges for soliciting bribes for political appointments. Most notably, Blagojevich was taped by the FBI stating about Barack Obama's vacant U.S. Senate seat when he ran for the office of President, "I've got this thing, and it's fucking golden. I'm just not giving it up for fucking nothing." Further, conspiracy charges were brought up against the governor for his part in soliciting the racetrack for kickbacks to ensure casinos continued to front their percentage.

The owner of the track was also held liable on three counts in a civil racketeering case involving conduct engaged in by former Governor Rod Blagojevich; $26.3 million each was awarded in damages to four Illinois riverboat casinos, including the Hollywood Casino Joliet and the Hollywood Casino Aurora. In total, the recovery was over $78 million.

The litigation took years until a verdict was reached, forcing both area tracks under management into bankruptcy — rocking the horse racing industry and all those involved to the core. Thousands went

Growing A Backbone

on to lose their jobs when both tracks closed indefinitely and were then liquidated. As of this writing, Rod Blagojevich is still serving out a fourteen-year sentence in Englewood, Colorado while President Trump considers a pardon to the disgraced Governor.

In all fairness it was a dying sport. Nostalgia drew me back a few years later, and I snuck into what was once my thriving kitchen, now eerily silent. The rows of ovens and glistening stainless steel tables now sat empty, and the hanging chef utensils remained indolent. I looked on with a mixture of remorse and sadness. All the concession stands in repose, and thousands of seats now empty, while row upon row of silent TV monitors remained dormant. If you stood silent and focused, you could hear the roar from the crowd, decades earlier during more innocent times. Each man wearing his Fedora hat and dressed in his suit, and women in their finest dress. The stands empty, I looked over to the area of the track as a light wind blew raising dust off the oval course. One of the billboard signs rusted and tilted off its hinge, I imagined the millions of horses trained to circle the track for our entertainment.

Twenty-five years later, not including those years operating Peppercorns, I would soon be forced to muster enough courage like all those years on the line before. The fight of my life was just about to begin.

CHAPTER ELEVEN

Inaptitude

Well over a year now into litigation, months became the same, offering no clear indication as to my case status, impending court dates, or Pepper's whereabouts. Phone calls from my counsel went unreturned and emails for the most part left me questioning. Most of my personal items were still intentionally being held back at the house, and I would be reminded repeatedly that any material items were to be considered marital property and decided upon in the final decree, despite the possibility it could take years. Forced to live without my personal belongings, in addition to not having Pepper by my side, was intransigent to say the least.

Questions continued to linger. What was the status of Pepper and the subsequent petition efforts for visitation? How was I to acquire any news about Pepper, his well-being, or who was taking care of him? Once again, I was instructed that no such criteria for visitation had yet been established for domesticated household pets, much less custody laws. Exasperated, I found myself at a loss, regretfully forced heeding the advice of my attorney. Each time I had made an inquiry, would set me back another $250 per hour, clearly a deliberate practice, keeping the client in the dark, forcing queries, and billing each time.

Resorting back to my own research, I continued questioning my attorney's efforts, or lack thereof. Why had no temporary divorce order been specified? This would have certainly provided me the groundwork to inquire why Pepper was being hidden. While I had completed my own discovery, our request for production on their behalf intentionally dragged on unnecessarily, and upon completion, was grossly incomplete when finally submitted. I then questioned where were the interrogatories that I was allowed as part of discovery? Initially given thirty days, this would turn into sixty days, then ninety, and finally 120, motion after motion filed.

Hearings continued, each purposely prolonging the case and my separation from Pepper, month after month, and then years spent apart from my best friend. In the eyes of the court, based on case evidence history, the longer we remained apart falsely suggested my being content and to some degree uncaring or passive. After all, in the eyes of many, I could just, "get another dog."

Inaptitude

After months of insistent prodding and heated exchanges with my counsel, a motion for visitation had finally —while reluctantly— been filed; seldom heard of in cases of household domesticated animals. Despite the chagrin of my attorney, my suspicion for his reluctance in filing the motion for visitation, was embarrassment on his behalf. Having to acknowledge what he felt was a capricious request, warranting no legal grounds, submitted before a sitting circuit court judge. This, while everyone involved was cognizant that no such laws existed and any introductory motion granted would certainly set precedence, however, we all knew would not stand a chance.

Filing the motion, we all knew would fail, was also a risky move on my behalf that could've been construed as making a mockery of the courtroom, wasting both the court's time, and taxpayers' money. It was suggested by many that perhaps my time be better served focusing on the house or monetary investments in the traditional sense during the divorce rather than a mere dog who you most likely will never see again. But what was there not to understand? Clearly, Pepper *was* my primary motivation and investment.

No surprise, on the day following the hearing, the expected news had been delivered that the motion had been thrown out. Castigating my efforts, my counsel viewed it as a waste of time to have even made such an attempt, however, complacent taking my money for his services. I was not only wasting my own money, but perhaps caused humiliation on his behalf as everyone was fully aware of the state's promulgation. With tensions elevated, I was pressured to entrust my counsel, never questioning his legal course of action again.

As the case continued gaining attention, I was questioned countless times why I was spending my time and effort, in addition to thousands of dollars, on one dog. "You could buy a hundred dogs or empty out a shelter for that matter!" I reminded each individual that those dogs are not my dog, and not my companion who waited for me countless nights, weeks, and years after grueling fourteen-hour days on the line for me to return home. On our first trek together in the forest with me when I was struggling, or laying aside my legs each night, ever loyal and uncomplaining. During those times of doubt, I reminded myself of that moment, years ago, lying on the bed with Pepper and assuring him, I would always be there. I was not about to simply walk away.

The motion stricken, unlike my representation, I knew it was a silent victory. Precedence had now been established, despite the motion being tossed. In the mind of the judge, and those in the courts, the validity of this case and the respondent's desire to be reunited with his dog made my willingness that I walk away unacceptable. I was determined to make this a common theme throughout the remainder of our hearings, both with my attorney and before the sitting judge. A man losing his dog and best friend was the drum I would repeatedly beat making our voices heard.

Had no motion request been made, it would have appeared I was uncaring or found the absence of my dog for two years nonessential, or that it never mattered. This, I knew, from the countless cases I discovered from those who had lost their companion through careless inaction while merely, hoping for the best. I was not about to remain idle despite the odds.

Before the motion had been submitted, as part of my research, I dug up several similar cases; pets that were used as tools and intentionally withheld from their primary caretaker. A useful tactic employed as leverage for bargaining, revenge, or deliberate cruelty; inherently it unfairly causes anguish on both the pet and the litigant. I noted that in every case example, that the party who failed to physically gain possession of the animal throughout the divorce proceeding eventually went on to lose permanent custody indefinitely. I could only find a few cases where the pet had been returned, but those cases typically involved sheer blackmail. The pet was eventually delivered under duress or in exchange for untold assets during bargaining.

Reservations aside, my aspirations towards Pepper were made apparent, placed on full display in an effort that the injustice be cited, not only for me and Pepper, but for all those individuals suffering from similar oppression. The unjust intentional separation had become much larger than my mere case alone. A risk I was willing, assured it was imperative establishing the theme that a man and his best friend is not separated without due process. Many times, I questioned what would happen to Pepper had I simply said nothing? I could not chance him being given up for adoption or worse yet, euthanized.

Had my tactic been revealed to my attorney, the ill-fated motion would have never made it to the courtroom floor to begin with. I held my convictions so strongly that I was days away from submitting my own visitation motion, risking losing my representation. However, not once during my time retaining his directive, was any tactic or exercise exhausted in the effort to have Pepper returned to me. Regardless of the court's decision and the failed motion, the seed had been planted. Viewed by my counsel as trivial and a waste of time, I began my search for alternative representation.

Even more months trailed, and life as it were was placed on an indefinite hiatus by the engrossing legal posturing. While I was breathing, it felt as if I weren't even alive and always in a state of suspension. My refuge included any Starbucks tapping into the WiFi while drinking countless cups of coffee. It became common for me to leave one Starbucks for another down the street, seeking the perfect combination of sunlight and a bustling crowd. The crowds offering a sense of belonging, and the sunlight hope.

My goal when working was to make it as work-like as possible; the table would be my cubicle, and the barista serving as the office coffee machine. Rarely would I dress down, despite having nowhere to go. My dress pants and button-down collared shirt would create a sense of urgency and focus, while helping me avoid complacency and my mind from wandering back to Pepper. Mornings gave way to night, ten hours later I was still at Starbucks, my body immune to the caffeine. When not working, I spent hours on end researching similar cases, animal law and welfare practices. A whole new world from my

Inaptitude

own case research was thrust upon me involving animal liberation issues, policies, and the lack thereof.

Never sought intentionally, the research I was subjected to brought upon a diverse and unbridled understanding that I had never given much attention. Always sensitive to animal welfare my whole life, however, I had dispatched little solicitude about frequenting zoos, Sea World, or tutelage for horse-drawn carriages, Yulin, and animal exploitation. Over time, it became increasingly near-impossible coping through the trials of my divorce, separation from Pepper, and the exposure I was subjecting myself, to the dark world of animal torture, abuse, testing, and incessant slaughter.

Despairingly, I'd pipe in sounds through my earbuds while at Starbucks augmenting those feelings of desolation and hopelessness. Headphones on, I'd stream looping sounds of rainfall or crashing ocean waves, hoping to drown out and avoid any conscious thoughts or feelings.

Shockingly, over 23 million animals are used for biomedical experimentation and genetic engineering annually, while much of the testing is performed unanesthetized. Seven million companion animals enter shelters every year, and on average 55% of those will be euthanized. It's estimated that over 1 billion dollars are spent annually in tax dollars for the collecting, transporting, housing and ultimate euthanizing of strays, those having escaped, or homeless pets. Felines accounting for 72% of those numbers.

A substantial majority of people exuberantly claim to have made great strides in animal welfare issues today, yet it was Charles Darwin who proclaimed almost 200 years ago: *"Animals, whom we have made our slaves, we do not like to consider our equal."* He further went on; *"There is no fundamental difference between man and the higher animals in their mental faculties. The lower animals, like man, manifestly feel pleasure and pain, happiness, and misery."* — *Charles Darwin*

This, circa 1837, yet only in the year 2018, was it finally made illegal to consume dog meat in the United States. While of course, most people frown upon consuming dog meat here in the U.S., one must question why it had taken so long placing into law? To this day, while laws have been passed to prevent unnecessary suffering, laws are also conveniently rewritten to allow *tolerable suffering* for the sake of experimentation, abuse, neglect, or for the benefit of humans.

While it's humans who enact these laws, in most cases they are written for self-appreciating dividends while denying the animals' cognitive wherewithal and ability to reason, thus, making it convenient. Closer to home for all of us, a recent bill respectively passed, frowns upon leaving a dog in a car on a hot day with the windows rolled up. However, until recently, it was acceptable for dogs to be literally chained for life to a stake in the ground or left outside in extreme elements. So long as they are provided food and water. It remained this way until finally in 2013, when in Oregon, House Bill 2783 was passed addressing dog tethering laws that

Inaptitude

dictates the length of time a dog can be tied up outside. While it certainly qualifies as neglect, the law is rarely enforced, nor do most municipalities have the funding or manpower to supervise each occurrence. I have personally witnessed this first-hand on several occasions.

Human history has always perpetuated our interests over the weak, both exploiting and leaving animals vulnerable to our whims. Billions of farm animals are bred and born while destined never to set foot on grass. On their way to the slaughterhouse, tens of thousands will arrive already dead, killed in transit due to trampling, suffocation, shock, or organ failure. Those dead, if not used for human consumption, will ultimately be butchered and processed for pet food in many cases. In the United States, while most cattle are stunned, and then brutally killed with a cap-bolt gun to the skull, many other countries merely deliver a single slit to the throat while they are still alive, leaving them to bleed out before butchering. These rituals are performed each day in the presence of the animals' siblings, or like-species, observing firsthand the same fate they too will experience.

As humans, our assumption is that their ignorance prevents any cognitive understanding or the ability to reason the real horror taking place before them. Almost 200 years after mere marginal laws were created, there remains a much larger resolution for recognizing the unethical treatment and intolerable practices of our kindred.

Those nonhuman creatures with blood coursing through their veins, the same as us, and hearts that pump blood for survival, the same as us, and mindful thoughts that are capable of reason, feeling, love, and empathy; characteristically the same as us, it has been proven we share innumerable traits. The ability to feel pain, experience joy, sadness, longing, and gratitude. The notion that animals are objects or mere property written into our laws conveniently avoids having to grant them rights or in many cases impassioned welfare practices. How can they be granted rights if they can't speak in order, they defend themselves? Unable to communicate, how are we then to understand their desires? It has always been the directive of humans that animals remain property, ignoring their fundamental right to life through our own process of artificial selection.

Recently, a tragic news story had the country following a grieving orca whale mother who carried her dead calf for over two weeks, refusing to let her go, her grief much the same as when humans experience the loss of a loved one.

We have all heard of cases where a dog is lost for months, hundreds of miles from home, and miraculously somehow finds his way back to his rightful owner. With no map or GPS to use for navigation, how can this be possible? In addition to their acute sense of smell, it has been long suspected that dogs have the ability to navigate via magnetism, orienting themselves using the earth's magnetic field. This on its own is remarkable, but their sheer dedication and loyalty should leave us to question: Why would they go back to their original home instead of merely settling with another welcoming family? They too, like humans, share that sense of belonging and need for familiarity and family bond.

Inaptitude

A grieving Labrador Retriever named Hawkeye made national headlines in 2011, recorded lying next to departed Navy SEAL Jon Tumilson's casket before 1,500 mourners, paying his last respects. Was he aware of his guardian's passing? If not, why the somber display, spending hours lying by his casket consumed with grief? These stories, while heartwarming indeed, also suggest the compassion and understanding animals share in the human-animal bond.

The objection to vivisection — the experimentation on living animals — is recorded as early as the mid-1600s. It wouldn't be until some 200 years later that the first animal protection laws were recognized, regulating the scientific use of animals during those barbaric practices. Many times, laws were introduced only when those overwhelmed with compassion could no longer stand idle, witnessing the extreme abuse. Similar to horses and mules used for transportation; steers were harnessed, their shoulders bloodied from the straps as they pulled plows through fields for days at a time. Pigs and cattle were mercilessly beaten and forced into pens, and their eventual slaughter would seldom be immediate or without suffering, often taking minutes or hours to succumb to their infliction. This was before automobiles existed and when farm animals were expected to perform the brunt of the work. Regretfully, many of these violent and cruel practices are still employed in several third world countries today.

On a lighter note, and fortunately for dogs, because of our kinship that began thousands of years earlier, there is a somewhat reciprocal understanding, mutual respect, admiration, and loyalty between canine and the modern human that wasn't always so. Remaining faithful to our auspice, our companion has come a long way.

From the grey timber wolf species, an apex predator, the house dog today maintains that same gene DNA upwards of 99% tracing back its lineage. To this day, they still display many of those same characteristics of their ancestors that we have come to admire. Once a human threat, the carnivores that they are, the grey wolf shared many of the same foods that we hunted for tens of thousands of years.

It is Suspected that they wandered onto our campsites, sharing our food, and from there worked on farms, perhaps as shepherds. They were then confined outside the home guarding against intruders, until finally, welcomed into our house, and for many of us, sharing our bed each night. You are essentially sleeping with a wolf! One could certainly question: What other nonhuman creature has gone through such a drastic, remarkable evolution, while also becoming such a trusted and loyal partner in alliance with us humans?

As court status hearings came up, most times it was unnecessary for either the defendant or plaintiff to be present. Regardless, I would religiously make the trek each time, my presence known in court, further driving a wedge between my attorney. Prohibited from speaking, I'd purposefully question aloud the status of Pepper within earshot of the judge making certain my pleas were transparent.

At one point it became so contentious that hearing dates were withheld from me. A nonissue, I had made a habit of checking the

Inaptitude

courts' docket for impending court dates. The whole process stunk of backroom deals, and handshakes between each counsel. Defendants who were used as tools of redistribution, with their open pocketbooks, forced into combat, eventually submitting when resources are depleted. Each time leaving the courthouse, I felt as though I needed to shower to wash off the stench of corruption and con artists at work, exploiting those less fortunate and gullible.

Despite my efforts, I could feel Pepper slipping away, my focused determination fading during those darkest of times. Making matters worse, work-travel, while offering the comfort of the road and being anywhere else, was now slowing. Back at Starbucks with my laptop, endless supply of coffee and work, I became a fixture. The four Starbucks within the three-square miles would become my home. Switching them up, I did my best at becoming obscure and somewhat less piteous; at times comforting, while mostly offering isolation.

Those long days on my feet as the defiant and unwavering chef now seemed so long ago and a completely different self than what I'd become. I questioned how I managed those years as a chef, now a shell of a man without my dog or my restaurant. With each passing month, the anxiety coupled with the fear of losing Pepper, obsessively encouraged a nasty habit where I would bite my own skin off from my fingers in layers. Starting from a hangnail, or sometimes from dry skin, red and bloodied, it became commonplace for me to carry around a small spool of white medical tape in my pocket so I could immediately tape over my fingers after having peeled off a layer. Ashamed, I'd intentionally keep my hands in my pockets or tucked behind me.

Arriving late to Starbucks one day and all the tables taken, forced me to grab one of the round circular tables that offered little room for my laptop, let alone any work documents. The bench was so short and uncomfortable that it forced me to reach up as I typed. The previous afternoon, I had suffered a setback in court, and was having a rough start to my day.

As even more people filled the store, two bearded men sat down beside me, offering a friendly gesture as they nestled into their chairs. To avoid being drawn into their conversation, I put on my headphones in effort to focus on my work. Tired of the canned rainfall and imaginary waterfalls that I would pipe into my headphones, I kept the volume down, thinking the headphones alone would drown out their voices.

Faintly I could hear their voices as my hands slowed over the keyboard. In between work and listening to their conversation, I learned that they were from a local church not far away and that one man's wife had been laid off from work, in addition, his trade as a carpenter was slowing. The conversation then trailed to Christian faith and the lack thereof during those most challenging of times in people's lives. Having caught my attention, their discussion then touched upon those people, who when faced with adversity, and the choice of taking one's own life, and the consequences of making that decision. My head turned towards the bookcase beside me to avoid being seen and so that I could maintain my composure. Shrouded in

Inaptitude

self-doubt, questioning who I had become, Pepper and my restaurant gone — this would be my darkest hour.

I stood up hurriedly heading to the bathroom, when upon my return and without notice, "John," rose to his feet taking it upon himself that we be introduced. With his lengthy, manicured greying beard, untucked thick plaid shirt, and large gripping calloused carpenter hands that enveloped mine when we greeted one another, John, was anything but menacing. A comfort exuded his presence, the type of man you felt you knew and could trust with a simple handshake. Exchanging introductions, I learned that while both men were working and things had slowed, they were still able to pay the bills and put food on the table back home. John held a role at the church, while the other man was a member of the congregation.

Despite those most challenging times they were both experiencing, one would have never known each's predicament. Their demeanor was unwavering, in fact, almost jovial. Was it their faith, or the simple fact that they were simply enjoying each other's companionship?

Returning to my seat, I seized the opportunity and summoned a burning question that had been allowed to torment my thoughts. Hesitating at first and doing my best at remaining anonymous, I questioned John with the straightest face I could muster; *"Is there forgiveness for the weak who ultimately decide taking their own lives?"* Uncertain how convincing with my words, I suggested that I was asking on behalf of a "friend." With sincere genuineness expressed on his weathered face, John exuded a feeling of comfort I will never forget. Patiently, he took the time and thought hard, answering my questions without passing judgment. That day, John, became my friend, and at the same time succeeded by gaining another to join his flock. The following Sunday would be the first time I had stepped into a church in years.

My spirit wavering, and simple things like the smell of sautéed onions escaping from restaurants or watching someone frolic with their dog in a park would trigger my emotions. Without my restaurant, a contentious divorce lingering, a doubtful attorney, and my longing for Pepper, each day became unbearable. The thought that I may never see Pepper again, those years together and miles of hiking now a memory, crippled me with raw emotions.

Determined from becoming an obscure statistic, I would dig deep, calling upon the strength and character I had championed all those years working under some of the most heinous of conditions. If you fail gaining any insight or hope from this book, know this; you are here for a reason, while each of us has been bestowed the gift of life. Just like those creatures I write about, the chance that you made it and were even born, the odds are staggering. It's up to you to make something of that gift and never, ever settle for less. It would take losing Pepper, my closest friend, and the travails I was subjected, before I understood the harsh reality of those words.

My daughter, family, and Pepper would prevent that lethal choice from being made in the end. While the unnerving exposure and the plight of those animals I had become familiar with was hampering my spirit, it reminded me that even at your lowest point, someone,

Inaptitude

some being, somewhere has it worse than you. That each challenge you face is an opportunity for growth and learning. That bliss is not defined as the absence of limitations, but rather, the opportunity to overcome those obstacles, while achieving the satisfaction of self-worth and accountability.

Checking out by your own hand not only shortchanges the gift of life provided, but it selfishly leaves a burden on those you leave behind. Your ultimate destination in life is not about your arrival, but rather relishing the road of your travels. Those welcoming moments, while only some may be victorious, all provide a chance to experience the gift of life offered, only to a select few. Never in my life had I taken the easy way out, nor was I about to then.

Searching through boxes, I pulled out photos taken of Pepper during unusual or special moments we shared together. I placed them on my dresser mirror, the dashboard of my car, and made a habit of always taking a couple photos with me whenever I traveled to keep me company. I would save clippings of random quotes from newspapers, offering hope or inspirational stories of people who had overcome extreme challenges.

They would be on my nightstand when I woke up, taped to my laptop, or inside books as a bookmark. Before putting my pants in the laundry, I'd check my pockets and find crumpled newspaper quotations I had forgotten that'd offer me newfound strength. If not indefinitely, at least for that moment it provided me with aspiration that would get me through yet another day. I'd purposely seek out ways to bring positivity back into my life. This is how I made it through each of my days, one hour at a time. Some of those adages I found inspirational:

"I have learned over the years that when one's mind is made up, this diminishes fear; knowing what must be done does away with fear." ~ Rosa Parks ~

"In times of great stress or adversity, it's always best to keep busy, to plow your anger and your energy into something positive."
~ Lee Iacocca ~

"Until one has loved an animal, a part of one's soul remains unawakened" ~ Anatole France ~

One of my favorites:

If you want something you have never had, you must do something you've never done. ~ Unknown ~

Surrounded by positive, I found was giving back positive in return. I would intentionally seek out ways to avoid any negative influence — be it people, politics, or surroundings. This focus required a conscious effort at first, but eventually would become second nature. Destructive people, negative discussions, criticizing, blame, and judgment; gave way to hope, encouragement, light and forbearance. Something greater was at stake, I had to remind myself.

For as long as the litigation continued, I had a glimmer of hope that we would eventually be reunited. Almost as if the door had not yet closed all the way, still offering Pepper and I a chance. Time,

Inaptitude

which had stood still for weeks and months, was now a ritual rather than an impediment. Slow at first to adjust my quiet, I began lifting myself. Time, while once an enemy, now instilled the hope I would need to propel me, us, forward. I now had nothing other than time. Assured, my focus would require me to be sharp; not only for myself, but for Pepper, if we were ever to see each other again.

CHAPTER TWELVE

Going All In

After spending the entire day in the law library, with heavy disinclination, I decided to drive by the house to see if any of my belongings may have been intentionally thrown into the garbage or left on the curb. Approaching the estranged neighborhood, I questioned, *was this place ever my home, or simply a setting where I was able to return each night, allowed to rest my head after working the restaurant each day?* I had always suspected my role while living there, most times leaving me feeling like a stranger in my own home. No longer any connection, the home now seemed like any other brick and mortar structure, however, colder and forbidding.

The account of what happened next was thoroughly dissected in heated discussion during a courtroom hearing, while the narrative varied, depending on who recanted the story. The first version, chronicalized as no one being home at the time, suggesting that I had entered the house and removed Pepper from the premises. Contradictory, my version found that Pepper had been locked out of the house, left wandering outside as I drove past.

Regardless of which version you subscribe; for the first time in two years I was finally able to witness Pepper. His jet-black coat and low stocky frame were unmistakable. Exiting the truck, I excitedly yelled for him in the distance. Arching his head back, he turned in the direction of my voice before sprinting into my arms to greet me. Licking, clawing, and spinning in place with his tail wagging profusely, I knew we had no time to waste.

Uncertain what had taken over me, frantically I fumbled with the passenger door, lifting him into the seat, racing back to the driver's side, and in a matter of seconds we were ghosts. Never, was it proven in court that I had entered the house nor if Pepper had merely been left outside unattended. If I was in that house, I didn't care about anything other than Pepper, but if he was outside, I was not about to leave him.

By now I had become a journeyman in the divorce game. Like a chess match, it became imperative, I remain mindful of two moves ahead and its repercussions, each time advancing my Pawn. With Pepper now by my side and adrenaline coursing through me, I decidedly alerted the local police department, explaining what had occurred and that Pepper was now safely in the hands of his guardian. What intruder in his right mind would notify the police *after* they had entered a home?

Going All In

While I could have easily hidden Pepper, I chose remaining transparent that he was in fact with me. A calculated move; either way the story unfolded, it was sending a clear message to the court and those involved the indisputable significance that Pepper, ultimately be returned to his rightful owner. A risk I was willing to take.

Driving for the next hour, my mind racing, curious what vengeance or retribution would there be in store for my actions? Filled with excitement and unable to remain seated, Pepper refused sitting alone in the passenger seat, whining to sit on my lap as I drove. After several attempts, I was forced into relenting all 80 pounds of him onto my lap as we both sat uncomfortably in the driver's seat barreling down the expressway.

Pepper staring at me as I drove, I was barely able to see over his head and steer properly. Shifting his body around, and allowing his claws to dig into my lap, we became totally reckless, however, loving every minute. No longer was there any doubt in my mind after being with Pepper that moment — finding newfound faith — that I would give up on our being reunited permanently.

With Pepper coming home, we immediately headed to the store for supplies since I no longer had any of his personal belongings. Purchasing food, a new leash, handsome collar, toys, and a huge memory foam bed; those items were in some small way my commitment to him, uncertain how long he'd be with me before *they'd* come knocking on my door. It became our reassurance that if he was taken away from me, that those new items would be waiting for his return.

Once in his new home, Pepper made a point to dutifully rummage from room to room, smelling each corner, under each couch, and every piece of furniture. As if it were yesterday, he would first stare at the front door and then back at me, messaging that it was time for us to resume where we'd left off two years earlier.

With plenty of hiking trails to choose from, we packed up and drove off, certain not to waste any time before *they* would arrive at the house. Finding a trail alongside a beautiful flat lake, Pepper, never missing a beat and like old times, took up the lead some 20 yards out front, every few steps turning his head back to ensure I wasn't far behind. After two hours into our hike and with dusk fast approaching, begrudgingly, we began our trek back.

Slowly circling the neighborhood twice, I first scanned the driveway and then each parked vehicle for anyone suspicious who was waiting in their car or that seemed out of place. Finding it safe to enter the house, and once back inside, Pepper followed me from room to room, and once again we become inseparable, each passing hour a gift knowing it was temporary. Relaxing together on the couch, we spent the remainder of the evening together, waiting expectantly for the eventual call or knock on the door that would separate us. The waiting giving way to exhaustion, like two old men, we made our way off to bed, climbing each step of the stairs, Pepper by my side. Once in bed, true to his character, Pepper, left me little room for comfortable sleep. Things were good, for *now*.

Going All In

Scheduled to work the following day, I found it impossible to focus on my efforts. With Pepper on the couch, and his head perched on the armrest, he would alternate between looking out the window at the squirrels taunting him, and then back at me staring into my laptop. Still, there were no phone calls, no knock on the door, nor any word, although I knew there was something imminent. After a midday walk around the neighborhood, the day once again gave way to night. Relaxing on the couch with Pepper by my side, the abrupt and menacing knock on the door was unmistakable. With his insistent barking, there would be no hiding Pepper, forced to lure him into a separate room with a slice of bologna, allowing me to answer the front door.

The unambiguous dark blue vest, badge, and Sheriff's car parked out front came as no surprise. Cautiously, I cracked the door open ever so slightly, greeting him with a solemn introduction. His demeanor while dispassionate, he delivered a series of questions that were followed by presenting a packet of documents.

Given only a moment to skim over all 25 pages, the paperwork would explain that a restraining order had been issued against me and that Pepper was to be returned immediately. *Seriously, a restraining order?* This, after being gone for two years and not at any time involved in a domestic disturbance or complaint? Not in any petition or on police record had there been any mention or indication of physical conflict or emotional distress either during the marriage or once estranged. For this very reason I left long ago; to avoid any false inflammatory inciting accusations. Sobering, I knew my lawyer was of little help at that moment, requiring me to make snap decisions based on what I'd read during similar cases.

With the door no more than one inch open, intuitively I kept an eye on the officer's shoulder movements. With each motion of the shoulder is followed by the arm; uncertain if he was going to cuff my wrist and arrest me or reach for the door. However, I knew he had no authority to enter my house, even had I refused relinquishing Pepper. Carefully, when I had moved my Pawn by bringing Pepper to the house, I had notified the police of his whereabouts, thus indicating he was never stolen. *How can I steal my own dog?* I could have simply hidden him as it had been done to me, however, I could not risk agitating the judge and possibly never see Pepper again. My actions would serve as an investment, gaining the trust of the court, and at the same time making my intentions clear. I had to reassure myself that my time would come, although now, with the stage set, *everyone* was going to hear Pepper's story.

Unsubstantiated, the restraining order would later be thrown out of court and stricken at the end of the trial, working in my favor. A shrewd technique at the time, however the OP had been fabricated, thus forcing me to part with Pepper.

Opening the bedroom door, Pepper sprinted past me, curious who was at the front entry. Pepper, unaware of what was going on, I said my goodbyes, uncertain if I would ever see him again. Slipping through the front door, he was taken away. Strange enough, once I got back inside there were no slamming doors, cursing, or tears shed. Maybe it was because I had a formal goodbye or more likely was because I was convinced things weren't over yet. That night, while I had plenty of legroom in bed, I managed to get little sleep without my buddy.

The next day, describing what had taken place with my attorney, the phone call lasted less than five minutes. Discussing my actions, he seemed less than surprised that I'd pull such a stunt. Even less surprising was that he offered no legal course of direction, nor interest in filing a motion that the falsified order of protection be expunged. I was essentially on my own.

As the trial was heating up, I had never been briefed on the pending deposition nor once offered guidance instructing me on what I should willingly submit during oral testimony or how best to formulate any of my responses. Rather than a deposition upon written questions, we were to provide as part of the discovery a deposition while sworn in under oath. With the date upon us, I was the first to be deposed and sworn in by the court reporter prior to direct examination. Despite no pre-deposition coaching and lack of any preparation, I couldn't wait to begin. For 30 long years, I worked side by side with kitchen grunts in some of the most confrontational, stress filled environments imaginable. This would be a cakewalk.

Behind closed doors in a solemn boardroom with the litigants and attorneys present from both sides, and the stenographer ready, I had nothing to hide that could possibly be self-incriminated. With my attorney next to me, I could not, however, help but feel all alone. Hours later, never once forced to refer to my attorney, the only revealing question, — obvious to everyone — was: "do you want

Pepper?" I sat there waiting before I would answer, hoping my attorney would offer an assert privilege objection. However, there was nothing. Clearly, the question posed had been propagated to get under my skin to provoke me. My response would have no merit or any usefulness as part of the discovery in the forthcoming trial and had been asked out of sheer cruelty. Everyone knew that the question posed, was an indirect inquiry about how much I was prepared to give up in exchange for Pepper. *That's okay, I thought. Remain calm. I got this.*

While Depositions can be raw and emotional; they are seemingly designed to harass the deponent in an effort that evidence be revealed that can then be used later in court. With the deposition now complete and the stenographer putting away her equipment, everyone began to rise from the table. It should be noted that the opposing counsel's stature had always struck me as being borderline anorexic, almost as if she was always swimming in her oversized suit.

Assuming her tactics would make the deposition personal and disrespectful to Pepper, I came ready. Preparing a delicious bologna sandwich at home and placing it in a zip-lock bag before the deposition, I removed it from my suit pocket and tossed it on the center of the boardroom table. In the presence of everyone, I then suggested aloud: *"You appear to be rather pale and tense. Perhaps you should eat something."* Stunned, everyone silently stared at the sandwich and then back at me, unprepared for what I might do next. Had the question about Pepper never been asked, I would've never produced that bologna sandwich on that day.

Going All In

Silently riding the elevator down with my attorney, he was completely caught off guard by what had just taken place. I wanted to yell, *"Have you not gotten it yet? I want my fucking dog!"* Failing to coach me, nor during the deposition declare an objection, he left me dumbfounded. Reluctantly, I would be forced to guard my words as we were too far in our proceedings for me to seek alternative representation.

Equally, as part of the deposition process and as part of the discovery, cross examination was then scheduled. Reaching out to my attorney, I wanted to know the date, in addition to the list of questions he would be proposing as part of our defense. Instructed it was to take place in two weeks, however, he highly *suggested*, I not be present. Suspecting he thought I'd be recklessly unpredictable, yet at the same time, I knew he would apathetically walk through the interrogation tossing softballs to the litigant. I would agree, on the condition he introduced a series of questions that I would provide. Once again, I would find out later, I had mistakenly placed my trust in him.

Two weeks following the cross examination, when finally, able to get through to his office, I was simply instructed; "the deposition went well." *"That's it, it went well. No revelations, no additional discovery that you care to share?"* Oblivious at the time of my rights as his client, I was never supplied with the booklet of the deposition nor any supporting documents of what had taken place. The silence had become deafening, clear that we had reached an impasse.

Rudderless after years of litigation, Pepper was now a memory, and an Order of Protection was embarrassingly hanging over my head. Time was escaping, and I considered I'd never see Pepper again. With only a couple of months before trial, it was clear that I may be losing Pepper, and a strong likelihood that I'd be without counsel during the impending trial.

Rather than feeling sorry for myself, I decided to take things to a whole new level. After using Facebook and Twitter as a tool medium for Peppercorns when marketing, I understood their potential power. Creating a Facebook for Pepper, I then backtracked for months, posting past photos and excerpts of my own experience while going through the court process. The story line was that of a man unjustly separated from dog. Remaining cautious to avoid any derogatory slander, I posted only those issues pertinent to my case and those efforts to be reunited with Pepper. Next came Twitter, Instagram, and eventually, blog chronicles that described related tribulations and stories of those having experienced similar misfortune.

Subsequently, Pepper's Twitter feed was at first followed by hundreds, and then thousands. I became relentless, despite begrudging each post, feeling as if I had somehow become an exhibit on display. Gaining momentum, I would remind myself it had to be done if I wanted any chance of getting Pepper back. Finding a higher calling, I began posting similar cases from people who had reached out to me, and stories of animal liberation and neglect.

Answering emails and corresponding with animal rights advocates and those involved in grassroots efforts of like causes eventually

Going All In

became common. Suddenly, I felt as if I'd found true meaningful support in a group that had a common cause, people of a similar mindset, instilling what I'd been missing all along. Emails began arriving from various parts of the world, the story morphing into a much larger purpose, more importantly, it was no longer selfishly just about the return of Pepper.

The Chicago Sun-Times newspaper would be the first to reach out. The narrative, now becoming familiar, would describe a man going through a divorce struggling to be reunited with his best friend. Next was the Chicago Tribune, Daily Southtown News, L.A. Times and numerous other publications after the story had been picked up by the Associated Press. Calls then originated from multiple media outlets, followed by a barrage of despondent people confronted by similar circumstances. Far from over, I had one more tool I had been contemplating using.

From my own research about animal law and liberation stewardship efforts, I became intrigued by a birthing trend where dog owners going through divorce had been experimenting by retaining the use of an Animal Arbitrator. A dog owner as well, I had heard of a passionate local arbitrator who focused primarily on animals. Reaching out to Aleksandra Nejman of Royale Litigation, she welcomed the opportunity. Back in my office at Starbucks, we immediately were able to empathize over similar issues, sharing our stories and solicitousness for animals. I felt confident she would welcome the exposure and at the same time provide a knowledgeable voice.

In a definitive moment that would set precedence for the remainder of the trial, I went on to have one last court date with my counsel. Summoned into an empty courtroom before the judge, my attorney then submitted that he would be withdrawing from the case and immediately stepping down as my legal representation. Something I had yet to witness, the judge was speechless. In all her years on the bench, proclaimed, she could not recall an attorney removing themselves from a case with an impending trial only weeks away. Highly unusual and uncertain, the judge had to refer to court protocol whether the request could be granted. Pushing for an answer, without going into further detail, my attorney then cited irreconcilable differences, thus causing an irreversible breakdown between client and counsel. Requested to speak before the bench, I found it unnecessary, as we both were in unmitigated agreement.

We both knew this day had become unpreventable, our relationship souring years ago. His removal was both necessary and a relief if I were to ever have a chance of getting Pepper back. Nevertheless, with the impending trial only weeks away, the timing could not have been more perfect.

Somewhat apologetic under such peculiar circumstances, the judge then granted so many days allowing me to retain new representation. Losing my counsel, a week before the story would unfold, had been carefully orchestrated, making certain he would in no way benefit from any ensuing media exposure. Suspecting then, he may have taken my case seriously, it was too late. Regardless, it had now become water under the bridge.

Going All In

Back at Starbucks, Alexa and I formed our strategy. Welcoming her intuition and voice, I invited her on press junkets where she'd further address unfair animal practices, not only for the pet owner, but also bringing to light what was in the best interest of the animal. While not my attorney, she agreed to appear with me in court at the next hearing as an official arbitrator.

Alone with no legal counsel other than Alexa, I was summoned before the bench for what was supposed to be a simple status hearing. Confident I was now qualified in creating a better world for all animals, arrogantly, I approached the bench. "Mr. Barthel, you are here in representation of yourself?" I then instructed the judge that while I had not yet retained my new counsel, would like to submit before the courts, an impartial arbitrator who was willing to hear our case and help decide the fate of the animal in question. *Very well stated*, I thought.

In front of a courtroom overflowing with people, some reporters, I was then immediately schooled on courtroom etiquette. "Mr. Barthel, if you have yet to hire an attorney on record, you cannot present to the court, especially during what is only a case status hearing, with just any person before the bench other than your representation. In addition, because she is not registered on record, your *friend* must take a seat! I strongly suggest that you take the next thirty days to engage representation and begin to prepare yourself for trial."

And Just like that, we were finished, and my budding career as a lawyer now in jeopardy. Harshly, I was reminded that the courts have no tolerance for leniency due to ignorance of the law or simply because you're held at a disadvantage. Deflated, I then realized I was in over my head. Making matters worse, a TV crew was waiting outside who had sent a reporter inside the courtroom, fully aware of what had taken place.

Undecided about my course of action, I spent the next week interviewing a handful of lawyers, doing press interviews, meeting with Alexa, and began taking the time to learn basic courtroom practices. I was determined that my next attorney understood the imperative nature of my case, have an animal case history or may have even been a contributing author for existing State animal legislation. Meanwhile, I filed my Pro Se appearance, allowing me to stay current on any case developments.

Not long after filing my appearance, I received notice that the case had been transferred to a different judge and the proceedings would now be taking place in an entirely different courtroom. Happening to be in the law library that same day, I decided to ride the elevator down to the divorce floor and observe a case that the new judge was presiding over.

Packed with casualties, upon entering the courtroom was silently deafening and only standing room left available. Each soul was prudently cautious as they approached the bench, litigants and lawyers alike. His voice boomed over each victim, repeatedly berating and reminding each person brave enough to stand before him that this was his courtroom, demanding respect. Fifty feet away, standing at the back of the room, eyes unblinking and filled with trepidation, I stared at the same predestination I knew was waiting for me.

Without an appointment, I hurriedly went across the street for a second meeting with a lawyer I was considering on hiring. Unrecognizable without her robe, by chance, I ran into my previous judge who was leaving the same building. Seizing the opportunity, I questioned her about why she had been pulled from my case, allowing it to move into a separate courtroom. Neither confirming nor denying, she speculated was because of all the media attention that the case had been getting. The new judge known for not allowing any nonsense and caring less about any *cause,* refusing that his courtroom be made into a mockery.

Despite the new judge and his jarring undertones, I never did hire an attorney that day. Rather, I decided it was simply too late in the proceedings and any attorney I did hire would only serve as a strawman. For hours I weighed the pros and cons of that decision. The previous female judge, who perhaps held some bias, was the same judge who had issued the Order of Protection against me. I questioned; would it perhaps work in my favor me with the new *male* judge? A male judge, who more than likely was a dog owner?

"Never trust a man who doesn't like dogs" ~ Unknown ~

Never conventional, I decided to double down and take my chances. I would stay on record as Pro Se and represent myself for the duration of the trial. Suddenly, with access to all the court documents, I was appalled at what had been lacking in my previous counsels' efforts. Never was there any effort seeking dissipation, and disclosures were found to be either incomplete, grossly understated or never even challenged. In addition, the questions I had proposed for the deposition were simply ignored. Shame on me for not acting sooner. I then immediately filed a motion seeking further disclosure upon noticing several unaccounted-for missing documents. Next, I then filed a motion for dissipation, followed by a separate motion for a continuance, requesting additional time so I could properly prepare for trial.

Nowhere in the mounds of court documents was I able to find any settlement offer that had been drafted on my behalf. Using the template provided by the opposing counsel in their offer, I then outlined my own counter-settlement in response to theirs, knowing full well that it would be rejected. However, my demonstrated willingness to settle, further preventing wasting the court's valuable time, was now on record. This would be viewed by the judge, disputing the unfounded claims of intentionally dragging the case out. Preparing for my first court date under the new judge, I then sat through numerous trials in his courtroom, knowing full well of his unforgiving disposition, especially since my first request was for a continuance. I could only imagine how he would respond.

Summoned to the bench by the bailiff, his Honor immediately let it be known he was fully aware of the case due to the media exposure, and by no means was he going to allow his courtroom be, "turned into a circus." Addressing the judge, I introduced that I needed more time since filing Pro Se, allowing me to prepare for my case. His thunderous voice burgeoned, "Mr. Barthel, what have you been doing with all your time since your last appearance?" I attempted to reply, *"Your Honor, due to--,"* Interrupting, he would have nothing of it. "Request denied, you have 30 days to prepare for trial. I would suggest you seek legal representation. Fast!"

Left relatively unscathed, I anticipated that the judge would come down harder, needing to set precedence in what was becoming a distraction in his courtroom. I never intended on seeking new counsel, however, at the time, I was unable to muster the courage to inform the judge that I was going to continue alone. Thus, granted an additional 30 days, and all the time I would need to assemble my case. A small victory, nonetheless.

Unwavering, I continued my efforts by pouring over all the documents and stacks of paperwork acquired from my previous counsel. I became a fixture in the clerk's office, submitting requests for documents or when in the law library. Through filed motions, I now had discovery including bank records, receipts, and previous settlement offers I had no previous knowledge. From there, I began to build my case, my focus that I substantiate the verity that Pepper live his remaining days with his rightful owner.

A regular in the courtroom, I watched several divorce cases, studied courtroom etiquette, and learned much of the vocabulary that would be used when presenting my case. More importantly, a subtle connotation, to ensure the judge was aware of my presence. My efforts would cost nothing other than clerk copy fees to produce documents, and the gas used to drive there each time. Each motion I filed, and the subsequent court date would require the opposing attorney's appearance.

Estimated at $250 per hour combined with the costly billed drive time from Chicago, I knew was making for an expensive defense. Considering that it could have been settled years ago, with the simplest of requests that my dog be returned to me. Going all in, it was no longer negotiable.

Anxious, I sat in Starbucks, working my regular job while the impending trial date was now only two weeks away. With the court date looming came another TV interview. Compelling with her message, I wanted to provide Aleksa more camera time that would allow her to shed some light on a more important subject. Much larger than Pepper and I, stood the world of animal welfare awareness. Together, we became cautious with our message, determined not to be distracted. While we weren't chaining ourselves to trees, expounding on rainforests or lying on roadways blocking traffic, our goal was to remain consequential and true to the travails of animal exploitation.

The interview taped late that afternoon and was to be shown on the 10:00 p.m. evening news. Weary from the all-consuming impending hoopla, I refused to sit at home and avoided the temptation to turn on the TV. Feeling as if I'd been selling a bit of me each time, I had become estranged by the circus that was now my life.

Aimlessly driving around, I pulled into a parking lot at some dive bar. Sitting alone amongst complete strangers, stood a bank of five

50" TVs along the back of the bar. Caving to temptation and pissing off some drunk, I asked for one of the channels be changed to the station that would be showing the interview. Ten minutes passed until the first teaser appeared about "a man losing his dog in divorce." Commercials, weather, second teaser, more commercials... Finally, the story played out; four minutes of a 30-minute newscast. The background music was turned down at the bar when complete strangers began coming over, introducing themselves and wishing me luck, telling me stories about their own pets, and how they too would do the same.

The TV crew also shot some video of Pepper walking around, wagging his tail, smiling the way he smiled, while completely oblivious to all the attention. Now going on three years, I watched my buddy on the screen who seemed so far away, almost unrecognizable. Both of us now older; no hikes, no cramped beds, and the seasons slipping away. Such short lives we all share with our dear friends.

Discussing my case with at least two dozen lawyers, I was tempted to change my mind on several occasions and pick one at the last minute. My confidence high, I felt I had sufficiently amassed enough of a defense to perhaps strike a chord with the judge on my own. It may have been those same lawyers interviewed that provided me with confidence, most in agreement that I had a good chance of winning. In truth, it was simply too late to pick a lawyer; my decision made months ago.

Win or lose, I would be forever grateful for the free advice many of those lawyers offered me, and many, I can now say have become close friends. Many dog owners themselves, they'd become impassioned by this common thread we shared, graciously devoting hours offering free legal advice.

After having witnessed several trials, how to plead your case, call witnesses, and present evidence; in the days before the trail, I made a bullet list of those facts pertinent, details, and who I'd call to the stand. Each piece of evidence was numbered, corresponding to my bullet list with various notes inscribed on each document. Dozens of photos of personal items, copies of canceled checks, including home financial records and documents taken from the restaurant had been collected and ready to produce. My opening dialogue, in addition to closing statement, had been carefully drafted, detailing an intentionally prolonged case littered with unnecessary motions and a concerted effort, keeping me from both my personal belongings and Pepper.

Knowing I would be called to the stand, I practiced my speech, how to answer questions, and what demeanor best to use. While depositions can be revealing, they can also disclose essential tools based on the questions asked. I already knew the questions they would ask based off my answers during the deposition. From this, I was able to prepare my responses.

Predictably, I would be labeled a workaholic who chose for years to operate a struggling restaurant, refusing to concede, forsaking his family, home and dog. Along the lines: "How can the man dare to submit to the court that he cared for his dog when he was working all the time?" The "reckless funding spent operating the restaurant" and "failure to recognize the needs of his family" would provide a common theme in the courtroom.

My argument had always been simple. Never did I give up or throw in the towel during those times when things became challenging. This *was* for the family. However, my unwavering work ethic and determination, that *we* succeed — found little understanding. Strange, is it not, we discover our true friends only while struggling, however, most are eager to be your acquaintance once thriving. Ironically, a dog would never do that.

With no sleep, I climbed out of bed at 3:00 a.m. Downing a coffee, I went over some final documents, scribbling last minute notes and practicing what I would say in my head. Finding it difficult to work from home, I suited up several hours before trial and headed off to Starbucks. Sitting in my car, I watched the lights come on in the store, the staff warmly greeting me when I entered. Checking emails, I couldn't help but notice one from California. Customarily, I'd get several emails a day, either from inquiries, causes, or people experiencing similar situations. However, I noticed this one had come from the Dr. Phil Show. Having already told my story, time had finally run out with nothing left to discuss other than what would take place after the trial.

Leaving the parking garage, I could see the courthouse in the distance and couldn't help but look upwards. Rising above the concrete were satellite dishes extended into the air, attached to several news trucks. Channels 2, 5, 7, 9, and a couple of cable trucks, all parked outside. Stopping in my tracks, my heart sank into my stomach; since the trial date was of public record, everyone knew when it would take place.

Intentionally, I had never discussed the actual trial date, hoping no coverage would show and they simply forget about us. Fortunately for me, today was also the arraignment for a noted murderer, his trial taking place in a separate courtroom. While the murder trial served as a welcome distraction, finally, almost three years later, Pepper's fate was to be decided.

CHAPTER THIRTEEN

Coming Home

After feeding tens of thousands of hungry souls, many times in some of the most godforsaken, wretched kitchens, and times with some of the most truly eccentric, interesting of characters, (another book) I am now on the outside of those kitchen cinderblock walls 30 some odd years later for the first time ever. Celebrations, everything from birthdays, funerals, Christmas gatherings, New Year's parties, weddings, and oddly enough, even divorce parties. Shamefully joining the ranks of countless chefs going through a divorce, I am now part of the two-time divorce club. Renowned chef, Grant Achatz of Alinea in Chicago, said it best, as a matter of fact: "A chef is married to his restaurant." The person they married at the altar, however, is at home.

Restaurants to this day remain notorious for fatalistic repercussions on relationships. More precisely, for those who live and die, bringing the restaurant to life each day, the restaurant can be a marriage killer. Compounded exponentially if your partner has never worked in the hospitality sector. Despite their reassurance in the beginning, few will never grasp the dedication and time required that each day demands. Eventually wearing on their staying power, the days, nights, and weekends homogenize into months and years. Missed birthdays, holidays, vacations postponed; there is always another urgent dinner party or compulsion that requires attention inside those walls. Always in a rigid state of consciousness, never allowing those to rest on their laurels while striving for excellence.

Charlie Trotter, went on to say, "The best you can do is reach for excellence, while never yet really achieving it." Even while dining out, most chefs cannot help but critique the dining room's ambiance, flatware, menu choices, quality of service, and most importantly the food. Countless times I found myself taking the long way to the restroom when dining out, hoping to get a glimpse into the kitchen through an open door or maybe over the pass. Chefs acknowledging one another like a secret brotherhood, all knowing the brutality of the business with a simple gesture — almost code-like. Hating it, we love it at the same time like a drug. The restaurant and all that it entailed had conveniently become my excuse for my failed marriage.

Riding the elevator up to the divorce floor for one of the very last times, I found relief no reporters or journalists waiting. Knowing where the courtroom was by heart, surprising even myself, I made my way without hesitation or fear. Perhaps because I had prepared for this day for years, a sense of calm had washed over me. Opening the double doors, once again, I was pleasantly surprised by the absence of the press inside the courtroom; evidently, Pepper had just as quickly become old news. There was a murderer on the other floor who had stolen his thunder.

Once inside, I noticed the court reporter, clerk, and bailiff, were already busy preparing for their day. After checking in, I then learned our trial was the only one scheduled that day to allow for what was an anticipated lengthy hearing. Alone at the litigant's desk in front of the jury box, on the boardroom sized table, I opened my boxes and began pulling out relevant exhibits spreading them out in the way I planned to present my case.

As part of my preparation, I had made multiple copies for each exhibit to avoid any objections by the opposing counsel. Appendix A included all the evidence that I had accumulated. Appendix B had all my exhibits, and finally Appendix C held my cross-examination inquiries, opening statements, and final closing testimonial. Each document laid out had a corresponding number in the right-hand corner matching the appropriate appendix once needed for reference. Looking somewhat unorthodox, eventually the entire desk was completely covered with nuances of the last three years. Finally, I placed one of my favorite photos of Pepper next to my pad and paper as a reminder to myself of my lofty goal.

My mind wandered as I worked alone arranging the documents. Had I done enough to prepare? Was it wise being so cavalier in doing this on my own, or was I merely a lamb being let out for slaughter? Remorseful for having to plan against someone who was once a part of my life, I had to remind myself that I had made several civil attempts to end this amicably, all to no avail. Countless times I had proposed shared custody of Pepper, which would've saved tens of thousands of dollars, allowing us to have finished years ago. In addition, with the fabricated Order of Protection fresh in my mind, make no mistake, this was no time to be soft. I could not afford to lay down now, nor question my motives, otherwise be devoured. Better to fight and have a chance than lay down and assuredly be beaten.

Sitting at the adjacent table, the other parties had finally arrived while two of the witnesses I'd suspected would show were also present. So far so good. The courtroom which had grown silent other than ruffling of papers was then suddenly interrupted. "All rise." With those words, we all stood while the judge was then introduced, and parties sworn in. "You know, for months I have presided over this case, with no clear indication of any type of settlement. Are both parties prepared for trial, and certain you have exhausted all efforts at reconciliation?"

It was at that moment, what I had seen him do before at the onset of every trial, I was provided with the window of opportunity I had been expecting. To avoid wasting any additional resources with the backlog of pending cases, it was customary that one final plea be made to avoid costly and lengthy trials, thus, further tying up the court.

His Honor pressed on; "Have all efforts been exhausted?" Before the opposing counsel could speak, I then seized the opportunity by expressing to the court that it was my desire and willingness to have settled months ago. By doing so, felt I then demonstrated my sincerity in avoiding wasting His Honor's and the court's valuable time before the trial began. Looking in my direction, the opposing counsel appeared stunned, having no other choice than to oblige, lest appear contentious. *Is this for real?* I thought. *Are these the same people?* The same people who, for almost three years, intentionally dragged this on indefinitely. Uncertain if His Honor was now smiling or perhaps had indigestion, he next rose from the bench, announcing a recess, giving us one hour to arrive upon an agreed settlement.

No secret, at an estimated $250 an hour for each lawyer, the travel time from Chicago, possibly another eight hours in the courtroom, and another two hours to draft up the divorce decree, it would easily cost thousands of additional dollars for the opposing representation. This, for one day alone. *You're damn right they were willing to discuss settlement!* My investment for the day set me back $10 in gas to drive to the courthouse and $2.50 for parking. *They had taken the bait.*

If they had declined an attempt to settle the impasse, they would have appeared rigid and unwilling, while disrespectful to the courts offer. My only concern was their genuineness in effort or were they more eager standing trial and billing their client another $5000 for the day?

Adjourned, we then left the courtroom seeking an open office allowing us to negotiate face to face. Once outside the courtroom in the hallway, there were people crying, pacing, some yelling, while each corridor was littered with fools once having subscribed to utopian dreams, now shattered. It was so busy that lawyers and clients alike were left to negotiate with their clients while standing or sitting on the scattered benches. Benches so worn that the finish stain had worn off from years of unsuspecting gullible fools who waited in line for their judgment day with their open checkbooks at the ready.

Finding an open space on a bench, we sat for the very first time. Three attorneys versus one man that had never practiced law a day in his life who simply wanted his dog back. You would have thought the fortunes of Jeff Bezos were at stake. Not once, prior to that day had we ever sat down in an attempt at reconciliation or any type of settlement. One must wonder, who really got milked and taken advantage of?

Breaking the ice, I reminded them of my willingness that we could have settled months ago. *"You do realize that, don't you?"* Curious, I then questioned whether they had even conveyed my settlement offers to the plaintiff or simply passed them over only to collect more billing hours? And now, on the midnight hour, why were they suddenly willing to discuss a settlement after having bled the turnip?

Comparing notes, we began listing each asset and any remaining liabilities. One by one, each item was picked over like crows over roadkill, items either sacrificed or someone refusing to part with. With the draft complete, perhaps they assumed I was prepared to surrender Pepper, strangely there was no mention of him verbally or in writing. With no discussion of the elephant in the room, I then bluntly and affirmatively stated, *"Pepper comes with me."* The draft was then taken back to the plaintiff and discussed with the conglomerate of lawyers for the next twenty minutes consulting in private. Similar when you purchase a car and the salesman excuses himself because he must *speak to his manager*, this continued for two hours with each revised settlement. Back and forth it went.

With tensions flaring, and at a standstill, it appeared as if we would be giving up any additional efforts and heading back to the courtroom to begin trial. Already well past the allotted time we had been granted by the judge, the clerk found us in the hallway offering us one last half-hour before we would be forced to return with our opening remarks.

My plan seemed to be falling apart. As much as I fooled myself into thinking I was prepared for trial, subconsciously knew I was out of my element. Like asking the opposing counsel to prepare a 12-course degustation for 40 people, in comparison, I was no lawyer. Each offer had been refused that Pepper be returned, and each time I rejected. I came here for nothing less.

Mere minutes before we would be called back inside the courtroom, the group of attorneys disappeared for almost the entire half-hour. Expecting the same outcome upon their return, we once again went over each item line by line, adjusting percentages, terms, how much, and who got what. As usual, further examining the columns and listing of assets, Pepper had been left out and his name was nowhere to be found. Concluding our time was up, I rose from the bench prepared to head back inside the courtroom. Expecting the same answer, I half-heartedly jested, "And what about Pepper?"

Refusing to cave, my mind trailed off. I thought back to those years Pepper would cramp my legs when he hogged the bed, our travels on the road leaving one hotel for the next, his selfish insistence that he always lead when hiking, and his dirty paws tracking up the house after each excursion. His gentleness when he offered his paw or when he nudged my face when I was troubled. The hours he spent watching me, his nose hanging over the couch armrest when I worked on menus, now almost three years later.

After hours of negotiations, our papers were now a hodgepodge of notes, scribbles, and figures, while I was barely able to read our latest exchange. Expressionless, her face limestone, she reiterated the final proposition, leaving me to assume once again that Pepper had been left out of the equation. Again, I pressed. "And what about Pepper?"

Initially failing to fully grasp what was said and unable register her words, time would stand still. Catching my breath, in disbelief, she uttered the words I would never forget. "…It would include Pepper." A fervor erupting inside of me, I put forth my best effort to mask my emotions, holding close any outburst or retort. After a brief pause and a moment to collect myself, I of course agreed to the settlement without hesitation and before any retractions. By no means was I obligated nor willing to exchange any gratitude or share my exultation openly. Never given to me, they had kept my dog from me for three years, costing thousands of dollars, and placing my life indefinitely on hold. Pepper coming home was no favor, but rather what was moral and ethical, belonging nowhere else.

At that moment the clerk appeared demanding our answer, seeming pleased upon the news that she could finally adjourn and have her lunch. She then requested we submit the final settlement draft to be presented before the judge. Excusing myself to go the restroom, once inside I closed the door to the stall behind me. In disbelief, a feverish, exuberant rush of emotions flowed through my body. I wanted to cry but was unable to muster any tears, I wanted to yell but had to remind myself where I was. As simple as that, as the case was drawing near to an end, reminded me that I was never more certain of anything in my life more than wanting Pepper to come home.

To this day, the courts remain backlogged with similar cases as lawyers get richer, eagerly legitimizing estranged spouses fight over Fido. Families are left torn apart, and pets, like children, suffer from being used as pawns. During the process, everyone's life is indefinitely placed on hold as they squabble over possessions nonsensically spending thousands of dollars. Pepper, however, was no object, and while I was grateful for the outcome, I could not help but feel disgusted with the system and all the players in the cogs of the wheel. Walking out of the stall, over to the sink, I stared into the mirror in disbelief. My baby is coming home!

Boiled down after three long years, the final decree was rewritten for presenting to the judge, taking all of ten minutes to prepare. I could not help but notice, while it had been agreed verbally that Pepper would be returned to me, any mention was suspiciously absent on the document. Uncertain if intentional or an oversight, my faith and trust having left long ago, I was not taking any chances. I then demanded before heading back into the courtroom that the settlement include his custody arrangement, and more precisely, that his name be added in the final determination.

His name on the document in some small way bearing significance for all the other tens of thousands of pets exploited in the court system. With Pepper being older, and with the little time left we might have together, I understood the odds I was taking by agreeing to sign the final papers. Regardless, I would provide the best remaining years of his life, despite how much time we had left together.

Pepper's name now inscribed on the agreement, once again we were summoned back inside the courtroom where the judge was presiding. "The court understands you have reached an agreement. I would first like to thank both parties after this long and arduous trial for your reaching a settlement, respecting the court's time." Sworn in, our final enforceable order, line by line, each item, was then torturously read aloud.

The last item addressed, of course, would be Pepper, an awkward pause following his name once read for everyone to hear. I recall the oddity, an animal's name being spoken in a courtroom of law, and the significance it held. Unable to be present, of course, I so desperately wanted Pepper to hear his name that day, unaware of what he represented and the struggles that were waged over his well-being.

Allowed to imagine, if only for a brief moment that day, when animals are no longer mere objects or personal possessions, and humans as their guardians are held to a greater moral obligation, accountable for their welfare and sanctity. No longer owned as property, however, recognized for the living, breathing beings they are, with as much right to life. If we could only hope for and imagine such a time. We never did change any laws on that day, however, a grassroots firestorm began soon after, further questioning the legitimacy of pets viewed as objects in the State of Illinois.

With the settlement granted and the final determination read, we were then asked if we had anything to say. For the first time in years, after my eyes had gone dry long ago waiting for this day, I could not help but feel a sense of regret and shame, finding the moment bittersweet. Acknowledging the judge, I mustered an offering. *"Your Honor, I'd have no problem if she still wanted to see Pepper."* With tears in the clerk's eyes, and the judge at a loss for words, despite Pepper coming home with me, I was offering what I had suggested long ago, that we both share custody. Suggesting that we work it out on our own if that were ever to happen, the judge then adjourned the court. There were no winners that day.

Back out in the hallway waiting for the decree to be completed, the trio of lawyers and I worked out an agreed rendezvous to retrieve both my personal belongings and Pepper. Two weeks an eternity, I questioned my logic for allowing 14 whole days before I could be reunited with Pepper. Concerned for his well-being and safety, I was pissed at myself for failing to demand his immediate return. Choosing not to press my good fortune, I resigned to praying that he would not be conveniently lost or mistreated before the scheduled pickup date.

Driving back to the house, I decided to stop by the Starbucks where all my planning and preparation had taken place earlier. Reflecting, maybe now I could look out the window and enjoy the view over my coffee without imperative dates or being forced to put on earbuds. *Were it even be possible?* Managing to get out of one fire after selling the restaurant, only to be thrown back into the flames with an additional three years of hell, it made those years at the restaurant seem like a picnic.

Still in my divorce suit and coffee in hand, for the first time, I ventured to the outside patio at Starbucks, inhaling the fresh air and enjoying my coffee al fresco. Melancholic and completely unorthodox, I dialed the plaintiffs' attorney whom I had just spent the entire day with. The hostility and contention now behind us, I decided offering an olive branch by apologizing for that day months ago after tossing the sandwich on the boardroom table and the insensitive comment.

Regardless of our disparity, my actions on that day had always bothered me. With the contentious case behind us, we spoke freely and without caution. Accepting my apology, she offered in closing that I had done well presenting a good defense. To her and the firm she represented, humbly suspected, I was just another brief annoyance, win or lose, making no difference to them, so as long those billable hours were assigned. A matter of business; just the same, I too did what was required to achieve the desired end result.

Back at home there was no celebration, no calls to reporters, no champagne, nor any banners celebrating my victory as one might imagine. I was still without my buddy, and only when he came home would I feel complete. With more work to do, I had one remaining motion that would have to be filed: To clear my name and the fabricated Order of Protection against me. The OP would have little bearing on my daily life and eventually expiring on its own, however, made no difference. My name had been falsely slandered, solely with the intention of having Pepper taken away, and later used as leverage. By now routine, I knew how to draw up the motion for dismissal, select a date, notify the defendant, and then submit to the clerk's office.

Approaching the courthouse, my stomach once again knotted up with its familiar sense of gloom and uncertainty. Motioned before the bench for the last time, I would first be allowed to plead my case, offering evidence why the OP should be removed, followed by the defendant justifying why the OP remain in effect.

After my brief statement and pleas failing to understand why the OP even existed, I then rested my case. Startled, I then stood and watched uncomfortably as His Honor unloaded a series of incendiary questions directed at the defendant. "Are there any substantiating police records? Any witnesses? Any recorded theft or list of items missing from the house? Does Mr. Barthel have any recorded instance of domestic abuse or priors?" Not even in the divorce summons were there any claims of abuse, he reminded the court.

From there, it only proceeded to get worse. Yelling, he went on, "I watched Mr. Barthel and his attempt at being an attorney as he struggled to defend himself, but he made every effort. If this order of protection had *ever* been filed in *my* courtroom, it would have been thrown out and ceased to exist in the first place." Without any further explanation, the Order of Protection was then stricken from the records and my name vindicated.

Cautiously, I thanked the judge, and for the very first time, turned and walked out of the courtroom with confidence, never looking back again. Crossing the line, the vacated Order of Protection should have served as a reminder that it never had to sink that low. The lambasting by the judge, while unfortunate and harsh for the defendant, certainly could have been avoided. Little did I know at the time, I never should have taken the OP so lightly. While it remains on record, it can enforce counseling, revoke my privilege from owning a firearm, and raise a red flag with law enforcement, questioning my stability.

The courthouse by now was a sea of familiar faces; attorneys, judges, police officers, and courtroom employees. One face alone stood out as I waited in line to file the vacated order down in the clerk's office. How ironic that on my last day I'd run into my former lawyer, months after our parting. Like old friends who hadn't seen each other in a long time, impervious how contentious we had become, he inquired, "Hey, how's the case going?" Without hesitation, I bluntly responded, *"I got my dog back."*

Passing me one last time on his way out, he would go on, "Ya know—" Interrupting, I finally summoned the confidence in my bearing, taking control of our dialogue and how I would allow myself to be treated. *"I suggest you get the fuck away from me!"* Overheard by several people around us, I couldn't care less. I had just accomplished *alone* what he failed at as my former attorney.

After the time, money, unscripted hostilities, and representing myself, not only had I gotten my best friend back, I had also successfully defended my integrity against false accusations. Our dissolvement as attorney and client was the best thing that could have happened in my fight that I be reunited with Pepper. Convinced, that had I kept him through the trial, not only would I be out tens of thousands of dollars, but would never have seen Pepper again. *Of this I'm certain.*

The sun was shining as I pushed open the exit door, leaving the decrepit and depressing courthouse for the last time. I am now forever cautiously obeying the speed limit when in that same county, unknowing if I could stomach a return to that hellish of a building. Finally, there was one last step before being reunited with Pepper.

Like a child filled with anticipation before Christmas, the remaining days before the big date dragged on incessantly. Intentionally, all my emails confirming our rendezvous time went unanswered. No replies or any indication of the date or time and only days before the two weeks would expire. Not only was Pepper to be returned, but it would also be necessary to rent a U-Haul large enough to retrieve all my remaining personal items.

On what would be the final day of the two weeks, I received a threatening email stating that if everything was not picked up, it would all be thrown out as garbage, with no mention of Pepper. *Seriously!?* By now I had grown accustomed to such antics. Already dressed, and full of caffeine, I had rented a U-haul prepared for such a stunt, and within minutes, I was barreling down the expressway. Apparently, we were still playing chess, however unbeknownst, the game had already ended.

Preferring to head off any additional scheming or theatrics, I then placed a call requesting the presence of a police officer during our final barter. In addition, I made a point to bring the final decree outlining the return of both my personal items and of Pepper, taking no chances of provocation. Assuming, that *conveniently* no one would be at the house, I purposely made no indication when nearing, with police in tow. As the officer knocked on the front door of the house, the garage door slowly began opening, and I notice all my belongings not seen in years, heaved into a massive pile. Items carelessly tossed on top of each other, countless possessions either missing, broken, or intentionally destroyed. Strangely, I made no mention, nor would I protest; there was only one thing on my mind at that time.

As the police officer idly stood by while each item was loaded, I could not help but smile when a familiar sound from a long-lost friend echoed from inside the house. Awakened from the noise inside the garage and barking profusely, we could hear the ever-curious Mr. Pepper wanting to come out and investigate all the commotion. With only a few feet separating us, under my breath and in my spirit, I silently reminded Pepper that we remain patient; our time was at hand.

Feeling sentimental looking at many of those items I placed inside the truck, my pace quickened as Pepper's barking became more urgent. Years later, each piece I loaded seemed so unimportant and no longer offered any personal attachment. I then began refusing items, no longer having a need or desire for each material object, leaving many items for trash. No longer chefing, purposely, I'd leave behind the dated restaurant equipment to be sold for pennies on the dollar, and volumes of cookbooks I no longer had a need for. Demanding the return of these items for years, I now felt foolish, realizing their worthless and insignificant value.

As Pepper continued to cry, I carelessly began throwing items into the truck on top of one another. Finally, with the truck loaded, the moment had arrived where only one item was remaining. Pausing to catch my breath, bending over, hands on my knees, I spoke for the first time, *"And now Pepper."* The officer who was somewhat puzzled, assuming he was there to supervise the final exchange of property between two divorcing parties, was completely unaware of Pepper and his significance. Producing the documents from the cab of the truck, I then handed over the decree to the officer outlining Pepper's return.

In one last radical attempt, spitefully, it was then suggested that Pepper was not part of the agreement, and that mention of Pepper was nowhere to be found in the final decree. In producing the final copy; to my dismay, the lawyer had left Pepper off, and we each held different copies. Calm up until that moment, I finally revealed my true sentiments; *"every fucking item that I just loaded into the truck can be placed on the curb. In all honesty, I only came here for one item."*

Sensing potential conflict, the officer then abruptly radioed for backup, and I immediately dialed the attorney; *"What kind of bullshit are you pulling now!"* I reminded her that regardless of what final settlement decree was provided, would not match the recorded transcript in court before the judge, and if necessary, I will have it pulled and you will be found in contempt. She then suggested that I calm down and asked if she could call me back.

With three squad cars now in front of the house, the officers had now become aware of Pepper's story as we all silently waited inside the garage. Back inside the house on the phone, the lawyer spoke with the plaintiff. A light rain now coming down, one officer spoke offering support, "no one could separate me from my labs. I would have done the same thing." Finding his comments reassuring, I knew for certain I had sufficient grounds for legal recourse should Pepper be denied.

Fifteen minutes passed. Silent in the garage other than the occasional police radio crackle and light rain falling. Without notice, we all turned to look at the garage door leading into the house as it slowly opened. With a crack in the door, everyone stared at the nose protruding from the bottom. A long, black, hairy nose sniffing profusely struggling to be let out. Pepper. Wincing and forcing his body through the gap in the door, I called out his name. Holding back my tears from escaping in front of everyone, never was it my intention to grandstand us reuniting or coming out victorious. Nor was it about defeating or having the upper hand over anyone, rather, what was just and impartial. Pepper clearly belonging with me.

Forcing the door open and running over to me, Pepper continued making circles in place as I tried to pet him, his tail wagging uncontrollably, contorting his body. Curious, he went from one police officer to the next, smelling and barking at each one, and then returning to his daddy. *I remember wondering, does he remember me? Did he ever long for me as I for him? What feelings did we share at that moment after being separated for so long?*

The poor last-minute attempt at keeping us apart, coupled with the fabricated Order of Protection, made leaving without guilt that much easier. As it turns out, while I had the final decree, my copy had never been certified. This warranted no significance; since the courts held both the official decree and transcripts, and could have easily been produced.

The rain now a steady drizzle, I lifted Pepper into the cab and started the truck. Before leaving, I thanked each officer before we then drove off, never looking back. In every essence of the word, it was finally over. Preferring to be alone, never was the press notified of the court's decision or when Pepper and I were to be reunited.

Prepared to settle into the quiet that would be our life together, there were no banners, champagne, or reporters.

 Leaving the subdivision, passing the archetypal row of homes, manicured lawns, and white picket fences of suburbia, we drove onto the expressway. While the rain continued lightly and my wipers steady, I focused on the road and Pepper beside me. Almost human-like sitting in the cab seat, he looked out the window, then back at me as I talked to him almost the entire way home. Alone with my dog, tears filled my eyes for the first time as the enormity slowly began setting in. Overjoyed we were no together, I was equally disgusted with how ugly it had gotten. Three years in the making, I felt appalled with both the system and who I allowed myself to become. There were no winners. Certainly, it was a day to be celebrated, however, bittersweet, was also a day for humility and a new beginning to perhaps find my decent self again.

 Once home, Pepper was welcomed into his new house unceremoniously; the whole experience leaving me exhausted. Holding his own little celebration, Pepper ran through the house, jumping on and off couches and smelling his new, unfamiliar territory. The rain subsiding, we made it a priority to hit the trails in our newfound time becoming reacquainted. As if it were yesterday, Pepper was his familiar self by insisting on leading and every so often glancing back like a child making sure I was watching and following. Hiking for two hours, it didn't take long for us to pick up where we had left off. At night, like two old men after a long evening, we climbed the staircase, preparing for bed. Once settled under the covers, like old times, Pepper would hog the base of the bed, choosing to lay horizontally, cramping my legs as we both struggled to find our place for the night.

After three years. In the U-Haul on our way home

Without the strains of the restaurant, the urgency to prepare for trial or the continuous impending court dates; I hadn't experienced a calm of this proportion in over thirty years, and with this refreshing normalcy we began our new life. I was reminded of those instances and things once taken for granted, now embracing each moment with welcoming pause. Similarly, being released from solitary confinement or miraculously healed from a terminal disease. Grateful, life once again became precious, finding most challenges an opportunity rather than a hindrance. Each obstacle, either mundane or a minor irritant while easy to overcome.

Once again, we became inseparable and if work allowed, I would take him with me on the road the same as before. Colorado, Wyoming, Montana, or South Dakota; taking photos along the way. While Pepper had become quite the experienced traveler, eventually I would be forced to curtail his travel due to the stress it placed on him going from one place to the next. Once closed and jaded, our reuniting and my new-found insight began to soften and unravel the discord I had been commandeering for years.

Out of *the business* and my kitchen knives carefully tucked away — although ready at a moment's notice — I was saddened and reminded once again the foreboding nature of the food industry. Taking no prisoners, bankruptcies and closures would take their hold on many once infamous eateries. Moto in Chicago, Grace, Trio and Tru, and of course, after twenty-five years, Charlie Trotters would close its doors for good. Attending Trotter's funeral was like the Oscars of chefs. Emeril Lagasse, Rick Tramonto, Gail Gand, Daniel Boulud; the list went on. Mayor Rahm Emanuel would address those in attendance. Only a couple years later the culinary world would be rocked once again after the suicides of famous chef's Anthony Bourdain and Homaru Cantu.

Coming Home

Anthony Bourdain

To this day, I still respond to random emails from strangers seeking advice or volunteer for causes requesting support. My experience through my own travails and the plight of those animals, awakened in me an itching desire to make a difference or somehow help curtail those areas of abuse, neglect, and intentional mistreatment.

On our farms, in our legislation, the way we hunt, careless breeding practices, inhumane transport, barbaric caging, forced feedings and exploitation those living and breathing beings for our own benefit and amusement. Shamefully, while we ignore or choose not to believe their own consciousness is unequivocal and parallel to ours, like us, they also possess the ability to reason, love, experience joy, and suffer, the same as we do. There should no longer be any irresolution.

Legislation created by humans to protect animals, for the most part, are composed merely to mask the rights of those animals while allowing for their legal exploitation suited for our own benefit. Those inequitable instances of misguided suffering are then conveniently concealed to achieve our own subterfuge, oftentimes as a commodity for consumption, clothing, examination, or blood trophy.

By estimation, the earth's population is nearly eight billion people, while over two billion animals are tortured and slaughtered every week. Fifteen million warm-blooded animals are still being used for scientific research, and five billion dollars spent annually on experimentaton and observation practices. Closer to home, thirty percent of domesticated animals are subject to regular domestic abuse, and 1.5 million dogs are euthanized each year.

While we certainly have come a long way from those early days of mistreated carriage horses on the streets of New York City, animal welfare remains in its infancy. Over ten million dogs in China alone are slaughtered every year for their meat. Many are boiled alive, their throats slit, or thrown directly into a fire while still breathing. Ten thousand bulls on average are killed every year in bullfights. Here in the states, while humans for the most part are fortunate enough to escape deadly natural disasters, on the other hand, we inhumanely leave behind tens of thousands of livestock trapped in pens or stables, unable to escape the rising waters, or ravaging fires. Too costly to transport to a safer haven, they are left for their own demise to drown, burn or die of starvation.

On a smaller scale, from my own experience after losing Pepper and recognizing the lack of resources available, I sought the guidance of those attorneys who had assisted me drafting a bill for introduction to the Illinois General Assembly, recognizing pets in divorce or domestic cases. From this, Pepper's Bill was created and petitions, seeking the support of constituents and lawmakers alike. The Bill seeking to acknowledge and discern living and breathing beings involved in domestic issues, and when contested, that mandatory arbitration be mandated.

Like child custody matters, the best interest of the animal be determined. It further outlined that the arbitrator be compensated by the litigants, forgoing any tax burdens or waste of valuable court time and need for bench trial discovery. This bill would not only assist with the judge's ruling, but more importantly recognize that animals and our pets are no longer inert objects of ownership, rather, a term now popularized as *living property*. Taking into consideration, while not in so many words, the difference between an object, and the living.

Around that same time, Illinois Senator, Linda Holmes, would be the first to sponsor a similar legislation, Senate Bill 1261, which successfully went on to revise the following sections of the Illinois Marriage and Dissolution of Marriage Act recognizing pets in divorce. Section 5/503 of the Illinois Marriage and Dissolution of Marriage Act was amended as follows. In summary:

> *If the court finds that a companion animal of the parties is a marital asset, it shall allocate the sole or joint ownership of and responsibility for a companion animal of the parties.*
> *In issuing an order under this subsection, the court shall take into consideration the well-being of the companion animal. Judges have the power to issue Orders of Protection which protect pets from abuse.*

On January 1, 2018, family law in Illinois included changes regarding the custody of pets, or as it is referred to: *The pet custody law.* Illinois would proudly be one of the first few States recognizing pets during litigation and eventually encourage other States to question enacting similar legislation. A small step, however, resounding, now provides for the best interest of the animal; one that I and Pepper are proud to have been part of. Had it already been law, may have prevented ours and countless others, the unnecessary alienation suffered during due process.

Exchanging emails with Senator Holmes, she went on to say: "I'm pleased my bill, Senate Bill 1261 passed in Illinois in 2017 (signed into law as Public Act 100-0422) and hope it may serve as a model for other state legislatures to consider for the best welfare of the pet and its family." Further: "I have a long record of animal legislation in my career in the Illinois State Senate, including the welfare of animals in circuses, medical and cosmetics testing, attempting to ban bobcat hunting, and the health and safety of pets in shelters, pet stores and homes."

During the writing of this book, another bill she sponsored went on to pass: Senate Bill 241, amends the Food, Drug and Cosmetic Act to prohibit importation or sale of cosmetic products or ingredients that use animal testing after the effective date of the act. It's efforts like these and conscientious lawmakers who take a stand, realizing the long overdue compulsory egalitarian representation for those animals.

Proudly, I now belong to a larger and ever-growing group. Those who dare to recognize and have the courage demanding necessary change. We are united by our belief in creation, be it by science or God, and from that our existence and universal right to life, all creatures big and small. Whatever your subscription, that if man does have *dominion* as suggested, brandishing a larger stick, this should hold no cause for the infliction, mistreatment, or neglect we subject those animals on our farms, in the wild who walk and crawl, or those that swim in our oceans, and certainly, those animals we share our homes with. This one earth we share is not ours to impose our assumed superior intelligence for the benefit of one species, but rather should be used to understand with compassion and empathy the gift of life we have all been bestowed.

As new animal laws and recognition continues to sweep our country, it painstakingly has been through slow and arduous efforts. Doing my part in many small ways, I am now one of those strange people you see that pulls over when driving out of respect to move those lifeless creatures off the street to the side after being struck, or encouraging deer back into the forest when they get too close to the highway. I will petition and appeal for proper and equitable treatment of our friends. That new laws be created and brought to the table, furthering those efforts for fair and equitable welfare practices. I will shun needless and disregardful exploitation, volunteer, and shelter those without a home, and beseech means of ethical and moral equality for those who cannot speak in our language.

Still in its infancy, *Voices For Pets* was created soon after losing Pepper in an effort to provide a voice and share stories of similar experiences. A grassroots effort that has steadily grown and has supported many of the newer laws we see today. Seeking its 5013c nonprofit status, we continue locally to push for similar laws in those states surrounding Illinois; Ohio, Indiana, Michigan, and Iowa. Puppy Mill legislation, spay and neutering laws, ban of cosmetics when tested on animals, humane treatment laws, and of course pet recognition during domestic matters.

The time consumed and experiences I endured after losing Pepper can be accredited in providing a much deeper sense and awareness of the brief, precious time we have been given. The days I now have with Pepper, however brief — to enjoy his exuberant, child-like demeanor, his hogging the bed, and refusing to leave the poor squirrels alone. That he never complains, remains ever loyal, never judgmental, and always inviting, has become infectious. Something we should all take to heart.

After spending decades on kitchen lines surrounded in isolated quarters, head buried, and ignorant of the larger picture, my impetus is much more focused today and my collection of chef knives stored away. When traveling in unfamiliar cities on foreign streets, many times those familiar scents from area restaurants still offer me pause. Each time, I find that same urge to burst inside the kitchen, helping my brothers and sisters get out of the weeds or to share a kitchen story. However, I now understand my place is back home, somewhere on a trail with my companion who waited for me. Perhaps never speaking and walking for miles, however totally understanding and appreciating our company without words. That this home and the space we share belongs to us all.

I saw deep in the eyes of the animals the human soul look out upon me. I saw where it was born deep down under feathers and fur, or condemned for a while to roam four-footed among the brambles, I caught the clinging mute glance of the prisoner and swore that I would be faithful.
~ Henry David Thoreau ~

Paul Barthel

Acknowledgments

Only Proper, I must thank Jessica A. Vaillancourt first for her patience, and above all her acute editing skills, support, and encouragement during the arduous editing process. Without her assistance would not have been possible.

"The dictionary is the only place that success comes before work. work is the key to success, and hard work can help you accomplish anything." — Vince Lombardi —

While I am a true believer in that analogy, I later found that one must also take the time to smell the roses. That realization would not have been possible were it not for the love and devotion of "Chub Chubs," aka., Pepper, for who I am indebted for awakening my heart with a deeper understanding, the larger picture.

My first debt of gratitude is owed to my family. My beautiful daughter Amy, whom I love with all my heart. My parents, James and Joyce Barthel. I wish we could do it all over again. My big brother Nick, I think of you every day. My brother Jim, whom I am eternally grateful for being there when I needed you most. Your inspiration and wisdom have always humbled me. It's just us now. Karin and the sunshine that you bring into everyone's life. My buddy Parker, Kaylee, Steve, Jeramiah, Addy, Abbi, Kylie, Jim, Katie, Brittnee, Kaitlynn, Megan, Molly, Barb, John, Roxie, Amanda, Ralph,

Dick, Geegee, Mike, Linda. My dear uncle Ray, whose courage was profound. I miss you. Too numerous to mention.

Back home, of course, I would like to thank Nancy for tolerating my waking her every day at 3a.m., to write this book and the support she offered. Angelina, Mike, Mike junior, Aviola, Joe, Toni. Sara, for bringing "Chub Chubs" into my life. Larry Yellen, Marc Ching and his devoted love to those Yulin Dogs, Chefs Stephanie Izard, Charlie, Jimmy, Rick, Tony, Gail, Mindy, Art, Joel. Radio legend Scott Allen, WJJG staff, Peter Zheutlin who inspired me, Wayne Pacelle, David Grimm. All my loyal customers who supported Peppercorns. Jimmy, George, Ed, Chuck, Gene, Bill, Sam, Lou, Jack, Ted, Steve, the Slick Brothers, Joe, "oh my goodness," Sam, Terry, Crazy Joe, Beverly, Cindy, Tina, Leslie, Larry. Simply too numerous to mention. Senator Linda Holmes, major props, and those lawyers who helped me when I needed you most.

Never too late, although no longer with us, I cannot forget my best friend and mentor Ken Kiwior. The hardest working chef I ever knew. I wish you knew how much you meant to me. Jill, Adam.

A big thank you to Aleksandra Nejman for her devoted compassion to animal rights issues.

The Humane Society, PETA, Spay Illinois, PAWS Chicago, The Puppy Mill Foundation, The Animal Welfare Institute, Best Friends Animal Society, The Farm Sanctuary, Stop Yulin. Too many....

— Paul Barthel

About the Author

Paul Barthel was born in Chicago. He grew up in Illinois and Wyoming. A Chef entrepreneur and restaurant owner who worked behind the scenes in kitchens for over thirty years. He is also an Animal Rights advocate who pushed to establish an Illinois law recognizing pets in domestic law.

He is the founder of Voices for Pets and currently pursuing Michigan, Iowa, and Ohio further establish identical laws in addition to puppy mill legislation, and furthered anti-cruelty measures. Barthel is also a strong opponent and activist against the Yulin Dog Festival. He currently volunteers for a variety of welfare organizations. Mr. Barthel is currently working on his next publication.

Learn more at: www.pepperstale.com.

Editor
Jessica A. Vaillancourt

www.ingramcontent.com/pod-product-compliance
Lightning Source LLC
Chambersburg PA
CBHW071233290426
44108CB00013B/1402